Arthur F. Klin Jr.

Margaret Jabo

Hi!.

HAMLET

Enter Critic

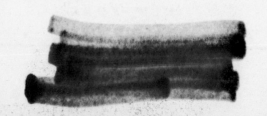

HAMLET
Enter Critic

Edited by

Claire Sacks

BROOKLYN COLLEGE

and

Edgar Whan

OHIO UNIVERSITY

APPLETON-CENTURY-CROFTS

NEW YORK

ACKNOWLEDGEMENTS:

To St. Martin's Press, for permission to reprint A. C. Bradley's Shakespearean
Tragedy.

To Browne & Nolan Ltd., for permission to reprint Thomas M. Kettle's "A
New Way of Misunderstanding *Hamlet*" in *The Day's Burden.*

Preface

Hamlet: Enter Critic cues the critic onstage. In the theater of his mind, the student is invited to witness and to judge a series of performances by critics who, from the time of Samuel Johnson to the time of Sir Laurence Olivier, interpret the puzzles and pleasures of *Hamlet*.

Hamlet: Enter Critic is designed to serve the student in two ways. As a controlled selection of critical material about Hamlet, it presents the beginning student with a small library in which he can conduct research about a perdurable and controversial literary work. It also presents the advanced student of Hamlet with supplementary reading material. It allows the instructor to discuss the techniques of documenting and organizing the research paper through material the entire class knows—the basic document remains the same for each student. Consequently, not only is the instructor better able to judge student progress and performance, but the student can learn from his fellow as he cannot when each member of the class concentrates on a different subject.

The critical selections are arranged alphabetically, so that the student must find and order the material pertinent to his own paper. To arrange the selections chronologically, for example, is to impose a prior pattern and so to editorialize for the student. The present arrangement does not give the student direction; it forces him to seek out and evaluate critical information on his own.

Whether one is dismayed or encouraged by the incredibly large corpus of Hamlet criticism (nearly 2000 items were published about Hamlet between 1877 and 1935 alone), that corpus is one indication of the varied, persistent, and profound response Hamlet has excited and continues to excite in us. That is why it is an apt choice for our intention: to provide the student with divergent and even contradictory solutions to a particular problem. Some selections were deliberately chosen because they are far-fetched by responsible critical standards. Such selections, we hope, will provoke the student to a reasoned rejection of his own. Out of controversy, out of a multiple focus, critical thinking is more likely to issue.

Therefore, by its subject matter and organization, *Hamlet: Enter Critic* involves the student in material which encourages the use of his critical intelligence. Furthermore, in his concentration upon the seemingly infinite responses to Hamlet, the student may discover or rediscover that literature is alive: it has been, it is, and it will continue to be.

For particular help in the preparation of this volume we should like to thank Mrs. Betty Addington, Mr. Robert T. Willard, Mr. Donald Cam of the New York Public Library, and Professor Warren Susman.

C. S.
E. W.

Contents

CONTENTS

PROBLEMS FOR INVESTIGATION

SUGGESTIONS FOR FURTHER READING

ROBERT ORNSTEIN
TM. Moral of Hamlet from *An Abstract Soldier, 19?* 195

EDGAR ALLAN POE
Review of "The Characters of Shakespeare," by William Hazlitt, 1845 199

W. TEIGNMOUTH SHORE
from *Shakespeare's Self*, 1920 235

CAROLINE SPURGEON
from *Shakespeare's Imagery and What It Tells Us*, 1935 207

A. C. SWINBURNE
from *A Study of Shakespeare*, 1880 258

A. J. A. WALDOCK
from *Hamlet: A Study in Critical Method*, 1931 248

JOHN WEISS
from *Wit, Humor, and Shakespeare*, 1876 234

KARL WERDER
from *The Heart of Hamlet's Mystery*, 1859-1860 243

REBECCA WEST
The Nature of Will, 1957 254

J. DOVER WILSON
from *What Happens in Hamlet*, 1935 266

PROBLEMS FOR INVESTIGATION

SUGGESTIONS FOR FURTHER READING

Selections

Die Shakespearomanie

By Roderich Benedix

Roderich Benedix, from *Die Shakespearomanie* (Stuttgart, 1873), in *A New Variorum Edition of Shakespeare*, IV. *Hamlet*, vol. II. Appendix. Horace Howard Furness, ed. (Philadelphia, J. B. Lippincott Company, 1877).*

ALL THESE ingenious theories of numberless critics for solving the mystery of Hamlet's character are wholly superfluous; the inexplicable mystery is simply due to Shakespeare's having fallen into a couple of gross faults of composition.

These faults of composition furnish us with the key by which we may explain this mysterious unintelligibility of Hamlet. Take out these, and his character is as plain and simple as any other.

These faults are pre-eminently a series of unusual, superfluous episodes, which have not the slightest influence on the action of the tragedy, nay, have scarcely any connection, or none, with it, and which must be pronounced, without qualification, faults.

There is, first, the despatch of an embassy to Norway, and its return. Neither the purpose nor the result of this proceeding has the slightest interest for us. But weeks, perhaps months, pass before the return, which we have to wait for, of this embassy.

The second episode is the journey of Laertes to Paris, with which the third is connected, the sending of Reynaldo after Laertes. All the long-winded instructions given by Polonius to Laertes and Reynaldo are wholly devoid of any dramatic character; they have not the remotest relation to the action of the piece, and accordingly

---

* Throughout the text, numbers in brackets indicate pagination in original source.

they leave us perfectly indifferent. Until the return of Laertes, months must pass away. And this return we have also to wait for.

The fourth episode is the journey of Fortinbras through Denmark to Poland. As this is not possible without ships, months must go by before he returns. And this return also we have to wait for.

The fifth episode is the embarking of Hamlet for England, which comes in just when the action promises to be lively, and is tending towards a conclusion. This departure of Hamlet is flung, like a drag-chain, right around the action. And we have to wait for Hamlet's return also. We thus see four persons travel away out of the piece, and not till late do they come back again. These journeys are wholly superfluous episodes.

They cause the time of the action to be extended through many months, and to these episodes, and to them alone, is it due that Hamlet's slowness becomes such a mystery. When Hamlet, most urgently summoned as he is to avenge his father's death, wanders about for months without doing anything, it is indeed unintelligible, and, to speak politely, mysterious and profound. But strike out those five episodes, which have not the least connection with the essential action of the piece, and all becomes clear and simple. The action then takes only a few days, and of Hamlet's mysterious irresolution there is no trace. It is true he proceeds only hesitatingly, but for this there are very good reasons. . . . In order to do away with all doubt, Hamlet gets up the play. He obtains certainty, and immediately sets to work, stabbing Polonius, whom he mistakes for the King. Where now is the irresolution? The Ghost appears to him again, and now we look for him to proceed against the King, whereupon the poet shoves in the journey to England, and creates a new delay. The whole fourth act looks like an interpolation, introduced to make out five acts.[351]

. . . Shakespeare is inconsequent in the delineation of character, and in *Hamlet* more than anywhere else. This inconsequence often appears strange enough, but as people do not venture to pronounce their idol inconsequent, they call his inconsequence, profundity. But let me mention some instances.

There is, in the first place, Hamlet's behavior to Ophelia. He has truly, ardently loved the maiden, but in his feigned madness he treats her shamefully. Here the poet has allowed himself to make a blunder. In the story from which this drama is fashioned, there is an intriguing lady of the court who endeavors, at the instance of the King, to act the spy upon Hamlet. This person is probably the prototype of Ophelia. The poet has added the incident of Hamlet's being in love with Ophelia, and thus comes the false stroke in the drawing. Hamlet's behavior would have been perfectly justifiable towards the court lady, but it was not justifiable towards Ophelia.

The second false stroke is Hamlet's rage at the way in which the courtiers treat him. The *Shakespearomaniacs* have not failed to find this rage very fine, and to applaud the poet for the surpassing skill with which he has delineated the pitiable behavior of the court people. But how is it? Hamlet represents himself as crazy, and they treat him accordingly. They do not contradict him, they flatter him, give in to his wildest conceits. But does not every sensible person do the same when he has to deal with a madman? Who would excite an insane person, and drive him to acts of violence by contradiction? This groundless rage is most fully spoken out when he has killed Polonius . . . So is it also with Laertes. He first appears before us as a true and noble knight. In his demand of vengeance for his murdered father, he is seen in the finest light. And yet this noble person enters into a plot to allow, in a sham fight, the point of his rapier to be secretly sharpened, and poisons the point. Horrible baseness! Here is the greatest inconsequence in character-drawing that can possibly be. The delineation of character is certainly not the strong side of the piece. There is not a person in it, save Hamlet, who knows how to awaken in us any interest. The King is an unmitigated rascal, and we can find no passion in him that renders his rascality intelligible.

The Queen is one of the—well, least agreeable of women. Polonius, with his pedantic garrulity, is one of the prettiest figures that the poet has drawn. Only his verbosity is somewhat wearisome. Ophelia is a maiden not so very agreeable, but her madness has made the role a favorite one. In representing insanity, an actress can make use of all the tones which she has in her power; she can utter any trifles, and draw upon all the registers. Thus some impression may be made, and it is not particularly difficult. Horatio is a thoroughly agreeable, graceful person, one of the best of Shakespeare's characters. Here we have done. The remaining per-

sons of the piece belong to the supernumeraries, and are mostly
very dull roles. In them the actor must be every inch an artist, if
he would awaken in us the slightest interest.

. . . I will grant that the death of Polonius serves a dramatic
purpose, inasmuch as it is the cause of Ophelia's madness, although
it is not a sufficient cause. No girl ever becomes insane because her
father dies, least of all Ophelia, whose relation to her father we
know was rather formal, lacking all heartiness. Besides, insanity [352] is a physical evil. If we are to believe that it is due to psychological causes, they must be very strong and manifest. We can
see how Gretchen, in *Faust*, becomes insane upon psychological
grounds; but not Ophelia. Yet granting that it is so, why, I ask,
does she become crazy and die? She is wholly guiltless. I ask still
further, why does Hamlet die? What conceivable guilt has he in-
curred? The *Shakespearomaniacs* say, indeed, his weakness of will,
his irresolution, was his fault, and he atones for it by dying. Without regard to the fact that weakness of will is a quality and no sin,
I have shown that this is not in the character of Hamlet. In letting
Hamlet perish, Shakespeare departs from the story upon which he
constructed his drama. In that story Hamlet is a bold, energetic
man, who comes back victorious from England, conquers the king
and his party, and gains the throne. It is from this deviation from
the original legend that the uncertainty, the inconsequence in
Hamlet's character comes. It is one half the good, substantial hero
of the old story, and the other half the creation of the poet.
Shakespeare was not perfect master of his materials. That he lets
Hamlet die without any necessity is simply unintelligible. No, there
is not a syllable of poetic justice here. Fortinbras says at the conclusion: "O proud Death! What feast is toward," &c. This is the
solution of the riddle. A banquet for death it was, suited to the
steeled nerves of a public delighting in blood.

Notwithstanding all I have said, there is still much good in
the piece. But as the *Shakespearomaniacs* seek out the good, and
even endeavor to turn the bad into good, I seek, on the contrary,
to set forth the bad. Of the poor economy of time, of the inconsequence of the characters, of the tediously long episodes, I have
now spoken. But, apart from all these, the piece is badly constructed. The Ghost apears twice in the first act. Why? Once were
enough. It has to speak to Hamlet only, therefore the first appear-

ance of it, as it is described at length in the second scene, is all the
more superfluous.

. . . Hamlet appears with the actors, and delivers a long lecture to them upon the art of speaking and acting. In this lecture
Shakespeare, at all events, sets forth his own principles in regard
to the player's art. But does this belong to a deep tragedy? And
these very respectable principles Shakespeare has, as a poet, by his
bombast and verbosity directly contradicted, for these characteristics of his must needs produce the very manner of delivery which
he blames. . . .

In Act IV, the King and the Queen, Rosencrantz and Guildenstern, are on the stage. The Queen says at the beginning to the
two latter: "Bestow this place on us a little while," whereupon
they retire. After eight-and-twenty verses they are again called in,
receive a commission, and go off again without speaking a word.
This is clumsy. Are the actors puppets, drawn hither and thither by
wires?

. . . The result of the fight between Hamlet and Laertes is
brought about in the strangest manner. *In the heat of the fight* the
combatants exchange weapons. Is this a conceivable possibility?
When a man knows how to handle a weapon, he never in a fight
lets it go. And had it been possible, would not Laertes have stopped
the fight under one pretext or another, since he knew that the
slightest wound from the poisoned rapier in the hand of Hamlet
would be certain death?

. . . After Hamlet is dead, there are fifty more lines spoken;
persons altogether unknown appear. I find this conclusion as
clumsy as that of *Romeo and Juliet*. What do we care, after Hamlet's death, for Rosencrantz and Guildenstern? What, for English
ambassadors? for Fortinbras? What is to us the succession to the
throne in Denmark? We have concerned ourselves only with Hamlet. With his [353] death our interest is at an end. We do not want
to know anything more.

It is true this drama has been a stock-piece on the German
stage for a century. Its influence is easily explained. In the first
place, the subject of it is very interesting. It had already been used
by others before Shakespeare. In the second place, the chief character is a role unusually telling. Hamlet feigns madness, and so
makes many striking and acute speeches, which are the chief charm

of the piece, and have always given especial pleasure. This poet pleases all the more, because the poet has so portrayed the other parts, the court people particularly, that they furnish food for Hamlet's satire. Furthermore, the piece has considerable dramatic effects. I reckon Hamlet's feigned madness among them, although it is too much spun out; Ophelia's insanity, on the other hand, is a more theatrical effect. Such purely theatrical effects are numerous in the piece, and have always charmed play-goers. Among these effects belong the three appearances of a ghost with the necessary, imposing accidents, a play upon the stage, a churchyard with graves and a burial, a fight and half a dozen corpses, and an abundance of fustian phrases withal.

That it is not piece itself particularly which impresses the public is evident from the fact, that for several decades the play has been given in different places in different shapes. Every one who has undertaken to alter the piece has picked out such parts as he considered especially effective, and left out other portions. . . . The fact that a piece has admitted of so many alterations shows how very loosely it is constructed.

. . . The tragic issue of a drama must be in the drama itself, in its essential necessity; there must be no other possible. *Richard III* and *Macbeth* must needs end tragically,—a reconciliation is in them not possible. In *Hamlet* no tragic issue is necessary.[354]

The Impediment of Adipose

By E. Vale Blake

E. Vale Blake, "The Impediment of Adipose," *Popular Science Monthly*, XVII (May 1880).

FROM THE DAYS of Hippocrates, intelligent medical observers have noticed that an unusual accumulation of fat, far from adding to the strength of a person, was a source of physical weakness, and, to a certain extent, an outward sign of incapacity; that it limited activity and shortened life. It is only in comparatively modern times that scientific experimentalists have ascertained precisely how the system generally, and the heart particularly, is affected either by the overloading or infiltration of superfluous fatty matter upon or in its muscular substance. In fact, it was not until the microscope was carefully applied to the investigation that the disease now known as "fatty degeneration" was really understood.[60]

. . . our principal object in these pages is to show that a *redundance of adipose matter essentially weakens and impedes the power of the will.* We know that it disinclines to activity, produces shortness of breath, palpitation of the heart, and comparative weakness in proportion to size, and is often accompanied by anaemia. We can make this clearer, perhaps, by an illustration. The normal weight of a man five feet in height is 120 pounds; of a man five feet ten inches, 169 pounds. Now, suppose the latter really weighs 300 pounds by accumulation of fat, what results but that all this superfluous matter has to be supplied with capillaries, and these have to get blood from vessels only constructed to circulate the original quantity? No wonder is it that the circulation is enfeebled and impeded! By this increase of adipose there is no increase of propelling force. Hence, the overstrain upon the capillaries and the ensuing comparative weakness in the vital functions are explained, and also why external injuries are less easily repaired. . . .[61]

But, to turn from the purely physical aspects of adipose, we wish to invite the reader's attention to a celebrated case of the impediment of adipose in affecting the mental character, and the action or inaction superinduced by this malady.

One of Shakespeare's famous characters—we should say perhaps his supreme portrait—is described thus with one dash of the pen:

He's fat and scant of breath!

The character of Hamlet has suffered such constant distortion at the hands of commentators, and has been made unintelligible and mysterious through a very natural but fatal oversight, namely, the habitual neglect of the annotators to take into account the physical organization of the Danish Prince—an oversight which the poet never made. He never failed to make the *physique* conform to the character.[62]

Every shade of capacity and ingenuity has been expended on the consideration and explanation of Hamlet's mental traits, but unfortunately with an essential factor left out. Not one, of all the numerous writers who have essayed to enlighten the world on the meaning and intent of this "consummate flower" of the poetic insight, has thought to inquire whether the body was not that "unknown quantity" which confounded Schlegel, and which Goethe thought he had found in the lines—

> The time is out of joint; O cursed spite!
> That ever I was born to set it right!

that is, that the Prince was overborne by the too great pressure of an Herculean task with which he was conscious he had not the ability to cope. But that there was really no insufficiency of mental power appears patent at every forward movement of the play. He perceives the situation clearly, argues about it rationally, notes all the circumstances and acknowledges his own duty in the premises; but he does not do the thing which he sets before himself to perform.

Why? Because "he's fat and scant of breath"—in other words, is weighted down with a non-executive or lymphatic temperament.

Painters, as well as actors, have done much to foist a false Hamlet upon the public imagination. He has habitually been represented by both as possessing a nervous, bilious, saturnine temperament, for which there is no warrant in the poet's description of him. Artists have portrayed him as fleshless and dark-hued. Fechter, the sole exception, did indeed remember his nationality to the extent of introducing the novelty of a flaxen wig, which was barely tolerated by the audience, so counter to the truth was the ill-taught popular fancy. But who has yet dared, on canvas or the stage, to present a true Shakespearean Hamlet "grunting and sweating under his weary load of life"?—so fat really as to need the "napkin" which the queen offers him to wipe the perspiration from his brow.*

Yet is this "fat" the keynote and solution of the "mystery of Hamlet."

Remembering that he was fat and scant of breath, we can

---

* Profuse perspiration is a recognized symptom of one form of heart disease—endocarditis.

readily understand many things which are otherwise certainly per-
plexing; particularly the inconsistency between his thoughts and
desires and his chronic inaction. He would represent in modern
life those persons whose cerebral developments are put down at
maximum figures by the expert phrenologist, and who exhibit to
admiring friends their large brain-power as thus indicated, but
who never do anything to confirm to diagnosis. Again why? because they lack the energizing temperament without which the
brain is but a dumb mass of latent possibilities.[63]

The character of Hamlet is generally conceded to be the most
wonderful production amid all that vast galaxy of dramatic figures
which has enchanted the world for three hundred years, and if one
new to the subject inquires why it thus takes precedence of Lear,
Othello, Macbeth, Shylock, and their proximate peers, we must
first answer negatively that it is not because there is so much deeper
philosophy in Hamlet than may be found, scattered pearl-like,
throughout all the plays by the same masterhand, nor because any
single passion is therein better delineated—but, affirmatively, because in the Prince of Denmark there is combined the greatest
complexity of mental acumen, allied to an unparalleled variety of
passional influxes, and bound, alas! to an inefficient temperament.
It is not one master passion which stirs, nor one affection alone that
is outraged; not one sole grief that afflicts, or one emotion which
reigns supreme over that great but erratic mind: it is a com-
mingling of jarring elements, most difficult to reconcile in the
formation of a characteristic individuality.

In the rising tide of the Moor's jealousy we have the most
vivid description of a half-savage tornado of mental suffering,
produced by the uncontrolled agonies of a strong but simple and
ill-balanced mind: in Lear, an already tottering intellect, quite
overthrown by the cruel irritations of unimagined ingratitude; in
Macbeth, an unsafe ambition troubled with a conscience; in Shylock, a member of an outraged race, essaying an hereditary revenge, stimulated by avarice: but in Hamlet we have a whole circle
of passions, a complication of emotions to draw into one converg-
ing action, like an engine required to run on a main road with
many branches, and no steam in the boiler. . . .[64]

Hamlet's "too too solid flesh" caused him to procrastinate.
Had it not been for that weight of adipose substance he "were

simply the most active fellow in Europe"; but the inertia of fat was like gyves upon his hands and feet, and could not be overcome except under extra-ordinary provocation, and then, the sudden impulse subsided, flagged again, mastered by the chronic habit of (let us give the right word, though the heavens fall!)—laziness!— the result of his "fatty degeneration.". . . .

In the very first scene of the first act we get an intimation, though no description, of Hamlet's physical temperament. Why, we may well ask, should the poet represent the Ghost as first appearing to certain officers of the guard, to whom it had no communication to make, and to whom none was necessary, unless it was to show a certain lack of sensitiveness to spiritual influences in the Prince, an absence of that refinement of nerve which originates, by attraction, spiritual influences? This preliminary stalking suggests a certain grossness of material texture in the Prince not present, for instance, in Horatio. The son of the royal Dane needed, it seems, a better attuned medium to put him *en rapport* with his own father's spirit. Here we have the succeeding events, that in everything which was to be really accomplished [65] others must take the initiative. The very expression which Hamlet uses in that frenzied burst of passion on parting with the Ghost, "While memory holds a seat in this distracted *globe*," is suggestive of a rotund and corpulent person. We can not conceive of the phrase-culling poet applying it to the narrow *caput,* for instance, of Master Slender, but must believe that Shakespeare kept well in mind the *personnel* of his hero; in fact, when did he ever forget that important item in the description of his creations! Indeed we are very soon again reminded of the characteristic physical development of the Prince by the expression Ophelia makes use of when she applies the term "bulk" in her sad description of Hamlet's visit to her closet.

> He raised a sigh* so piteous and profound
> As it did seem to shatter all his bulk.

Bulk! the very word Shakespeare employs to describe the ponderous Wolsey—"His very *bulk* takes up the rays o'the beneficial sun."

---

* Medical men indicate frequent sighing as a sign of heart-disease, caused by superfluous fat.

Ophelia had taken an accurate survey—she notes the disorder of his garments, mentions that he is pale (a symptom of anaemic adipose), but gives no hint that he has "fallen away vilely," which would have been the first thing to attract the attention of a young lady who believed one mad for the love of her. No, his "bulk" is evidently undiminished either by love or lunacy.

As with Ophelia, so with all the persons who address or describe him, none make any comment which would suggest a thin or haggard appearance. When Polonius describes to the King the course of the seeming madness, he confines himself exclusively to the mental analysis, and makes no mention that the Prince's body has succumbed to the malady. When the King drinks to him, it is not to his better health or better wits, but to his "better breath"! And the Queen-mother, watching him anxiously during the passage-at-arms with Laertes, makes the exclamation which we have taken as the keynote of our theory, "He's fat and scant of breath." And then, with instinctive maternal tenderness calls to him: "Here, Hamlet, take my napkin, rub thy brow"; which he not heeding, she repeats, "Come, let me wipe thy face."

Can we not see the perspiration trickling over the broad, heavy cheeks as we read these lines? It was surely from experience that he spoke of "sweating and grunting under a weary life.". . .[66]

Again, he evidently feels the drag-anchor of his heavy mold, and the consequent ill-cooperation of his bodily frame with his discerning spirit, when even under great excitement he stops to explain that he "is not splenetic and rash," though yet there is a sort of ground-swell of "something dangerous" in him. Yes, dangerous if sufficiently aroused; but his was a kind of nature which could endure a great deal of arousing before it culminated in action. When he takes his leisurely walk in the hall this quiet exercise goes under no other name with his than a *"breathing-time";* and, once familiarized with his true physical picture, how apt appears his reply to Osric: "Sir, I will walk here in the hall; if it please his Majesty, this is the *breathing-time* of day with me." [67]

. . . toward the close of the play, we get another insight into the torpid constitution of the Prince. In the preliminary discussion with Horatio as to his fitness for the duel with Laertes, his friend says:

You will lose the wager, my lord.

And Hamlet replies: "No, I shall win at the odds; but thou wouldst not think *how ill all's here about my heart;* but it's no matter." Just such an answer as a person might make who was suffering from "fatty degeneration." Evidently, in the opinion of the writer, the consideration of the unpleasant possibilities of the duel had brought the action of the heart almost to a standstill— the result of a chronic, sluggish circulatory system. Had his blood been accelerated, as would naturally have occurred in a nervous temperament, other expressions would have been more fitting; but the phrase quoted above better indicates partial stagnation than anything else. His philosophy, indeed, "defies augury," but his physical organization can not choose but respond to the near presence of a fatal venture. With the one not surprising exception of the first sight of the Ghost, Hamlet is throughout like the obese class generally which he represents, sufficiently careful of his personal safety. He puts himself to no bodily risk. . . .[69]

The medley of the last scene, including the death of the King, though the latter is finally slain by Hamlet, is all brought about by the management of other heads and hands, and its conclusion evidently unforeseen by the Prince. From first to last he accomplished nothing of set purpose. He moralizes by temperament and habit, but acts only *when inaction is the more difficult resource.* The fine spirit, the clear insight, the keen reader of other men's thoughts, is *imprisoned in walls of adipose,* and the desire for action dies out with the utterance of wise maxims, philosophic doubts, and morbid upbraidings of his own inertness. Hamlet is like one of those persons (to be met with in every community) who can relieve themselves by talking. This is a kind of character well understood by Shakespeare. In the third Richard's conference with the murderers of Clarence, one replies to him:

> Tut, tut, my lord, we will not stand to prate;
> Talkers are no great doers.

Again, in describing a character the very opposite to that of Hamlet—one of few words, Cordelia—the poet makes her say, "what I well intend, I'll do't before I speak." Now, of all the characters drawn by Shakespeare, Hamlet is preeminently the man of words;

not only his famous soliloquies but his dialogues take up unwonted space; he is the most prolific moralizer of the dramatist's conception, and thus all practical manhood is allowed to ooze out in words.

To judge the better whether Shakespeare intended in this play to show how the body may clog the aspirations of the mind, we have only to observe that whenever the physical appearance of any character is described by him, we find that leanness is an element of the executive man, and "bulk" or fatness of the dilatory and procrastinating, just as we see it in every-day life. Says Prince Henry to Falstaff:

> What! stand'st thou idle here? Lend me thy sword!

And the fat knight replies:

> O Hal, I prithee give me leave to breathe awhile—

the very expression used by both the King and Queen in regard to Hamlet, and in which he also describes his own case.

On another occasion Prince John addresses the pseudo-hero of Salisbury Plain:

> Now, Falstaff, where have you been all this while?
> —When everything is ended, then you come.

And the inimitable old rogue, knowing that he must be pardoned for his fat, answers:

> Do you think me a swallow, an arrow, a bullet?

So also Caesar, recognizing the physiological improbability of a fat man actually carrying out a treasonable conspiracy, says:

> Let me have men about me that are fat.[70]

And of Cassius—

> Would he were fatter!
> If my name were liable to fear,
> I do not know the man I should avoid
> As soon as that spare Cassius.

Macbeth was not fat, nor Richard III., nor Henry V., nor Harry Hotspur. They did the things which they planned to do.

They did not have to stop to "breathe" themselves like the Prince of Denmark. Who can possibly conceive of a fat Coriolanus? The fat man may be greedy and avaricious like Cardinal Wolsey, or witty and sensual like old Jack, or brooding and melancholy like Hamlet: but he who can vault into his saddle "like feathered Mercury" will ever win the day by action.

Hamlet's uncle-father might confidently have left the unhappy philosopher to his questionings and musings; had he not set his own trap he might have finished his reign in safety, if not in peace, for the Hamlet of Shakespeare, unlike the real Hamlet of Saxo Grammaticus, would no more have set the palace on fire than he would have produced a conflagration of the Skager Rack—for he was "fat and scant of breath," impeded at every step by a superfluity of adipose.[71]

Shakespearean Tragedy

By A. C. Bradley

A. C. Bradley, from "Hamlet," (1904), in *Shakespearean Tragedy*. (New York, The Macmillan Company, 1949).

SUPPOSE YOU WERE to describe the plot of *Hamlet* to a person quite ignorant of the play, and suppose you were careful to tell your hearer nothing about Hamlet's character, what impression would your sketch make on him? Would he not exclaim: 'What a sensational story! Why, here are some eight violent deaths, not to speak of adultery, a ghost, a mad woman, and a fight in a grave! If I did not know that the play was Shakespeare's, I should have thought it must have been one of those early tragedies of blood and horror from which he is said to have redeemed the stage'? And would he not then go on to ask: 'But why in the world did not Hamlet obey the Ghost at once, and so save seven of those eight lives?'

This exclamation and this question both show the same thing, that the whole story turns upon the peculiar character of the hero. For without this [89] character the story would appear sensational and horrible; and yet the actual *Hamlet* is very far from being so, and even has a less terrible effect than *Othello, King Lear* or *Macbeth*. And again, if we had no knowledge of this character, the story would hardly be intelligible; it would at any rate at once suggest that wondering question about the conduct of the hero; while the story of any of the other three tragedies would sound plain enough and would raise no such question. It is further very probable that the main change made by Shakespeare in the story as already represented on the stage, lay in a new conception of Hamlet's character and so of the cause of his delay. And, lastly, when we examine the tragedy, we observe two things which illustrate the same point. First, we find by the side of the hero no other figure of tragic proportions, no one like Lady Macbeth or Iago, no one even like Cordelia or Desdemona; so that, in Hamlet's absence, the remaining characters could not yield a Shakespearean tragedy at all. And, secondly, we find among them two, Laertes and Fortinbras, who are evidently designed to throw the character of the hero into relief. Even in the situations there is a curious parallelism; for Fortinbras, like Hamlet, is the son of a king, lately dead, and succeeded by his brother; and Laertes, like Hamlet, has a father slain, and feels bound to avenge him. And with this parallelism in situation there is a strong contrast in character; for both Fortinbras and Laertes possess in abundance the very quality which the hero seems to lack, so that, as we read, we are tempted to exclaim that either of them would have accomplished Hamlet's task in a day. Naturally, then, the tragedy of *Hamlet* with Hamlet left out has become the symbol of extreme absurdity; while the character itself has probably exerted a greater fascination, and certainly has been the subject of more discussion, than any other in the whole literature of the world. . . .[90]

The direct cause [of Hamlet's delay] was a state of mind quite abnormal and induced by special circumstances,—a state of profound melancholy. Now, Hamlet's reflectiveness doubtless played a certain part in the *production* of that melancholy, and was thus one indirect contributory cause of his irresolution. And, again, the melancholy, once established, displayed, as one of its *symptoms,* an excessive reflection on the required deed. But excess of reflection was not, as the theory makes it, the *direct* cause of the irresolution at all; nor was it the *only* indirect cause; and in the Hamlet of the last four Acts it is to be considered rather a symptom of his state than a cause of it.

These assertions may be too brief to be at once clear, but I hope they will presently become so.

Let us first ask ourselves what we can gather from the play, immediately or by inference, concerning Hamlet as he was just before his father's death. And I begin by observing that the text does not bear out the idea that he was one-sidedly reflective and indisposed to action. Nobody who knew him seems to have noticed this weakness. Nobody regards him as a mere scholar who has 'never formed a resolution or executed a deed.' In a court which certainly would not much admire such a person he is the observed of all observers. Though he has been disappointed of the throne everyone shows him respect; and he is the favourite of the people, who are not given to worship philosophers. Fortinbras, a sufficiently practical man, considered that he was likely, had he been put on, to have proved most royally. He has Hamlet borne by four captains 'like a soldier' to his grave; and Ophelia says that Hamlet *was* a soldier. If he was fond of acting, an aesthetic [108] pursuit, he was equally fond of fencing, an athletic one: he practised it assiduously even in his worst days. So far as we can conjecture from what we see of him in those bad days, he must normally have been charmingly frank, courteous and kindly to everyone, of whatever rank, whom he liked or respected, but by no means timid or deferential to others; indeed, one would gather that he was rather the reverse, and also that he was apt to be decided and even imperious if thwarted or interfered with. He must always have been fearless,—in the play he appears insensible to fear of any ordinary kind. And, finally, he must have been quick and impetuous in action; for it is downright impossible that the man we see rushing after the Ghost, killing Polonius, dealing with the King's commission on the ship, boarding the pirate, leaping into the grave, executing his final vengeance, could *ever* have been shrinking or slow in an emergency. Imagine Coleridge doing any of these things!

If we consider all this, how can we accept the notion that Hamlet's was a weak and one-sided character? 'Oh, but he spent ten or twelve years at a University!' Well, even if he did, it is possible to do that without becoming the victim of excessive thought. But the statement that he did rests upon a most insecure foundation.

Where then are we to look for the seeds of danger?

(1) Trying to reconstruct from the Hamlet of the play, one would not judge that his temperament was melancholy in the present sense of the word; there seems nothing to show that; but one would judge that by temperament he [109] was inclined to nervous instability, to rapid and perhaps extreme changes of feeling and mood, and that he was disposed to be, for the time, absorbed in the feeling or mood that possessed him, whether it were joyous or depressed. This temperament the Elizabethans would have called melancholic; and Hamlet seems to be an example of it, as Lear is of a temperament mixedly choleric and sanguine. And the doctrine of temperaments was so familiar in Shakespeare's time—as Burton, and earlier prose-writers, and many of the dramatists show—that Shakespeare may quite well have given this temperament to Hamlet consciously and deliberately. Of melancholy in its developed form, a habit, not a mere temperament, he often speaks. He more than once laughs at the passing and half-fictitious melancholy of youth and love; in Don John in *Much Ado* he had sketched the sour and surly melancholy of discontent; in Jaques a whimsical self-pleasing melancholy; in Antonio in the *Merchant of Venice* a quiet but deep melancholy, for which neither the victim nor his friends can assign any cause. He gives to Hamlet a temperament which would not develop into melancholy unless under some exceptional strain, but which still involved a danger. In the play we see the danger realised, and find a melancholy quite unlike any that Shakespeare had as yet depicted, because the temperament of Hamlet is quite different.

(2) Next, we cannot be mistaken in attributing to the Hamlet of earlier days an exquisite sensibility, to which we may give the name 'moral,' if [110] that word is taken in the wide meaning it ought to bear. This, though it suffers cruelly in later days, as we saw in criticising the sentimental view of Hamlet, never deserts him; it makes all his cynicism, grossness and hardness appear to

us morbidities, and has an inexpressibly attractive and pathetic effect. He had the soul of the youthful poet as Shelley and Tennyson have described it, an unbounded delight and faith in everything good and beautiful. We know this from himself. The world for him was *herrlich wie am ersten Tag*—'this goodly frame the earth, this most excellent canopy the air, this brave o'erhanging firmament, this majestical roof fretted with golden fire.' And not nature only: 'What a piece of work is a man! how noble in reason! how infinite in faculty! in form and moving how express and admirable! in action how like an angel! in apprehension how like a god!' This is no commonplace to Hamlet; it is the language of a heart thrilled wtih wonder and swelling into ecstasy.

Doubtless it was with the same eager enthusiasm he turned to those around him. Where else in Shakespeare is there anything like Hamlet's adoration of his father? The words melt into music whenever he speaks of him. And, if there are no signs of any such feeling towards his mother, though many signs of love, it is characteristic that he evidently never entertained a suspicion of anything unworthy in her,—characteristic, and significant of his tendency to see only what is good unless he is forced to see the reverse. For we find this tendency elsewhere, and find it going so far that we must call it a disposition to idealise, to see something better than what is there, or at least to ignore deficiencies. He says to Laertes, 'I loved you ever,' and he describes Laertes as a 'very noble youth,' which he was far from being. In his first greeting of Rosencrantz [111] and Guildenstern, where his old self revives, we trace the same affectionateness and readiness to take men at their best. His love for Ophelia, too, which seems strange to some, is surely the most natural thing in the world. He saw her innocence, simplicity and sweetness, and it was like him to ask no more; and it is noticeable that Horatio, though entirely worthy of his friendship, is, like Ophelia, intellectually not remarkable. To the very end, however clouded, this generous disposition, this 'free and open nature,' this unsuspiciousness survive. They cost him his life; for the King knew them, and was sure that he was too 'generous and free from all contriving' to 'peruse the foils.' To the very end, his soul, however sick and tortured it may be, answers instantaneously when good and evil are presented to it, loving the one and hating the other. He is called a sceptic who has no firm belief in anything, but he is never sceptical about *them*.

And the negative side of his idealism, the aversion to evil, is perhaps even more developed in the hero of the tragedy than in the Hamlet of earlier days. It is intensely characteristic. Nothing, I believe, is to be found elsewhere in Shakespeare (unless in the rage of the disillusioned idealist Timon) of quite the same kind as Hamlet's disgust at his uncle's drunkenness, his loathing of his mother's sensuality, his astonishment and horror at her shallowness, his contempt for everything pretentious or false, his indifference to everything merely external. This last characteristic appears in his choice of the friend of his heart, and in a certain impatience of distinctions of rank or wealth. When Horatio calls his father 'a goodly king,' he answers, surely with an emphasis on 'man,'

> He was a man, take him for all in all,
> I shall not look upon his like again. [112]

He will not listen to talk of Horatio being his 'servant.' When the others speak of their 'duty' to him, he answers, 'Your love, as mine to you.' He speaks to the actor precisely as he does to an honest courtier. He is not in the least a revolutionary, but still, in effect, a king and a beggar are all one to him. He cares for nothing but human worth, and his pitilessness towards Polonius and Osric and his 'school-fellows' is not wholly due to morbidity, but belongs in part to his original character.

Now, in Hamlet's moral sensibility there undoubtedly lay a danger. Any great shock that life might inflict on it would be felt with extreme intensity. Such a shock might even produce tragic results. And, in fact, *Hamlet* deserves the title 'tragedy of moral idealism' quite as much as the title 'tragedy of reflection.'

(3) With this temperament and this sensibility we find, lastly, in the Hamlet of earlier days, as of later, intellectual genius. It is chiefly this that makes him so different from all those about him, good and bad alike, and hardly less different from most of Shakespeare's other heroes. And this, though on the whole the most important trait in his nature, is also so obvious and so famous that I need not dwell on it at length. But against one prevalent misconception I must say a word of warning. Hamlet's intellectual power is not a specific gift, like a genius for music or mathematics or philosophy. It shows itself, fitfully, in the affairs of life as unusual quickness of perception, great agility in shifting the mental attitude, a striking rapidity and fertility in resource; so that, when

his natural belief in others does not make him unwary, Hamlet easily sees through them and masters them, and no one can be much less like the typical helpless dreamer. It shows itself in conversation chiefly in the form of [113] wit or humour; and, alike in conversation and in soliloquy, it shows itself in the form of imagination quite as much as in that of thought in the stricter sense. Further, where it takes the latter shape, as it very often does, it is not philosophic in the technical meaning of the word. There is really nothing in the play to show that Hamlet ever was 'a student of philosophies,' unless it be the famous lines which, comically enough, exhibit this supposed victim of philosophy as its critic:

> There are more things in heaven and earth, Horatio,
> Than are dreamt of in your philosophy.

His philosophy, if the word is to be used, was, like Shakespeare's own, the immediate product of the wondering and meditating mind; and such thoughts as that celebrated one, 'There is nothing either good or bad but thinking makes it so,' surely needed no special training to produce them. Or does Portia's remark, 'Nothing is good without respect,' i.e., out of relation, prove that she had studied metaphysics?

Still Hamlet had speculative genius without being a philosopher, just as he had imaginative genius without being a poet. Doubtless in happier days he was a close and constant observer of men and manners, noting his results in those tables which he afterwards snatched from his breast to make in wild irony his last note of all, that one may smile and smile and be a villain. Again and again we remark that passion for generalisation which so occupied him, for instance, in reflections suggested by the King's drunkenness that he quite forgot what it was he was waiting to meet upon the battlements. Doubtless, too, he was always considering things,[114] as Horatio thought, too curiously. There was a necessity in his soul driving him to penetrate below the surface and to question what others took for granted. That fixed habitual look which the world wears for most men did not exist for him. He was for ever unmaking his world and rebuilding it in thought, dissolving what to others were solid facts, and discovering what to others were old truths. There were no old truths for Hamlet. It

is for Horatio a thing of course that there's a divinity that shapes
our ends, but for Hamlet it is a discovery hardly won. And
throughout this kingdom of the mind, where he felt that man,
who in action is only like an angel, is in apprehension like a god,
he moved (we must imagine) more than content, so that even in
his dark days he declares he could be bounded in a nutshell and yet
count himself a king of infinite space, were it not that he had bad
dreams.

If now we ask whether any special danger lurked *here,* how
shall we answer? We must answer, it seems to me, 'Some danger,
no doubt, but, granted the ordinary chances of life, not much.'
For, in the first place, that idea which so many critics quietly take
for granted—the idea that the gift and the habit of meditative and
speculative thought tend to produce irresolution in the affairs of
life—would be found by no means easy to verify. Can you verify
it, for example, in the lives of the philosophers, or again in the
lives of men whom you have personally known to be addicted to
such speculation? I cannot. Of course, individual peculiarities being
set apart, absorption in *any* intellectual interest, together with
withdrawal from affairs, may make a man slow and unskilful in
affairs; and doubtless, individual peculiarities being again set apart,
a mere student is likely to be more at a loss in a sudden and great
practical [115] emergency than a soldier or a lawyer. But in all this
there is no difference between a physicist, a historian, and a philosopher; and again, slowness, want of skill, and even helplessness
are something totally different from the peculiar kind of irresolution that Hamlet shows. The notion that speculative thinking specially tends to produce *this* is really a mere illusion.

In the second place, even if this notion were true, it has appeared that Hamlet did *not* live the life of a mere student, much
less of a mere dreamer, and that his nature was by no means
simply or even one-sidedly intellectual, but was healthily active.
Hence, granted the ordinary chances of life, there would seem to
be no great danger in his intellectual tendency and his habit of
speculation; and I would go further and say that there was nothing
in them, taken alone, to unfit him even for the extraordinary call
that was made upon him. In fact, if the message of the Ghost had
come to him within a week of his father's death, I see no reason
to doubt that he would have acted on it as decisively as Othello

himself, though probably after a longer and more anxious deliberation. And therefore the Schlegel-Coleridge view (apart from its
descriptive value) seems to me fatally untrue, for it implies that
Hamlet's procrastination was the normal response of an over-
speculative nature confronted with a difficult practical problem.

On the other hand, under conditions of a peculiar kind,
Hamlet's reflectiveness certainly might prove dangerous to him,
and his genius might even (to exaggerate a little) become his
doom. Suppose that violent shock to his moral being of which I
spoke; and suppose that under this shock, any possible action being
denied to him, he began to sink into melancholy; then, no doubt,
his imaginative and generalising habit of mind might extend the
effects of this shock through his whole being [116] and mental
world. And if, the state of melancholy being thus deepened and
fixed, a sudden demand for difficult and decisive action in a matter
connected with the melancholy arose, this state might well have
for one of its symptoms an endless and futile mental dissection of
the required deed. And, finally, the futility of this process, and
the shame of his delay, would further weaken him and enslave
him to his melancholy still more. Thus the speculative habit would
be *one* indirect cause of the morbid state which hindered action;
and it would also reappear in a degenerate form as one of the
symptoms of this morbid state.

Now this is what actually happens in the play. Turn to the
first words Hamlet utters when he is alone; turn, that is to say, to
the place where the author is likely to indicate his meaning most
plainly. What do you hear?

> O, that this too too solid flesh would melt,
> Thaw and resolve itself into a dew!
> Or that the Everlasting had not fix'd
> His canon 'gainst self-slaughter! O God! God!
> How weary, stale, flat and unprofitable,
> Seem to me all the uses of this world!
> Fie on't! ah fie! 'tis an unweeded garden,
> That grows to seed; things rank and gross in nature
> Possess it merely.

Here are a sickness of life, and even a longing for death, so intense that nothing stands between Hamlet and suicide except religious awe. And what has caused them? The rest of the soliloquy

so thrusts the answer upon us that it might seem impossible to
miss it. It was not his father's death; that doubtless brought deep
grief, but mere grief for some one loved and lost does not make a
noble spirit loathe the world as a place full only of things rank
and gross. It was not the vague suspicion that we know Hamlet
felt. Still less was it the loss of the crown; for though [117] the
subserviency of the electors might well disgust him, there is not a
reference to the subject in the soliloquy, nor any sign elsewhere
that it greatly occupied his mind. It was the moral shock of the
sudden ghastly disclosure of his mother's true nature, falling on
him when his heart was aching with love, and his body doubtless
was weakened by sorrow. And it is essential, however disagreeable, to realise the nature of this shock. It matters little here
whether Hamlet's age was twenty or thirty: in either case his
mother was a matron of mature years. All his life he had believed
in her, we may be sure, as such a son would. He had seen her not
merely devoted to his father, but hanging on him like a newly-
wedded bride, hanging on him

> As if increase of appetite had grown
> By what it fed on.

He had seen her following his body 'like Niobe, all tears.' And
then within a month—'O God! a beast would have mourned
longer'—she married again, and married Hamlet's uncle, a man
utterly contemptible and loathsome in his eyes; married him in
what to Hamlet was incestuous wedlock; married him not for
any reason of state, nor even out of old family affection, but in
such a way that her son was forced to see in her action not only
an astounding shallowness of feeling but an eruption of coarse
sensuality, 'rank and gross,' speeding post-haste to its horrible
delight.[118] Is it possible to conceive an experience more desolating to a man such as we have seen Hamlet to be; and is its result
anything but perfectly natural? It brings bewildered horror, then
loathing, then despair of human nature. His whole mind is poisoned. He can never see Ophelia in the same light again: she is a
woman, and his mother is a woman: if she mentions the word
'brief' to him, the answer drops from his lips like a venom, 'as
woman's love.' The last words of the soliloquy, which is *wholly*
concerned with this subject, are,

But break, my heart, for I must hold my tongue!

He can do nothing. He must lock in his heart, not any suspicion of his uncle that moves obscurely there, but that horror and loathing; and if his heart ever found relief, it was when those feelings, mingled with the love that never died out in him, poured themselves forth in a flood as he stood in his mother's chamber beside his father's marriage-bed. . . .[119]

'Melancholy,' I said, not dejection, nor yet insanity. That Hamlet was not far from insanity is very probable. His adoption of the pretence of madness may well have been due in part to fear [120] of the reality; to an instinct of self-preservation, a fore-feeling that the pretence would enable him to give some utterance to the load that pressed on his heart and brain, and a fear that he would be unable altogether to repress such utterance. And if the pathologist calls his state melancholia, and even proceeds to determine its species, I see nothing to object to in that; I am grateful to him for emphasising the fact that Hamlet's melancholy was no mere common depression of spirits; and I have no doubt that many readers of the play would understand it better if they read an account of melancholia in a work on mental diseases. If we like to use the word 'disease' loosely, Hamlet's condition may truly be called diseased. No exertion of will could have dispelled it. Even if he had been able at once to do the bidding of the Ghost he would doubtless have still remained for some time under the cloud. It would be absurdly unjust to call *Hamlet* a study of melancholy, but it contains such a study.

But this melancholy is something very different from insanity, in anything like the usual meaning of that word. No doubt it might develop into insanity. The longing for death might become an irresistible impulse to self-destruction; the disorder of feeling and will might extend to sense and intellect; delusions might arise; and the man might become, as we say, incapable and irresponsible. But Hamlet's melancholy is some way from this condition. It is a totally different thing from the madness which he feigns; and he never, when alone or in company with Horatio alone, exhibits the signs of that madness. Nor is the dramatic use of this melancholy, again, open to the objections which would justly be made to the portrayal of an insanity which brought the hero to a tragic end. The man who suffers as Hamlet suffers—and thousands go about their business [121] suffering thus in greater or less degree—is considered irresponsible neither by other people nor by himself: he is only too keenly conscious of his responsibility. He is therefore, so far, quite capable of being a tragic agent, which an insane person, at any rate according to Shakespeare's practice, is not. And, finally, Hamlet's state is not one which a healthy mind is unable sufficiently to imagine. It is probably not further from average experience, nor more difficult to realise, than the great tragic passions of Othello, Antony or Macbeth.

Let me try to show now, briefly, how much this melancholy accounts for.

It accounts for the main fact, Hamlet's inaction. For the *immediate* cause of that is simply that his habitual feeling is one of disgust at life and everything in it, himself included,—a disgust which varies in intensity, rising at times into a longing for death, sinking often into weary apathy, but is never dispelled for more than brief intervals. Such a state of feeling is inevitably adverse to *any* kind of decided action; the body is inert, the mind indifferent or worse; its response is, 'it does not matter,' 'it is not worth while,' 'it is no good.' And the action required of Hamlet is very exceptional. It is violent, dangerous, difficult to accomplish perfectly, on one side repulsive to a man of honour and sensitive feeling, on another side involved in a certain mystery (here come in thus, in their subordinate place, various causes of inaction assigned by various theories). These obstacles would not suffice to prevent Hamlet from acting, if his state were normal; and against them there operate, even in his morbid state, healthy and positive feelings, love of his father, loathing of his uncle, desire of revenge, desire to do duty. But the retarding motives acquire an unnatural strength because they have an ally in something [122] far stronger than themselves, the melancholic disgust and apathy; while the healthy motives, emerging with difficulty from the central mass of diseased feeling, rapidly sink back into it and 'lose the name of action.' We *see* them doing so; and sometimes the process is quite simple, no analytical reflection on the deed intervening between the outburst of passion and the relapse into melancholy. But this melancholy is perfectly consistent also with that incessant dissection of the task assigned, of which the Schlegel-Coleridge theory makes so much. For those endless questions (as we may imagine them), 'Was I deceived by the Ghost? How am I to do the deed? When? Where? What will be the consequence of attempting it— success, my death, utter misunderstanding, mere mischief to the State? Can it be right to do it, or noble to kill a defenceless man? What is the good of doing it in such a world as this?'—all this, and whatever else passed in a sickening round through Hamlet's mind, was not the healthy and right deliberation of a man with such a task, but otiose thinking hardly deserving the name of thought, an unconscious weaving of pretexts for inaction, aimless tossings on a sick bed, symptoms of melancholy which only increased it by deepening self-contempt.

Again, (*a*) this state accounts for Hamlet's energy as well as for his lassitude, those quick decided actions of his being the outcome of a nature normally far from passive, now suddenly stimulated, and producing healthy impulses which work themselves out before they have time ot subside. (*b*) It accounts for the evidently keen satisfaction which some of these actions give to him. He arranges [123] the play-scene with lively interest, and exults in its success, not really because it brings him nearer to his goal, but partly because it has hurt his enemy and partly because it has demonstrated his own skill (III. ii. 286-304). He looks forward almost with glee to countermining the King's designs in sending him away (III. iv. 209), and looks back with obvious satisfaction, even with pride, to the address and vigour he displayed on the voyage (v. ii. 1-55). These were not *the* action on which his morbid self-feeling had centred; he feels in them his old force, and escapes in them from his disgust. (*c*) It accounts for the pleasure with which he meets old acquaintances, like his 'schoolfellows' or the actors. The former observed (and we can observe) in him a 'kind of joy' at first, though it is followed by 'much forcing of his disposition' as he attempts to keep this joy and his courtesy alive in spite of the misery which so soon returns upon him and the suspicion he is forced to feel. (*d*) It accounts no less for the painful features of his character as seen in the play, his almost savage irritability on the one hand, and on the other his self-absorption, his callousness, his insensibility to the fates of those whom he despises, and to the feelings even of those whom he loves. These are frequent symptoms of such melancholy, and (*e*) they sometimes alternate, as they do in Hamlet, with bursts of transitory, almost hysterical, and quite fruitless emotion. It is to these last (of which a part of the soliloquy, 'O what a rogue,' gives a good example) that Hamlet alludes when, to the Ghost, he speaks of himself as 'lapsed in *passion*,' and it is doubtless partly his conscious weakness in regard to them that inspires his praise of Horatio as a man who is not 'passion's slave.' [124]

Finally, Hamlet's melancholy accounts for two things which seem to be explained by nothing else. The first of these is his apathy or 'lethargy.' We are bound to consider the evidence which the text supplies of this, though it is usual to ignore it. When Hamlet mentions, as one possible cause of his inaction, his 'thinking too precisely on the event,' he mentions another, 'bestial oblivion'; and the thing against which he inveighs in the greater part of that soliloquy (IV. iv.) is not the excess or the misuse of reason (which for him here and always is god-like), but this *bestial* oblivion or '*dullness*,' this 'letting all *sleep*,' this allowing of heaven-sent reason to 'fust unused':

> What is a man,
> If his chief good and market of his time
> Be but to *sleep* and feed? a *beast,* no more.

So, in the soliloquy in II. ii. he accuses himself of being 'a *dull* and muddy-mettled rascal,' who 'peaks [mopes] like John-a-dreams, unpregnant of his cause,' dully indifferent to his cause. So, when the Ghost appears to him the second time, he accuses himself of being tardy and lapsed in *time;* and the Ghost speaks of his purpose being almost *blunted,* and bids him not to *forget* (cf. 'oblivion.' And so, what is emphasized in those undramatic but significant speeches of the player-king and of Claudius is the mere dying away of [125] purpose or of love. Surely what all this points to is not a condition of excessive but useless mental activity (indeed there is, in reality, curiously little about that in the text), but rather one of dull, apathetic, brooding gloom, in which Hamlet, so far from analysing his duty, is not thinking of it at all, but for the time literally *forgets* it. It seems to me we are driven to think of Hamlet *chiefly* thus during the long time which elapsed between the appearance of the Ghost and the events presented in the Second Act. The Ghost, in fact, had more reason than we suppose at

first for leaving with Hamlet as his parting injunction the command, 'Remember me,' and for greeting him, on reappearing, with
the command, 'Do not forget.' These little things in Shakespeare
are not accidents.

The second trait which is fully explained only by Hamlet's
melancholy is his own inability to understand why he delays. This
emerges in a marked degree when an occasion like the player's
emotion or the sight of Fortinbras's army stings Hamlet into
shame at his inaction. '*Why*,' he asks himself in genuine bewilderment, 'do I linger? Can the cause be cowardice? Can it be
sloth? Can it be thinking too precisely of the event? And does *that*
again mean cowardice? What is it that makes me sit idle when I
feel it is shameful to do so, and when I have *cause, and will, and
strength, and means,* to act?' A man irresolute merely because he
was considering a proposed action too minutely would not feel
this bewilderment. A man might feel it whose conscience [126]
secretly condemned the act which his explicit consciousness approved; but we have seen that there is no sufficient evidence to
justify us in conceiving Hamlet thus. These are the questions of a
man stimulated for the moment to shake off the weight of his
melancholy, and, because for the moment he is free from it, unable to understand the paralysing pressure which it exerts at other
times.

I have dwelt thus at length on Hamlet's melancholy because
from the psychological point of view, it is the centre of the tragedy, and to omit it from consideration or to underrate its intensity
is to make Shakespeare's story unintelligible. But the psychological
point of view is not equivalent to the tragic; and, having once
given its due weight to the fact of Hamlet's melancholy, we may
freely admit, or rather may be anxious to insist, that this patho-
logical condition would excite but little, if any, tragic interest if it
were not the condition of a nature distinguished by that speculative
genius on which the Schlegel-Coleridge type of theory lays stress.
Such theories misinterpret the connection between that genius
and Hamlet's failure, but still it is this connection which gives to
his story its peculiar fascination and makes it appear (if the
phrase may be allowed) as the symbol of a tragic mystery inherent
in human nature. Wherever this mystery touches us, wherever we
are forced to feel the wonder and awe of man's godlike 'appre-

hension' and his 'thoughts that wander through eternity,' and at the same time are forced to see him powerless in his petty sphere of action, and powerless (it would appear) from the very divinity of his thought, we remember Hamlet. And this is the reason why, in the great ideal movement which began towards the close of the eighteenth century, this tragedy acquired a position unique among Shakespeare's dramas, and shared only by Goethe's *Faust*.[127] It was not that *Hamlet* is Shakespeare's greatest tragedy or most perfect work of art; it was that *Hamlet* most brings home to us at once the sense of the soul's infinity, and the sense of the doom which not only circumscribes that infinity but appears to be its offspring.[128]

Shakespeare's Autobiographical Poems

By Charles Armitage Brown

Charles Armitage Brown, from *Shakespeare's Autobiographical Poems* (London, James Bohn, 1838).

*N*OTHING IN THE CHARACTER of Hamlet has given rise to more animadversion or critical disquisition than his apparent unfeeling behaviour to Ophelia; and actors [255] have, without distinction, represented him as guilty of unprovoked rudeness, or influenced by a touch of real madness in this scene. This I have frequently talked of as a mistake; and I once urged my reasons to an actor in London, when about to play it, but in vain. We are obliged to Mr. Skottowe for a valuable elucidation of the text on this subject. He points out that, in the original story, the usurping uncle, in order to discover if Hamlet's madness is feigned or real, causes him, attended by spies, to be met by a young lady, who had been already tutored to discover what was passing in his mind. Hamlet has long entertained a sincere affection for her, and was ready to fall into the snare, were he not timely advised of it by a friend; upon which he is careful to behave towards her as if distracted in his mind. Here, Mr. Skottwoe justly observes, recurring to the scene between Hamlet and Ophelia, "A satisfactory solution of the difficulty is derived from the history; whence it is learnt, what is not to be learnt from the play, that Hamlet was aware that Ophelia was purposely thrown in his way; that spies were about them; and that it was necessary, for the preservation of his life, to assume a conduct which he thought could be attributed to madness only." Those accustomed to examine the prototypes of Shakespeare's fables, may be satisfied with this solution, for they well know how artfully he could appropriate incidents or shades in character, while he partially or almost wholly differed from the story. But I cannot agree in the assertion, that such a solution is "not to be learnt from the play," because it has always been evident to me there. As it is now in [256] my power, with Mr. Skottowe's assistance, to remove a difficulty which has hitherto been beyond my skill, I will recall to the reader's mind the precise circumstances related in the text, and thence draw, what seems to me, the only conclusion that can be made.

In order to discover the real cause of Hamlet's seeming madness, Ophelia is placed in his way, while her father and the king conceal themselves within earshot as "lawful espials." Hamlet enters without observing her, absorbed in deep reflexion, and gives breath to the famed soliloquy of "To be, or not to be." At length, seeing her, he gently approaches, and salutes her in a tone suitable to her occupation, and to his serious state of mind:

> Nymph, in thy orisons
> Be all my sins remembered!

Unaccustomed to deceit, she doubtless acts according to her father's instructions, and rather suddenly offers back his remembrances of love. He, having just before been made aware that his two schoolfellows, Rosencrantz and Guildenstern, were employed as spies upon him, is naturally full of suspicion, looks furtively around if any one is near, and perceives the king and Polonius spying from their covert, and eagerly listening. The moment he has caught a

glance at them, he exclaims to himself "Ha! ha!" and half doubting the conduct of Ophelia, asks this searching question,—"Are
you honest?" She is surprised; and in self-defence he instantly
assumes his former mask of madness, though, as usual with him,
"there is method in it." As the dialogue proceeds,[257] a thought
crosses his mind respecting her participation in their treachery,
and he puts another question to her, completely suited to his purpose,—"Where's your father?" In compelled untruth, poor girl!
for she well knows he is listening close at hand, she faintly (I
suppose) replies,—"At home, my lord." His exclamation at this is
intended, if not to reproach her, to be loud in his ears;—"Let the
doors be shut upon him; that he may play the fool no where but
in's own house. Farewell." Scarcely has he left her, probably in
anger at her duplicity, when he returns for the purpose of adding
to the deception of the king, and talks in a higher strain of madness than before.

Thus it has ever appeared to me that our poet gives sufficient
hints of his intention in this scene.[258]

Second String

By Gould Cassal

Gould Cassal, "Second String," Brooklyn *Daily Eagle* (October 18, 1936), Section C.

MR. McCLINTIC has been too generous
in the matter of "Hamlet." He has given his scenic designer free
rein, has allowed his star the utmost freedom of expression; that
he is in complete accord with them I do not doubt, but between
them the triumvirate submerges a good deal of Shakespeare.
Though they are far from his best, Mr. Mielziner's sets will serve.
His costumes attract too much attention, almost as much as the
spotlights which played so beautifully on the cubic outlines of the

Bel Geddes production five years ago. The combination of McClintic and Mielziner is guarantee of a good show, but it is a partner-
ship that heads with increasing abandon towards a lush romanticism that first prettified "Romeo and Juliet," clad St. Joan in
Ziegfeldian silver armor, and has now swathed the hard, somber
outline of the Danish prince in voluptuous silks and satins.

The interpretation of the script from the director's view-
point seems to me a bit old-fashioned in its insistence on being
"modern," and its rigid avoidance of any hint of the classic in the
acting. Mr. McClintic has turned his people into typical human
beings. How human are Shakespeare's men and women? Stephen
Spender, in "The Destructive Element," remarks, ". . . the characters of Shakespeare are not people whom one would meet in
everyday life, but are yet symbols representing in their most significant form people who are real." One of the faults of the present
"Hamlet" is its devaluation of the people in it, an expression in
greasepaint terms of the modern fear of greatness. An austere,
murderous melodrama with the action pivoting on the mind of the
world's foremost neurotic intellectual, has been converted into a
glamorous play about a sensitive undergraduate who is more es-
thetic and hysterical than he is "proud, revengeful, ambitious."

Mr. Gielgud, like his colleagues, is obviously an intelligent
man, in addition to being a striking emotional actor, but neither
Shakespeare nor Jules Laforgue, among others, would recognize
his Hamlet. Mr. Gielgud sedulously omits the bitter wit of him
or reduces it to drawing room malice. In the quieter moments, in
the soliloquies, in the contemplation of the jester's skull, the part
is finely conceived, but one feels that Mr. Gielgud would profit by
some experience here where theatrical politeness and reserve carry
less weight than they do in London.

That Mr. Burdett and I took to the aisle after the second
scene of the second act (the courtesy I felt due Mr. McClintic kept
me a bit longer in the lobby) should not be construed as a deliberately contramundum gesture. This "Hamlet" is effective in its
way, but I wish it had more vigor and less gilded decor. Many
people consider it a thrilling experience. I'd be interested in hearing from any one on the other side of the fence.[2]

Unravelling the Mystery
of Shakespeare's 'Hamlet'

By Samuel C. Chew

Samuel C. Chew, "Unravelling the Mystery of Shakespeare's 'Hamlet'" [review of J. Dover Wilson, *What Happens in 'Hamlet'* (New York, The Macmillan Company—Cambridge University Press)] New York *Herald Tribune* Books, February 9, 1936).

IN AN ESSAY which, because of its author's prestige, has provoked an amount of discussion disproportionate to its value, Mr. T. S. Eliot asserted that "so far from being Shakespeare's master-piece" Hamlet is "most certainly an artistic failure"; and after showing himself astonishingly familiar with the contents of the nonextant pre-Shakespearean drama on the same subject, Mr. Eliot reached the conclusion that if we do not understand Hamlet it is because Shakespeare himself did not understand it. Mr. Eliot spoke, as usual, as one having a direct revelation from on high, though in this particular case what little revelation he possessed had come to him from the late J. M. Robertson. The author of "The Waste Land" has always exacted a considerable amount of cerebral effort from his readers; and what we vouchsafe to Eliot shall we deny to Shakespeare? From our own lack of understanding is it safe to argue that the dramatist did not know what he was about? This is not the attitude of Dr. Dover Wilson (who, by the way, disposes of Mr. Eliot neatly and quickly, gently but firmly, in an appendix). Dr. Wilson lays no claim to speak with any authority save that which comes from many years of patient study and meditation. He has wrestled with the problem of Hamlet ever since, away back in 1917, he read an article by Dr. W. W. Greg (not one of Greg's happiest efforts) in

which it was argued from the curious fact that King Claudius witnesses the performances of the Dumb Show without evincing by a
single tremor the possession of a guilty conscience that he was not
rendered uneasy by the pantomimic poisoning because he did not
recognize in it the representation of his own crime; that consequently the ghost must have lied to Hamlet; and that consequently
what Hamlet thought he saw was no "honest ghost,"but a mere
hallucination, a figment of his own fancy already warped by suspicions of his uncle's guilt. The ingenious part of Dr. Greg's
paper was that it accounted for the otherwise almost incredible
coincidence that the company of actors who visited Elsinor had in
their repertory "The Murder of Gonzago," a play closely analo-
gous in plot to the actual murder committed by Claudius. According to Dr. Greg this was the very play (and we know that Hamlet
has read it) which put into the Prince's head the notion that his
uncle had killed his father by pouring poison into his ear!

Of course, all this is specious reasoning; and Dr. Wilson had
no difficulty in disposing of it in a subsequent issue of the same
journal in which Greg's article had been published. But it is worth
recalling that indiscretion of the learned (but not quite sufficiently
learned) editor of the Malone Society Publications because it was
this article which started Dr. Wilson upon the long Road to Elsinor. Upon the way he shares with his readers excitement as delightful as that which, under other equally expert guidance, they
experience on the Road to Xanadu. With the publication of his
present volume he has reached the end of a quest whose milestones
have been the two former volumes in which he studied the textual
problems of the play and advanced and defended his solutions of
them and his edition of Hamlet in the "New" Cambridge Shakespeare. Not till the text was established was he ready to set forth
his exposition of what happens in Hamlet. So much happens in
the greatest piece of dramatic illusion ever fashioned by the mind
of man that it takes Dr. Wilson over three hundred pages of closely
packed exposition to set it forth; and even then he does not answer
quite all the questions nor give convincing answers to some others.

He does not resolve what seems to us the dramatic contradiction between his admission that the ghost is a "Catholic" come
from Purgatory and his argument that the Danish Court is Prot-
estant and the maimed rites at Ophelia's burial more or less Angli-

can. His attempt to differentiate between Hamlet's behavior toward Horatio and toward Marcellus in I, v, after the departure of the ghost, does not carry conviction. He does not account for the coincidence that the visiting players have in their repertory "The Murder of Gonzago." His argument requires him to assume that the First Player was "rascally" and probably deliberately treacherous to Hamlet: but he supplies no motive for this rascality and treachery. These are, however, minor and non-essential particulars in a tightly knit argument which is at once vastly entertaining (for Dr. Wilson writes with an infectious gusto) and delicately subtle. Some of his readers may object that so subtle are the dramatic effects, long obscured by traditions of the stage and the study, that it is impossible to believe that Shakespeare designed them for the public stage. The objection fails to take account of the fact, now recognized by all save those who, like Mr. Eliot, consider the play "an artistic failure," that Shakespeare worked upon two planes: the one comparatively low and crude and "easily understanded of the people," the other lofty and charged with delicate intentions and fine effects. In other words, he would appeal at once to the "general" and to the "judicious"; or, as some have preferred to hold, he had in mind not only the careless audience of the Globe Theater, but the scrutinizing attention of the thoughtful reader.

The crux of the problem, as Dr. Wilson sees it, is that same Dumb Show in the Play Scene which led Dr. Greg so sadly astray. To summarize Dr. Wilson's solution of this and many other problems would be as unfair as to give away the solution of a detective story. The reader of his book will experience entertainment somewhat similar to that afforded by a detective story and will derive from it much more profit. To whet his interest let us close with some questions. When did Hamlet first suspect the ghost of being the devil in disguise? Did Gertrude commit adultery? Was she privy to the murder of her first husband? Was Claudius legally a usurper and was the loss of his rightful heritage part of Hamlet's grief? At what exact point in the action does Hamlet become aware of the plot to plant Ophelia in his path? Is Horatio a stranger or a native of Denmark? What technical necessity forced Shakespeare to introduce the redundant Dumb Show? Why did it not startle the King's conscience? Why does Hamlet describe the

player-poisoner as "nephew to the King"? Why does Gertrude not
see the Ghost? In what manner are the foils changed in the duel
scene?

These as well as a score of other questions have, of course,
been adumbrated by earlier scholars, and there have been fumbling
answers often expanded into enormous monographs of misapplied
ingenuity. In no other book, however, known to the present re-
viewer have so many questions been lucidly proposed and reasonably answered. What is more important, they are not answered
singly but are tied together in one admirable sustained argument.
Dr. Wilson's interpretation of the play will interest every student
and lover of Shakespeare, and future producers will ignore it only
if they are content to miss the opportunity to restore to the modern
stage various fine effects which, though perhaps not apprehended
by the vulgar, surely delighted the judicious spectators at the
Globe.[5]

An Apology for His Life

By Colley Cibber

Colley Cibber, from *An Apology For His Life by Colley Cibber*
(1740) (London, J. M. Dent and Sons, Ltd., [1914?]).

YOU HAVE SEEN a Hamlet perhaps,
who, on the first appearance of his father's spirit, has thrown himself into all the straining vociferation requisite to express rage
and fury, and the house has thunder'd with applause; tho' the
mis-guided actor was all the while (as Shakespear terms it) tearing a passion into rags.—I am the more bold to offer you this
particular instance, because the late Mr. Addison, while I sate by
him, to see this scene acted, made the same observation, asking
me with some surprise, if I thought Hamlet should be in so violent a passion with the Ghost, which tho' it might have astonish'd,
it had not provok'd him? for you may observe that in this beautiful
speech, the passion never rises beyond an almost breathless astonishment, or an impatience, limited by filial reverence, to enquire

into the suspected wrongs that may have rais'd him from his peaceful tomb! and a desire to know what a spirit so seemingly distrest, might wish or enjoin a sorrowful son to execute towards his future quiet in the grave? This was the light into which Betterton threw this scene; which he open'd with a pause of mute amazement! then rising slowly to a solemn, trembling voice, he made the ghost equally terrible to the spectator as to himself! and in the descriptive part of the natural emotions which the ghastly vision gave him, the boldness of his expostulation was still govern'd by decency, manly, but not braving; his voice never rising into that seeming outrage, or wild defiance of what he naturally rever'd. But alas! to preserve this medium, between mouthing, and meaning too little, to keep the attention more pleasingly awake, by a temper'd spirit, than by mere vehemence of voice, is of all the master-strikes of an actor the most difficult [57] to reach. In this none yet have equall'd Betterton. But I am unwilling to shew his superiority only by recounting the errors of those who now cannot answer to them; let their farther failings therefore be forgotten! or rather, shall I in some measure excuse them? for I am not yet sure, that they might not be as much owing to the false judgment of the spectator as the actor. While the million are so apt to be transported, when the drum of their ear is so roundly rattled; while they take the life of elocution to lie in the strength of the lungs, it is no wonder the actor, whose end is applause, should be also tempted, at this easy rate, to excite it. Shall I go a little farther? and allow that this extreme is more pardonable than its opposite error? I mean that dangerous affectation of the monotone, or solemn sameness of pronunciation, which to my ear is insupportable; for of all faults that so frequently pass upon the vulgar, that of flatness will have the fewest admirers. That this is an error of ancient standing seems evident by what Hamlet says, in his instructions to the players, viz:

Be not too tame, neither, etc.

The actor, doubtless, is as strongly ty'd down to the rules of Horace as the writer.

Si vis me flere, dolendum est
Primum ipsi tibi—— *

* If you want me to weep, you must first grieve yourself.

He that feels not himself the passion he would raise, will talk to a
sleeping audience. But this never was the fault of Betterton; and
it has often amaz'd me to see those who soon came after him,
throw out in some parts of a character, a just and graceful spirit,
which Betterton himself could not but have applauded. And yet
in the equally shining passages of the same character, have heavily
dragg'd the sentiment along like a dead weight; with a long-ton'd
voice, and absent eyes, as if they had fairly forgot what they were
about. If you have never made the observation, I am contented
you should not know where to apply it.[58]

The Character of Hamlet

By Samuel Taylor Coleridge

Samuel Taylor Coleridge, "The Character of Hamlet" [1] (1813), in
Coleridge's Shakespearean Criticism, Thomas Middleton Raysor,
ed. (Cambridge, Harvard University Press, 1930), I.

SHAKESPEARE'S MODE of conceiving
characters out of his own intellectual and moral faculties, by
conceiving any one intellectual or moral faculty in morbid excess
and then placing himself, thus mutilated and diseased, under
given circumstances. This we shall have repeated occasion to re-
state and enforce. In Hamlet I conceive him to have wished to
exemplify the moral necessity of a due balance between our attention to outward objects and our meditation on inward thoughts
—a due balance between the real and the imaginary world. In
Hamlet this balance does not exist—his thoughts, images, and

[1] This manuscript is from a transcript by E. H. Coleridge of one of Coleridge's note-books. The original note-book has escaped the editor's search for
it. The transcript indicates that this is a lecture prepared for the Bristol series
of 1813. It may be compared with the third lecture as reported in the BRISTOL
GAZETTE. . . . The resemblance is incomplete, but sufficient for the necessary
date, even if no external evidence were available. The title of the lecture is
Coleridge's and is, therefore, printed without brackets. . . .

fancy [being] far more vivid than his perceptions, and his very perceptions instantly passing thro' the medium of his contemplations, and acquiring as they pass a form and color not naturally their own. Hence great, enormous, intellectual activity, and a consequent passionate aversion to real action, with all its symptoms and accompanying qualities.

Action is transitory, a step, a blow,[1] etc.

Then as in the first instance proceed with a cursory survey thro' the play, with comments, etc.

(1) The easy language of ordinary life, contrasted with the direful music and wild rhythm of the opening of *Macbeth*. Yet the armour, the cold, the dead silence, all placing the mind in the state congruous with tragedy.

(2) The admirable judgement and yet confidence in his own marvellous powers in introducing the ghost twice, each rising in solemnity and awfulness before its third appearance to Hamlet himself.

(3) Shakespeare's tenderness with regard to all innocent superstition: no Tom Paine declarations and pompous philosophy.

(4) The first words that Hamlet speaks—

A little more than kin, and less than kind.

He begins with that play of words, the complete absence of which characterizes *Macbeth* [2] . . . [?]. No one can have heard quarrels among the vulgar but must have noticed the close connection of punning with angry contempt. Add too what is highly characteristic of superfluous activity of mind, a sort of playing with a thread or watch chain or snuff box.

(5) And [note] how the character develops itself in the next speech—the aversion to externals, the betrayed habit of brooding over the world within him, and the prodigality of beautiful words, which are, as it were, the half embodyings of thoughts, that make them more than thoughts, give them an outness, a reality

---

[1] "Action is transitory—a step, a blow,

. . . .

Suffering is permanent, obscure and dark,
And shares the nature of infinity."
Wordsworth, THE BORDERERS, III.v.

[2] The first word, 'This' of the omitted phrase is all that is legible.

sui generis, and yet retain their correspondence and shadowy approach to the images and movements within.

(6) The first soliloquy [I. ii.

> O, that this too solid flesh would melt.]

[The] reasons why *taedium vitae* oppresses minds like Hamlet's: the exhaustion of bodily feeling from perpetual [38] exertion of mind; that all mental form being indefinite and ideal, realities must needs become cold, and hence it is the indefinite that combines with passion.

(7) And in this mood the relation is made [by Horatio, who tells Hamlet of his father's ghost], of which no more than [that] it is a perfect model of dramatic narration and dramatic style, the purest poetry and yet the most natural language, equally distant from the inkhorn and the provincial plough.

(8) Hamlet's running into long reasonings [while waiting for the ghost], carrying off the impatience and uneasy feelings of expectation by running away from the *particular* in[to] the *general.* This aversion to personal, individual concerns, and escape to generalizations and general reasonings a most important characteristic.

Besides that, it does away with surprizing [1] all the ill effects that the two former appearances of the ghost would have produced by rendering the ghost an expected phenomenon, and restores to it all the suddenness essential to the effect.

(9) The ghost [is] a superstition connected with the most [sacred?] truths of revealed religion and, therefore, O how contrasted from the withering and wild language of the [witches in] *Macbeth.*

(10) The instant and over violent resolve of Hamlet—how he wastes in the efforts of resolving the energies of action. Compare this with the . . . [?] of Medea; and [note] his quick relapse into the satirical and ironical vein [after the ghost disappears].

(11) Now comes the difficult task, [interpreting the jests of Hamlet when his companions overtake him].

The familiarity, comparative at least, of a brooding mind with shadows is something. Still more the necessary alternation when one muscle long strained is relaxed; the antagonist comes into

---

[1] That is, by means of the consequent surprise when the ghost appears.

action of itself. Terror [is] closely connected with the ludicrous; the latter [is] the common [39] mode by which the mind tries to emancipate itself from terror. The laugh is rendered by nature itself the language of extremes, even as tears are. Add too, Hamlet's wildness is but *half-false*. O that subtle trick to pretend the *acting* only when we are very near *being* what we act. And this explanation of the same with Ophelia's vivid images [describing Hamlet's desperation when he visits her]; nigh akin to, and productive of, temporary mania. [See II. i. 75-100, the speeches of] Ophelia, [which were just mentioned,] proved by [Hamlet's wildness at Ophelia's grave, V. i. 248-78].

(12) Hamlet's character, as I have conceived [it, is] described by himself [in the soliloquy after the players leave him—

O, what a rogue and peasant slave am I, etc.]

But previous to this, speak of the exquisite judgement in the diction of the introduced play. Absurd to suppose it extracted in order to be ridiculed from [an] old play. It is in thought and even in the separate parts of the diction highly poetical, so that this is its fault, that it is too poetical, the language of lyric vehemence and epic pomp, not of the drama. But what if Shakespeare had made the language truly dramatic? Where would have been the contrast between *Hamlet* and the play of *Hamlet?* [1]

(13) And then conclude with the objections; see the cover and first page of this book.[2] Schlegel,[3] III, 67, 69.

(14) After this whether it will not do to speak of the honest pride of our Englishmen—Milton, Shakespeare, Bacon, Newton, and now Wellington—and how the glorious events of the day [4] all are [?] deducible from the attack on England.[40]

---

[1] Cf. i. 27-28.

[2] A reference to the fragment on *Macbeth* in the same note-book. (Cf. i. 77-79.)

[3] Cf. i. 78 and note 3.

[4] Wellington was just beginning his invasion of southern France, after driving Soult out of Spain.

Lecture XII
Collier Report

By Samuel Taylor Coleridge

Samuel Taylor Coleridge, from "The Lectures of 1811–12, Lecture
XII (Collier Report)," in *Coleridge's Shakespearean Criticism*,
Thomas Middleton Raysor, ed. (Cambridge, Harvard University
Press, 1930), II.

WE WILL NOW PASS to "Hamlet," in
order to obviate some of the general prejudices against the author,
in reference to the character of the hero. Much has been objected
to, which ought to have been praised, and many beauties of the
highest kind have been neglected, because they are somewhat
hidden.

The first question we should ask ourselves is—What did
Shakespeare mean when he drew the character of Hamlet? He
never wrote any thing without design, and what was his design
when he sat down to produce this tragedy? My belief is, that he
always regarded his story, before he began to write, much in the
same light as a painter regards his canvas, before he begins to
paint—as a mere vehicle for his thoughts—as the ground upon
which he was to work. What then was the point to which Shakespeare directed himself in Hamlet? He intended to portray a
person, in whose view the external world, and all its incidents
and objects, were comparatively dim, and of no interest in themselves, and which began to interest only, when they were reflected
in the mirror of his mind. Hamlet beheld external things in the
same way that a man of vivid imagination, who shuts his eyes,
sees what has previously made an impression on his organs.

The poet places him in the most stimulating circumstances
that a human being can be placed in. He is the heir apparent of a

throne; his father dies suspiciously; his mother excludes her son from his throne by marrying his uncle. This is not enough; but the Ghost of the murdered father is introduced, to assure the son that he was put to death by his own brother. What is the effect upon the son?—instant action and pursuit of revenge? No: endless reasoning and hesitating—constant urging and solicitation of the mind to act, and as constant an escape from action; ceaseless reproaches of himself for sloth and negligence,[192] while the whole energy of his resolution evaporates in these reproaches. This, too, not from cowardice, for he is drawn as one of the bravest of his time—not from want of forethought or slowness of apprehension, for he sees through the very souls of all who surround him, but merely from that aversion to action, which prevails among such as have a world in themselves.

How admirable, too, is the judgment of the poet! Hamlet's own disordered fancy has not conjured up the spirit of his father; it has been seen by others: he is prepared by them to witness its re-appearance, and when he does see it, Hamlet is not brought forward as having long brooded on the subject. The moment before the Ghost enters, Hamlet speaks of other matters: he mentions the coldness of the night, and observes that he has not heard the clock strike, adding, in reference to the custom of drinking, that it is

> More honour'd in the breach than the observance.
> *Act I., Scene* 4.

Owing to the tranquil state of his mind, he indulges in some moral reflections. Afterwards, the Ghost suddenly enters.

> HOR.   Look, my lord; it comes.
> HAM. Angels and ministers of grace defend us!

The same thing occurs in "Macbeth": in the dagger-scene, the moment before the hero sees it, he has his mind applied to some indifferent matters; "Go, tell thy mistress," &c. Thus, in both cases, the preternatural appearance has all the effect of abruptness, and the reader is totally divested of the notion, that the figure is a vision of a highly wrought imagination.

Here Shakespeare adapts himself so admirably to the situation—in other words, so puts himself into it—that, though poetry, his language is the very language of nature. No terms, associated

with such feelings, can occur to us so proper as those which he
has employed, especially on the highest, the most august, and the
most awful subjects that can interest a human being in this sentient
world. That [193] this is no mere fancy, I can undertake to establish
from hundreds, I might say thousands, of passages. No character
he has drawn, in the whole list of his plays, could so well and fitly
express himself, as in the language Shakespeare has put into his
mouth.

There is no indecision about Hamlet, as far as his own sense
of duty is concerned; he knows well what he ought to do, and
over and over again he makes up his mind to do it. The moment
the players, and the two spies set upon him, have withdrawn, of
whom he takes leave with a line so expressive of his contempt,

> Ay so; good bye you.[a]—Now I am alone,

he breaks out into a delirium of rage against himself for neglecting to perform the solemn duty he had undertaken, and contrasts
the factitious and artificial display of feeling by the player with
his own apparent indifference;

> What's Hecuba to him, or he to Hecuba,
> That he should weep for her?

Yet the player did weep for her, and was in an agony of grief at
her sufferings, while Hamlet is unable to rouse himself to action,
in order that he may perform the command of his father, who had
come from the grave to incite him to revenge:—

> This is most brave!
> That I, the son of a dear father murder'd,
> Prompted to my revenge by heaven and hell,
> Must, like a whore, unpack my heart with words,
> And fall a cursing like a very drab,
> A scullion.
>
> Act II., Scene 2.

It is the same feeling, the same conviction of what is his duty,
that makes Hamlet exclaim in a subsequent part of the tragedy:

> How all occasions do inform against me,
> And spur my dull revenge. What is a man,[194]
> If his chief good, and market of his time,

---

[a] Cambridge editors, 'God be wi' ye' (Capell); $F_1F_2F_3$ 'God buy ye.'

Be but to sleep and feed? A beast, no more. . . .
. . . . I do not know
Why yet I live to say—'this thing's to do,'
Sith I have cause and will and strength and means
To do't.

Act IV., Scene 4.

Yet with all this strong conviction of duty, and with all this resolution arising out of strong conviction, nothing is done. This admirable and consistent character, deeply acquainted with his own feelings, painting them with such wonderful power and accuracy, and firmly persuaded that a moment ought not to be lost in executing the solemn charge committed to him, still yields to the same retiring from reality, which is the result of having, what we express by the terms, a world within himself.

Such a mind as Hamlet's is near akin to madness. Dryden has somewhere said,[1]

Great wit to madness nearly is allied,

and he was right; for he means by "wit" that greatness of genius, which led Hamlet to a perfect knowledge of his own character, which, with all strength of motive, was so weak as to be unable to carry into act his own most obvious duty.

With all this he has a sense of imperfectness, which becomes apparent when he is moralising on the skull in the churchyard. Something is wanting to his completeness—something is deficient which remains to be supplied, and he is therefore described as attached to Ophelia. His madness is assumed, when he finds that witnesses have been placed behind the arras to listen to what passes, and when the heroine has been thrown in his way as a decoy.

Another objection has been taken by Dr. Johnson, and Shakespeare has been taxed very severely. I refer to the scene where Hamlet enters and finds his uncle praying, and refuses [195] to take his life, excepting when he is in the height of his iniquity. To assail him at such a moment of confession and repentance, Hamlet declares,

Why,[a] this is hire and salary, not revenge.

Act III., Scene 3.[b]

---

[1] "Great wits are sure to madness near allied."
                                Absolom and Achitophel, 163.
[a] *Ff and Cambridge editors,* 'O'; *Qq* 'Why.'
[b] *Collier,* 'Act III. Scene iv.'

He therefore forbears, and postpones his uncle's death, until he can catch him in some act

> That has no relish of salvation in't.

This conduct, and this sentiment, Dr. Johnson has pronounced to be so atrocious and horrible, as to be unfit to be put into the mouth of a human being.[1] The fact, however, is that Dr. Johnson did not understand the character of Hamlet, and censured accordingly: the determination to allow the guilty King to escape at such a moment is only part of the indecision and irresoluteness of the hero. Hamlet seizes hold of a pretext for not acting, when he might have acted so instantly and effectually: therefore, he again defers the revenge he was bound to seek, and declares his determination to accomplish it at some time,

> When he is drunk, asleep,[c] or in his rage,
> Or in th' incestuous pleasures [d] of his bed.

This, allow me to impress upon you most emphatically, was merely the excuse Hamlet made to himself for not taking advantage of this particular and favourable moment for doing justice upon his guilty uncle, at the urgent instance of the spirit of his father.[2] [196]

Dr. Johnson farther states, that in the voyage to England, Shakespeare merely follows the novel as he found it, as if the poet had no other reason for adhering to his original;[3] but Shake-

---

[c] *Ff and Cambridge editors, 'drunk asleep.' Qq 'drunk, asleep.'*

[d] *Read 'pleasure.'*

[1] Cf. i. 32, and note.

[2] Both Richardson and Robertson anticipated Coleridge in his interpretation of this passage. William Richardson, "Additional Observations on Hamlet," ESSAYS ON SHAKESPEARE'S DRAMATIC CHARACTERS (1784); Thomas Robertson, "An Essay on the Character of Hamlet," TRANSACTIONS OF THE ROYAL SOCIETY OF EDINBURGH, vol. ii (1790). Robertson's note (p. 261) indicates that his criticism is independent of Richardson's.

[3] This is an error, I believe. It scarcely seems worth while to speculate regarding the actual source of Coleridge's recollection. But it may be said in passing that Malone quotes at the end of his notes on HAMLET the anonymous pamphlet, SOME REMARKS ON THE TRAGEDY OF HAMLET (1736). In this pamphlet (p. 33) there is a criticism of Shakespeare for Hamlet's feigned madness, which the critic explains as due only to Shakespeare's desire to keep to his source. The madness, he says, causes Hamlet's being sent to England.

speare never followed a novel, because he found such and such an incident in it, but because he saw that the story, as he read it, contributed to enforce, or to explain some great truth inherent in human nature. He never could lack invention to alter or improve a popular narrative; but he did not wantonly vary from it, when he knew that, as it was related, it would so well apply to his own great purpose. He saw at once how consistent it was with the character of Hamlet, that after still resolving, and still deferring, still determining to execute, and still postponing execution, he should finally, in the infirmity of his disposition, give himself up to his destiny, and hopelessly place himself in the power, and at the mercy of his enemies.

Even after the scene with Osrick, we see Hamlet still indulging in reflection, and hardly thinking of the task he has just undertaken: he is all dispatch and resolution, as far as words and present intentions are concerned, but all hesitation and irresolution, when called upon to carry his words and intentions into effect; so that, resolving to do everything, he does nothing. He is full of purpose, but void of that quality of mind which accomplishes purpose.

Anything finer than this conception, and working out of a great character, is merely impossible. Shakespeare wished to impress upon us the truth, that action is the chief end of existence— that no faculties of intellect, however brilliant, can be considered valuable, or indeed otherwise than as misfortunes, if they withdraw us from, or render us repugnant to action, and lead us to think and think of doing, until the time has elapsed when we can do anything effectually.[197] In enforcing this moral truth, Shakespeare has shown the fulness and force of his powers: all that is amiable and excellent in nature is combined in Hamlet, with the exception of one quality. He is a man living in meditation, called upon to act by every motive human and divine, but the great object of his life is defeated by continually resolving to do, yet doing nothing but resolve.[198]

Great Expectations

By Charles Dickens

Charles Dickens, from *Great Expectations* (1860–1861) (New York, Rinehart and Company, Inc., 1948).

[Pip Sees Mr. Wopsle As Hamlet]

ON OUR ARRIVAL in Denmark, we found the king and queen of that country elevated in two armchairs on a kitchen-table, holding a Court. The whole of the Danish nobility were in attendance; consisting of a noble boy in the wash-leather boots of a gigantic ancestor, a venerable Peer with a dirty face, who seemed to have risen from the people late in life, and the Danish chivalry with a comb in its hair and a pair of white silk legs, and presenting on the whole a feminine appearance. My gifted townsman stood gloomily apart, with folded arms and I could have wished that his curls and forehead had been more probable.

Several curious little circumstances transpired as the action proceeded. The late king of the country not only appeared to have been troubled with a cough at the time of his decease but to have taken it with him to the tomb, and to have brought it back. The royal phantom also carried a ghostly manuscript round its truncheon, to which it had the appearance of occasionally referring, and that, too, with an air of anxiety and a tendency to lose the place of reference which were suggestive of a state of mortality. It was this, I conceive, which led to the Shade's being advised by the gallery to "turn over!"—a recommendation which it took extremely ill. It was likewise to be noted of this majestic spirit that whereas it always appeared with an air of having been out a long time and walked an immense distance, it perceptibly came from a closely-

contiguous wall. This occasioned its terrors to be received deri-
sively. The Queen of Denmark, a very buxom lady, though no
doubt historically brazen, was considered by the public to have too
much brass about her; her chin being attached to her diadem by a
broad band of that metal (as if she had a gorgeous toothache),[256]
her waist being encircled by another, and each of her arms by
another, so that she was openly mentioned as "the kettledrum."
The noble boy in the ancestral boots was inconsistent, representing
himself, as it were in one breath, as an able seaman, a strolling
actor, a grave-digger, a clergyman, and a person of the utmost
importance at a Court fencing-match, on the authority of whose
practised eye and nice discrimination the finest strokes were judged.
This gradually led to a want of toleration for him, and even—on
his being detected in holy orders, and declining to perform the
funeral service—to the general indignation taking the form of
nuts. Lastly, Ophelia was a prey to such slow musical madness,
that when, in course of time, she had taken off her white muslin
scarf, folded it up, and buried it, a sulky man who had been long
cooling his impatient nose against an iron bar in the front row of
the gallery, growled, "Now the baby's put to bed, let's have
supper!" Which, to say the least of it, was out of keeping.

Upon my unfortunate townsman all these incidents accumu-
lated with playful effect. Whenever that undecided Prince had to
ask a question or state a doubt, the public helped him out with it.
As for example; on the question whether 'twas nobler in the mind
to suffer, some roared yes, and some no, and some inclining to both
opinions said "toss up for it"; and quite a Debating Society arose.
When he asked what should such fellows as he do crawling between earth and heaven, he was encouraged with loud cries of
"Hear, hear!" When he appeared with his stocking disordered
(its disorder expressed, according to usage, by one very neat fold
in the top, which I suppose to be always got up with a flat iron), a
conversation took place in the gallery respecting the paleness of his
leg, and whether it was occasioned by the turn the ghost had given
him. On his taking the recorders—very like a little black flute that
had just been played in the orchestra and handed out at the door
—he was called upon unanimously for Rule Britannia. When he
recommended the player not to saw the air thus, the sulky man
said, "And don't *you* do it, neither; you're a deal worse than *him!*"

And I grieve to add that peals of laughter greeted Mr. Wopsle on every one of these occasions.

But his greatest trials were in the churchyard: which had [257] the appearance of a primeval forest, with a kind of small ecclesiastical wash-house on one side, and a turnpike gate on the other. Mr. Wopsle, in a comprehensive black cloak, being descried entering at the turnpike, the grave-digger was admonished in a friendly way, "Look out! Here's the undertaker a-coming, to see how you're getting on with your work!" I believe it is well known in a constitutional country that Mr. Wopsle could not possibly have returned the skull, after moralizing over it, without dusting his fingers on a white napkin taken from his breast; but even that innocent and indispensable action did not pass without the comment "Wai-ter!" The arrival of the body for interment (in an empty black box with the lid tumbling open) was the signal for a general joy which was much enhanced by the discovery, among the bearers, of an individual obnoxious to identification. The joy attended Mr. Wopsle through his struggle with Laertes on the brink of the orchestra and the grave, and slackened no more until he had tumbled the king off the kitchentable, and had died by inches from the ankles upwards.

We had made some pale efforts in the beginning to applaud Mr. Wopsle; but they were too hopeless to be persisted in. Therefore we had sat, feeling keenly for him, but laughing, nevertheless, from ear to ear. I laughed in spite of myself all the time, the whole thing was so droll; and yet I had a latent impression that there was something decidedly fine in Mr. Wopsle's elocution— not for old associations' sake, I am afraid, but because it was very slow, very dreary, very up-hill and down-hill, and very unlike any way in which any man in any natural circumstances of life or death ever expressed himself about anything. When the tragedy was over, and he had been called for and hooted, I said to Herbert, "Let us go at once, or perhaps we shall meet him." [258]

Hamlet and His Problems

By T. S. Eliot

T. S. Eliot, "Hamlet and His Problems" (1919), in *Selected Essays:*
1917–1932 (New York, Harcourt, Brace and Company, 1932).

FEW CRITICS have even admitted that
Hamlet the play is the primary problem, and Hamlet the character
only secondary. And Hamlet the character has had an especial
temptation for that most dangerous type of critic: the critic with a
mind which is naturally of the creative order, but which through
some weakness in creative power exercises itself in criticism
instead. These minds often find in Hamlet a vicarious existence
for their own artistic realization. Such a mind had Goethe, who
made of Hamlet a Werther; and such had Coleridge, who made of
Hamlet a Coleridge; and probably neither of these men in writing
about Hamlet remembered that his first business was to study a
work of art. The kind of criticism that Goethe and Coleridge
produced, in writing of Hamlet, is the most misleading kind possible. For they both possessed unquestionable critical insight, and
both make their critical aberrations the more plausible by the sub-
stitution—of their own Hamlet for Shakespeare's—which their
creative gift effects. We should be thankful that Walter Pater did
not fix his attention on this play.

Two writers of our own time, Mr. J. M. Robertson and Professor Stoll of the University of Minnesota, have issued small
books which can be praised for moving in the other direction. Mr.
Stoll performs a service in recalling to our attention the labours of
the critics of the seventeenth and eighteenth centuries,[1] observing
that

"they knew less about psychology than more recent Hamlet critics, but
they were nearer in spirit to Shakespeare's art; and as they insisted on

---

[1] I have never, by the way, seen a cogent refutation of Thomas Rymer's
objections to *Othello*.

the importance of the effect of the whole rather than on the importance of the leading character, they were nearer, in their old-fashioned way, to the secret of dramatic art in general."

Qua work of art, the work of art cannot be interpreted; there is nothing to interpret; we can only criticise it according to standards, in comparison to other works of art; and for "interpretation" the chief task is the presentation of relevant historical facts which the reader is not assumed to know. Mr. Robertson points out, very pertinently, how critics have failed in their "interpretation" of *Hamlet* by ignoring what ought to be very obvious; that *Hamlet* is a stratification, that it represents the efforts of a series of men, each making what he could out of the work of his predecessors. The *Hamlet* of Shakespeare will appear to us very differently if, instead of treating the whole action of the play as due to Shakespeare's design, we perceive his *Hamlet* to be superposed upon much cruder material which persists even in the final form.

We know that there was an older play by Thomas Kyd, that extraordinary dramatic (if not poetic) genius who was in all probability the author of two plays so dissimilar as *The Spanish Tragedy* and *Arden of Feversham;* and what this play was like we can guess from three clues: from *The Spanish Tragedy* itself, from the tale of Belleforest upon which Kyd's *Hamlet* must have been based, and from a version acted in Germany in Shakespeare's lifetime which bears strong evidence of having been adapted from the earlier, not from the later, play. From these three sources it is clear that in the earlier play the motive was a revenge-motive simply; that the action or delay is caused, as in *The Spanish Tragedy,* solely by the difficulty of assassinating a monarch surrounded by guards; and that the "madness" of Hamlet was feigned in order to escape suspicion, and successfully. In the final play of Shakespeare, on the other hand, there is a motive which is more important than that of revenge, and which explicitly "blunts" the latter; the delay in revenge is unexplained on grounds of necessity or expediency; and the effect of the "madness" is not to lull but to arouse the king's [122] suspicion. The alteration is not complete enough, however, to be convincing. Furthermore, there are verbal parallels so close to *The Spanish Tragedy* as to leave no doubt that in places Shakespeare was merely *revising* the text of Kyd. And finally there are unexplained scenes—the Polonius-

Laertes and the Polonius-Reynaldo scenes—for which there is
little excuse; these scenes are not in the verse style of Kyd, and not
beyond doubt in the style of Shakespeare. These Mr. Robertson
believes to be scenes in the original play of Kyd reworked by a
third hand, perhaps Chapman, before Shakespeare touched the
play. And he concludes, with very strong show of reason, that the
original play of Kyd was, like certain other revenge plays, in two
parts of five acts each. The upshot of Mr. Robertson's examination is, we believe, irrefragable: that Shakespeare's *Hamlet,* so far
as it is Shakespeare's, is a play dealing with the effect of a mother's
guilt upon her son, and that Shakespeare was unable to impose
this motive successfully upon the "intractable" material of the old
play.

Of the intractability there can be no doubt. So far from being
Shakespeare's masterpiece, the play is most certainly an artistic
failure. In several ways the play is puzzling, and disquieting as is
none of the others. Of all the plays it is the longest and is possibly
the one on which Shakespeare spent most pains; and yet he has
left in it superfluous and inconsistent scenes which even hasty revision should have noticed. The versification is variable. Lines like

> Look, the morn, in russet mantle clad,
> Walks o'er the dew of yon high eastern hill,

are of the Shakespeare of *Romeo and Juliet.* The lines in Act v,
sc. ii,

> Sir, in my heart there was a kind of fighting
> That would not let me sleep . . .
> Up from my cabin,
> My sea-gown scarf'd about me, in the dark
> Grop'd I to find out them: had my desire;
> Finger'd their packet; [123]

are of his quite mature. Both workmanship and thought are in an
unstable position. We are surely justified in attributing the play,
with that other profoundly interesting play of "intractable" material and astonishing versification, *Measure for Measure,* to a
period of crisis, after which follow the tragic successes which cul-
minate in *Coriolanus. Coriolanus* may be not as "interesting" as
Hamlet, but it is, with *Antony and Cleopatra,* Shakespeare's most

assured artistic success. And probably more people have thought *Hamlet* a work of art because they found it interesting, than have found it interesting because it is a work of art. It is the "Mona Lisa" of literature.

The grounds of *Hamlet's* failure are not immediately obvious. Mr. Robertson is undoubtedly correct in concluding that the essential emotion of the play is the feeling of a son towards a guilty mother:

"[Hamlet's] tone is that of one who has suffered tortures on the score of his mother's degradation. . . . The guilt of a mother is an almost intolerable motive for drama, but it had to be maintained and emphasized to supply a psychological solution, or rather a hint of one."

This, however, is by no means the whole story. It is not merely the "guilt of a mother" that cannot be handled as Shakespeare handled the suspicion of Othello, the infatuation of Antony, or the pride of Coriolanus. The subject might conceivably have expanded into a tragedy like these, intelligible, self-complete, in the sunlight. *Hamlet,* like the sonnets, is full of some stuff that the writer could not drag to light, contemplate, or manipulate into art. And when we search for this feeling, we find it, as in the sonnets, very difficult to localize. You cannot point to it in the speeches; indeed, if you examine the two famous soliloquies you see the versification of Shakespeare, but a content which might be claimed by another, perhaps by the author of the *Revenge of Bussy d'Ambois, Act* v, sc. 1. We find Shakespeare's Hamlet not in the action, not in any quotations that we might select, so much as in an unmistakable tone which is unmistakably not in the earlier play.

The only way of expressing emotion in the form of art is by finding an "objective correlative" in other words, a set of objects,[124] a situation, a chain of events which shall be the formula of that *particular* emotion; such that when the external facts, which must terminate in sensory experience, are given, the emotion is immediately evoked. If you examine any of Shakespeare's more successful tragedies, you will find this exact equivalence; you will find that the state of mind of Lady Macbeth walking in her sleep has been communicated to you by a skilful accumulation of imagined sensory impressions; the words of Macbeth on hearing of his wife's death strike us as if, given the sequence of events, these words were automatically released by the last event in the series. The artistic "inevitability" lies in this complete adequacy of the external to the emotion; and this is precisely what is deficient in *Hamlet*. Hamlet (the man) is dominated by an emotion which is inexpressible, because it is in *excess* of the facts as they appear. And the supposed identity of Hamlet with his author is genuine to this point: that Hamlet's bafflement at the absence of objective equivalent to his feelings is a prolongation of the bafflement of his creator in the face of his artistic problem. Hamlet is up against the difficulty that his disgust is occasioned by his mother, but that his mother is not an adequate equivalent for it; his disgust envelops and exceeds her. It is thus a feeling which he cannot understand; he cannot objectify it, and it therefore remains to poison life and obstruct action. None of the possible actions can satisfy it; and nothing that Shakespeare can do with the plot can express Hamlet for him. And it must be noticed that the very nature of the *données* of the problem precludes objective equivalence. To have heightened the criminality of Gertrude would have been to provide the formula for a totally different emotion in Hamlet; it is just *because* her character is so negative and insignificant that she arouses in Hamlet the feeling which she is incapable of representing.

The "madness" of Hamlet lay to Shakespeare's hand; in the earlier play a simple ruse, and to the end, we may presume, understood as a ruse by the audience. For Shakespeare it is less than madness and more than feigned. The levity of Hamlet, his repetition of phrase, his puns, are not part of a deliberate plan of dissimulation, but a form of emotional relief. In the [125] character Hamlet it is the buffoonery of an emotion which can find no outlet in action; in the dramatist it is the buffoonery of an emotion which he cannot express in art. The intense feeling, ecstatic or terrible, without an object or exceeding its object, is something which every person of sensibility has known; it is doubtless a subject of study for pathologists. It often occurs in adolescence: the ordinary person puts these feelings to sleep, or trims down his feelings to fit the business world; the artist keeps them alive by his ability to intensify the world to his emotions. The Hamlet of Laforgue is an adolescent; the Hamlet of Shakespeare is not, he has not that explanation and excuse. We must simply admit that here Shakespeare tackled a problem which proved too much for him. Why he attempted it at all is an insoluble puzzle; under compulsion of what experience he attempted to express the inexpressibly horrible, we cannot ever know. We need a great many facts in his biography; and we should like to know whether, and when, and after or at the same time as what personal experience, he read Montaigne, II. xii, *Apologie de Raimond Sebond*. We should have, finally, to know something which is by hypothesis unknowable, for we assume it to be an experience which, in the manner indicated, exceeded the facts. We should have to understand things which Shakespeare did not understand himself.[126]

Scourge and Minister
A Study of Hamlet

By G. R. Elliott

G. R. Elliott, from *Scourge and Minister: A Study of Hamlet* (Durham, Duke University Press, 1951).

*T*HE *QUESTION* "Why does Hamlet delay, fatally for himself, the killing of Claudius?" is inseparable dramatically from another query: "Why does Claudis delay, fatally for himself, the killing of Hamlet?" Of course there is a very obvious ground of Claudius's delay so far as the first half of the drama is concerned. The new king conciliates his queen together with "the world" (I. ii. 108) by recognizing the son of her and the former king as crown prince. But soon we learn from the Ghost that Claudius had performed a quite unique feat: he had managed to murder his mighty predecessor with absolute secrecy. Surely he may very well do likewise to Hamlet later on. That is what we feel if we credit the specter's story and if we are as much interested (very many of us are not) as Shakespeare intended us to be in his fascinating Claudius. And our premonition is justified in the second half of the drama. There the king devises two clever schemes for disposing of his nephew without incurring suspicion on the part of the queen and Denmark: first, Hamlet's healthful voyage to England, to be climaxed by the beheading of him there; then his charmingly friendly, but fatal, fencing-match with Laertes. Both schemes are wonderfully specious, but especially the second; which is apparently so designed by the king as to rule out the unforeseen accidents, very regrettable from his standpoint, that nullified the first. The upshot is, however, that Hamlet is left alive long enough to unveil and destroy his enemy before he himself succumbs. Surely, then, we are intended to perceive that Claudius's second and last murder, in contrast with his first, is brilliantly unsuccessful. It is true that Hamlet dies because he postpones too long the killing of the king. But it is equally significant that Claudius dies because he postpones too long the killing of Hamlet.[xvi]

[An Analysis of Act III, Scene iii]

Now come two extraordinary and parallel soliloquies by king and prince, sudden, startling outbursts, yet all along carefully prepared for by the dramatist. Here the two men who [104] are the heads of the realm are heedless of that realm's fate and fortune.[25] They are morbidly concerned, each in his own way, with their private problems. And their self-centered emotions, though for the moment sincere, are strikingly unveracious. The two are not true to themselves and it follows "as the night the day" (I. iii. 79) that they are false to the interests of every man, of "those many many" (9) dependent upon them. The public spirit nobly shown by the prince in the first act, and by no means entirely lacking in the king, is here totally absent from both. The remorsefulness in which Claudius indulges is self-centered, irrelevant, and ineffectual. So is the revengefulness of Hamlet. The two protagonists are here swept by opposite waves of passionate feeling, which the poet

[25] The "massy wheel" above (17) would at once suggest to the Elizabethan audience the well-known Wheel of Fortune; and that audience would be keenly conscious of the king's and the prince's selfish disregard of the fortune of the kingdom, now in danger of "ruin" (22).

makes us understand fully and sympathize with—and condemn.

Claudius's preliminary fit of remorse (III. i. 49 ff.) gave
way quickly to his new sense of danger. His second and shattering
fit, at the close of the Play, has suffered much the same fate; so we
have gathered from his words to Rosencrantz and Guildenstern
above. Nevertheless, his present confession is very moving and, at
first, promising. In revulsion from his hypocritic mien to the devoted Polonius, "dear my lord" (35), who had unwittingly lashed
his conscience in III. i, he cries out suddenly, as soon as alone:

> Oh my offence is rank, it smells to heaven,
> It hath the primal eldest curse upon't,
> A brother's murther.

His "rank" sin, pervading with its stench the "undiscovered
country," the invisible realm of the spirit, has risen to "men's
eyes" (I. ii. 258) in the Play scene just because—the awed sinner
seeks now no further explanation of Hamlet's discovery—it is
known to and cursed by the "heaven" above, like Cain's uncon-
cealable crime. It is primarily a "fault to heaven" (I. ii. 101), not
to man, as Claudius has inwardly felt from the first. He admits
that fact plainly and fully now, laying aside [105] for the time being
all his accomplished hypocrisy. Prayer, therefore, is his "sharp"
and "strong" need (38-40). His guilt, however, is stronger. But it
can be overcome by the divine mercy. "Is there not rain enough in
the sweet heavens To wash it white as snow? [26] . . . Then I'll look
up, my fault is past."

But he knows he can have neither mercy nor any reality of
prayer unless he is willing to proceed from remorse to "repentance" (65).[27] Repentance means an entire turning away of his soul
from his sin, and therefore involves penance and restitution, a
giving up of the "effects" (54) for which he did the murder,
"My crown, mine own ambition, and my queen." Here his already
determined banishment of Hamlet recurs to us pointedly. The

---

[26] Mercy "droppeth as the gentle rain from heaven" (*Merchant of Venice*
IV. i. 185). Claudius's words reflect two passages in the Bible concerning
"rain" and "snow," Matthew 5:45 and Psalms 51:7.

[27] A very sharp distinction between remorse and repentance, as in orthodox
Christian thought, is prominent in Shakespeare's work from *Hamlet* on. The
theme culminates in the deadly remorse of Macbeth and his Lady, devoid of
any touch of real repentance. For a vivid allegorical treatment of the subject,
see *The Faerie Queene* I. x. 23-29.

present safety of Claudius requires it; but his soul's salvation, on
his own showing, requires the rescinding of it. He does not mention it, but it is certainly in the uneasy background of his mind
while he ponders, "May one be pardoned and retain th' offence?"
(56). Here the word "offence," finely prepared for in his opening
line (36), comprises both the sin and its "effects," notably the
throne, kept from Hamlet by "the wicked prize itself," i.e., by the
very power which the throne has conferred on Claudius:

> In the corrupted currents of this world
> Offence's gilded hand may shove by justice,
> And oft 'tis seen the wicked prize itself
> Buys out the law; but 'tis not so above:
> There is no shuffling, there the action lies
> In his true nature, and we ourselves compelled
> Even to the teeth and forehead of our faults
> To give-in evidence.

That keen image of the heavenly, above the earthly, justice is central in *The Tragedy of Hamlet, Prince of Denmark.* The speaker
uses the present tense: Judgment Day is here and now,[106] for all
men. It is so for Claudius himself. Not only does he confess his
past corruption; he is "compelled" by supernal power to give
"evidence" of his present "shuffling." He avoids all mention of
Hamlet. "What, then? What rests?" We know that the matter of
Hamlet's banishment, and of Hamlet's right to the throne, rests.
But Claudius shrinks from facing the "true nature" of the conduct now required of him by a real and just repentance.

Hence his climactic emotional agony. He tries to "repent"
without repenting (65-66). His "soul" is "limed," like a bird's
caught feet, with the yearning to retain his crown; that soul is only
the more "engaged" (69) by the beating of its wings. "Help,
angels"—those free and strong birds of heaven! We recall Hamlet's "Angels and ministers of grace" (I. iv. 39) as Claudius
kneels, perhaps before the crucifix where Ophelia (III. i. 89)
knelt and prayed for Hamlet, and as the prince himself enters the
scene, distantly. The king breathes "All may be well." Yes, it
still, though very doubtfully, "may be." For at the first his attitude in his ensuing prayer is "soft as sinews of the new-born
babe" (71).

And "how his audit stands who knows save heaven?" though "in our circumstance and course of thought 'Tis heavy with him" (82 ff.). These words, presently uttered by Hamlet in soliloquy regarding his dead father, apply realistically, for us, also to the present condition of Claudius, which (such is Shakespeare's art) is reflected unwittingly by the prince in his lines. And as Hamlet's soliloquy grows "horrid" (88), so, we are to observe, does the face of the kneeling king, unseen by Hamlet but visible to us. For now, doubly oblivious of the prince—of his bodily presence and of his right to the throne—the king listens more and more to the evil ambition within him. In commencing his prayer he adjured his "bosom black as death" (67); in the end, the prospect is open that, in Hamlet's words, "his soul may be as damned and black As hell" (94). For having seen the light, extraordinarily, he refuses to follow it, after painful "shuffling" (61). His fresh and firm evil determination is in the very rhythm of the two final lines of the scene: [107]

> My words fly up, my thoughts remain below;
> Words without thoughts never to heaven go.

In plain terms he will not do right to his nephew; he will not repent: his thoughts cannot "to heaven go."

Nor can the present thoughts of Hamlet himself "to heaven go." His soliloquy shows him at his lowest ebb, sharing in a remarkable degree the dishonesty that he hates in Claudius and in Claudius's Denmark. He enters this scene, as he left the preceding one, intent upon converting his mother before killing his uncle. Confronted by the kneeling figure, he recoils as violently as he did (I. v. 40) when he first learned from the Ghost that the murderer was the king of Denmark:

> Now might I do it pat, now he is praying,
> And now I'll do't; and so he goes to heaven;
> And so am I revenged: that would be scanned.

The three "now's" echo suggestively the three "now's" of his preceding speech, at the close of III. ii; and the heavy stress on the "might," sequel of the conditional "could" and "would" of that speech, lapses away as the sentence proceeds to its close like a falling wave. In fact his present speech is to be regarded as a continuation of the other: the two taken together form one soliloquy. At present we are shown, what we already know, that "now" is the time when he is precisely least inclined to "do't"; the third and final low-keyed "now," in the three lines quoted above, is in full tune with his "Soft, now, to my mother" (III. ii. 410). Hamlet's desire to go to her remains the most urgent of all his impulses since the Play scene. This impulse causes him to postpone the abhorrent regicide which is his public duty; and in regard to which he now becomes immensely dishonest with himself.

The postponement of his chief duty would not be fatal if Hamlet would frankly face the real cause of it. Instead he engages like Claudius in "shuffling," refusing to see "the action" in its "true nature" (61 f.). Blinded by pride, he will not admit to himself and to heaven that he is crucially evading the deed prerequisite for setting the time right. Instead he justifies himself by conjuring up an ideally *complete* revenge, to be [108] taken in the near future, a revenge *completely* out of keeping with his proper character and "course of thought" (83). Here, and here only, Hamlet is an absolute idealist, and a very bad one: his ideal, unlike himself, is blatantly trite, immoral, and unchristian. Yet he can throw his emotion into it fully, for the time being, because of his personal hatred of Claudius. Previously Shakespeare has shown us how natural, though bad, that hate was; here he shows us how extremely stultifying it can be. Hamlet has no jot of that charitable understanding of the wicked Claudius which Shakespeare has just given us so fully in the king's soliloquy. Accordingly the prince can make himself feel sincerely hesitant (85)

> To take him in the purging of his soul
> When he is fit and seasoned for his passage.

That time, in common charity, is exactly the right time for executing a criminal. But Hamlet's Christian humanity, as well as his sense of public justice, is overtopped by his personal hatred of the criminal. This hate bolsters emotionally his excuse for procrastination.

The gross outburst of that hate in the "bloody villain" passage (II. ii. 605-610), though quickly displaced by the just and temperate project of the Play, was, as we saw, not viewed by Hamlet in its "true nature" (62). He rebuked but did not uproot his primitive revengefulness. Therefore the gross passion remained latent in him. A few minutes ago it stirred in the "hot blood" verses (III. ii. 406-410); weakly, to be sure, but sufficiently to remind us of its existence. And now Hamlet can whip it up in support of an image more "horrid" (88) than the "horridly tricked" Pyrrhus (II. ii. 478) whom his soul abhorred. His imagination pictures Claudius taken in some act devoid of any "relish" of salvation (92):

> *Then* trip him, that his heels may kick at heaven
> And that his soul may be as damned and black
> As hell, whereto it goes.

This vision is as "rank and gross in nature" (I. ii. 136) as Claudius's own crime; it "smells to heaven" (36). Of course [109] it is factitious, a rationalization of the prince's present delay. But the pride that set him upon this invention and, more, the hate that inspires it are tragically real. Actually, then, it is Hamlet's absolute lack of charity for the man Claudius that prevents his timely execution of the criminal king.

In this scene, as a whole, Shakespeare displays the fact that true justice is charitable; that, in divine reality, "mercy seasons justice" (*Merchant of Venice* IV. i. 197)—tempers it and preserves its true quality. Both the protagonists manage to "shove by justice" (58), when it confronts them, by divorcing it from charity and mercy. Claudius, praying for mercy, is not taught by "that same prayer" to render to Hamlet a "deed of mercy" [28] which would also be a deed of plain justice. And Hamlet's conduct is as unjust as it is unmerciful. The ideal revenge which he proposes is not only blackly primitive but pettily domestic, irrelevant to his Denmark's needs: it is a substitute for just and timely action. The execution of Claudius here would have been at once just and merciful: it would have prevented his doing "further evil" (V. i. 70) to the commonweal and to his own soul. In short, this scene shows prince and king offending against "heaven"—against the spirit of just charity, of charitable justice.[29]

---

[28] *Merchant of Venice* IV. i. 201 f. Portia demonstrates that Shylock's procedure is equally unmerciful and unjust, but her legal details are unconvincing. In the present scene the principle is applied convincingly to the hero as well as to the villain of the piece. Shakespeare treats Hamlet with unswerving justice, consequently with a firmer and richer charity than appeared in the earlier play.

[29] Brutus, contrariwise, offends "heaven" by a theoretic imitation of charitable justice in killing Caesar. Brutus and Hamlet do not think too much: they think wrongly, each in his own way, each misled by unconfessed pride.

The close of the scene leaves us with acute premonitions as to what "heaven" and the two protagonists will do next. We perceive that the king is now ready to do a greater wrong than merely banishing Hamlet; for the contrite benevolence which he had previously maintained, though dwindlingly, for the prince is now, in effect, ended. And on the other hand the prince is prepared to perpetrate something violently rash. If he had deferred his regicide in that spirit of honest humility which he achieved before the Play, acutely aware of his own [110] shortcomings and his need of patient temperance, he would not have thrust his sword blindly through the arras in the next scene. At present he is indeed, this time without confessing it, in a mood that is "very proud, revengeful, ambitious, with more offences at my beck than I have thoughts to put them in" (III. i. 126 ff.). Now he is indeed, what he previously condemned, "passion's slave" (III. ii. 77). At this moment he can do a deed ruinously rash and wrong.[111]

Wilhelm Meister's Apprenticeship

By Johann Wolfgang von Goethe

Johann Wolfgang von Goethe, from *Wilhelm Meister's Apprenticeship* (1795–1796), Translated from the German of Goethe by Thomas Carlyle (1824) (London, Chapman and Hall Ltd., [187–]), 2 vols., vol. I; Book IV, Chapter XIII.

"CONCEIVE A PRINCE such as I have painted him, and that his father suddenly dies. Ambition and the love of rule are not the passions that inspire him. As a king's son he would have been contented; but now he is first constrained to consider the difference which separates a sovereign from a subject. The crown was not hereditary; yet a longer possession of it by his father would have strengthened the pretensions of an only son, and secured his hopes of the succession. In place of this, he now beholds himself excluded by his uncle, in spite of specious promises, most probably forever. He is now poor in goods and favour, and a stranger in the scene which from youth he had looked upon as his inheritance. His temper here assumes its first mournful tinge. He feels that now he is not more, that he is less, than a private nobleman; he offers himself as the servant of every one; he is not courteous and condescending, he is needy and degraded.

"His past condition he remembers as a vanished dream. It is in vain that his uncle strives to cheer him, to present his situation in another point of view. The feeling of his nothingness will not leave him.

"The second stroke that came upon him wounded deeper, bowed still more. It was the marriage of his mother. The faithful tender son had yet a mother, when his father passed away. He hoped, in the company of his surviving noble-minded parent, to reverence the heroic form of the departed; but his mother too he loses, and it is something worse than death that robs him of her. The trustful image, which a good child loves to form of its parents, is gone. With the dead [280] there is no help; on the living no hold. She also is a woman, and her name is Frailty, like that of all her sex.

"Now first does he feel himself completely bent and orphaned; and no happiness of life can repay what he has lost. Not reflective or sorrowful by nature, reflection and sorrow have become for him a heavy obligation. It is thus that we see him first enter on the scene. I do not think that I have mixed aught foreign with the piece, or overcharged a single feature of it.". . .

"Figure to yourselves this youth," cried he, "this son of princes: conceive him vividly, bring his state before your eyes, and then observe him when he learns that his father's spirit walks; stand by him in the terrors of the night, when the venerable ghost itself appears before him. A horrid shudder passes over him; he speaks to the mysterious form; he sees it beckon him; he follows it, and hears. The fearful accusation of his uncle rings in his ears; the summons to revenge, and the piercing oft-repeated prayer, Remember me!

"And when the ghost has vanished, who is it that stands before us? A young hero panting for vengeance? A prince by birth, rejoicing to be called to punish the usurper of his crown? No! trouble and astonishment take hold of the solitary young man; he grows bitter against smiling villains, swears that he will not forget the spirit, and concludes with the significant ejaculation:

> The time is out of joint: O cursed spite,
> That ever I was born to set it right!

"In these words, I imagine, will be found the key to Hamlet's whole procedure. To me it is clear that Shakespeare meant, in the present case, to represent the effects of a great [281] action laid upon a soul unfit for the performance of it. In this view the whole piece seems to me to be composed. There is an oak-tree planted in a costly jar, which should have borne only pleasant flowers in its bosom; the roots expand, the jar is shivered.

"A lovely, pure, noble and most moral nature, without the strength of nerve which forms a hero, sinks beneath a burden which it cannot bear and must not cast away. All duties are holy for him; the present is too hard. Impossibilities have been required of him; not in themselves impossibilities, but such for him. He winds, and turns, and torments himself; he advances and recoils; is ever put in mind, ever puts himself in mind; at last does all but lose his purpose from his thoughts; yet still without recovering his peace of mind." [282]

On the Use of Metaphors

By Oliver Goldsmith

Oliver Goldsmith, "On the Use of Metaphors" (1765), in *The Miscellaneous Works of Oliver Goldsmith,* James Prior, ed. (Philadelphia, 1875), vol. I.

*T*HE SOLILOQUY in *Hamlet* which we have so often heard extolled in terms of admiration, is, in our opinion, a heap of absurdities, whether we consider the situation,

the sentiment, the argument, or the poetry.[305] Hamlet is informed
by the ghost that his father was murdered and, therefore, he is
tempted to murder himself, even after he had promised to take
vengeance on the usurper and expressed the utmost eagerness to
achieve this enterprise. It does not appear that he had the least
reason to wish for death; but every motive which may be supposed to influence the mind of a young prince, concurred to render
life desirable—revenge towards the usurper; love for the fair
Ophelia; and the ambition of reigning. Besides, when he had an
opportunity of dying without being accessory to his own death;
when he had nothing to do but, in obedience to his uncle's command, to allow himself to be conveyed quietly to England, where
he was sure of suffering death; instead of amusing himself with
meditations on mortality, he very wisely consulted the means of
self-preservation, turned the tables upon his attendants and returned to Denmark. But granting him to have been reduced to the
lowest state of despondence, surrounded with nothing but horror
and despair, sick of this life and eager to attempt futurity, we
shall see how far he argues like a philosopher.

In order to support this general charge against an author so
universally held in veneration, whose very errors have helped to
sanctify his character among the multitude, we will descend to
particulars and analyse this famous soliloquy.

Hamlet, having assumed the disguise of madness, as a cloak
under which he might the more effectually revenge his father's
death upon the murderer and usurper, appears alone upon the
stage in a pensive and melancholy attitude and communes with
himself in these words:

To be, or not to be ? etc.

We have already observed that there is not any apparent circumstance in the fate or situation of Hamlet that should prompt
him to harbour [306] one thought of self-murder; and, therefore,
these expressions of despair imply an impropriety in point of
character. But, supposing his condition was truly desperate and he
saw no possibility of repose but in the uncertain harbour of death,
let us see in what manner he argues on that subject. The question
is: "To be, or not to be?", to die by my own hand, or live and
suffer the miseries of life. He proceeds to explain the alternative
in these terms: "Whether 'tis nobler in the mind to suffer, or

endure the frowns of fortune or to take arms and, by opposing, end them." Here he deviates from his first proposition and death is no longer the question. The only doubt is, whether he will stoop to misfortune or exert his faculties in order to surmount it. This, surely, is the obvious meaning and, indeed, the only meaning that can be implied in these words:

> Whether 'tis nobler in the mind to suffer
> The slings and arrows of outrageous fortune,
> Or to take arms against a sea of troubles
> And, by opposing, end them.

He now drops this idea and reverts to his reasoning on death in the course of which he owns himself deterred from suicide by the thoughts of what may follow death:

> the dread of something after death—
> That undiscover'd country, from whose bourne
> No traveller returns.

This might be a good argument in a heathen or pagan and such indeed Hamlet really was; but Shakespeare has already represented him as a good Catholic, who must have been acquainted with the truths of revealed religion and says expressly in this very play:

> had not the Everlasting fix'd
> His canon 'gainst self-murder.

Moreover, he had just [307] been conversing with his father's spirit, piping hot from purgatory, which we would presume is not within the *bourne* of this world. The dread of what may happen after death, says he

> Makes us rather bear those ills we have,
> Than fly to others that we know not of.

This declaration at least implies some knowledge of the other world and expressly asserts that there must be ills in that world, though what kind of ills they are we do not know. The argument, therefore, may be reduced to this dilemma: this world abounds with ills which I feel; the other world abounds with ills, the nature of which I do not know; therefore, I will rather bear those ills I have "than fly to others which I know not of": a deduction amounting to a certainty, with respect to the only circumstance that could create a doubt, namely, whether in death he should rest from his misery; and if he was certain there were evils in the next world, as well as in this, he had no room to reason at all about the matter. What alone could justify his thinking on this subject, would have been the hope of flying from the ills of this world, without encountering any others in the next.

Nor is Hamlet more accurate in the following reflection:

Thus conscience does make cowards of us all.

A bad conscience will make us cowards; but a good conscience will make us brave. It does not appear that anything lay heavy on his conscience and, from the premises, we cannot help inferring that conscience in this case was entirely out of the question. Hamlet was deterred from suicide by a full conviction that, in flying from one sea of troubles which he did know, he should fall into another which he did not know.

His whole chain of reasoning, therefore, seems inconsistent and incongruous.[308] "I am doubtful whether I should live or do violence upon my own life; for I know not whether it is more honourable to bear misfortune patiently, than to exert myself in opposing misfortune and, by opposing, end it." Let us throw it into the form of a syllogism, it will stand thus: "I am oppressed with ills; I know not whether it is more honourable to bear those ills patiently or to end them by taking arms against them; *ergo,* I am doubtful whether I should slay myself or live. To die is no more than to sleep; and *to say* that by a sleep we end the heartache, etc., 'tis a consummation devoutly to be wished." Now, to *say it,* was of no consequence unless it had been true. "I am afraid of the dreams that may happen in that sleep of death; and I choose rather to bear those ills that are almost insupportable in this life. I know not what is in the next, because it is an undiscovered country: *ergo,* I had rather bear those ills I have, than fly to others which I know not of." Here the conclusion is by no means warranted by the premises. "I am sore afflicted in this life; but I will rather bear the afflictions of this life, than plunge myself in the afflictions of another life; *ergo,* conscience makes cowards of us all." But this conclusion would justify the logician in saying, *negatur consequens;* for it is entirely detached from both the major and minor proposition.

This soliloquy is not less exceptionable in the propriety of expression than in the chain of argumentation. "To die—to sleep —no more," contains an ambiguity, which all the art of punctuation cannot remove; for it may signify that "to die" is to sleep no more; or the expression "no more" may be considered as an abrupt apostrophe in thinking, as if he meant to say "no more of that reflection."

"Ay, there's the rub," is a vulgarism beneath the dignity of Hamlet's character and the words that follow [309] leave the sense imperfect:

> For in that sleep of death what dreams may come,
> When we have shuffled off this mortal coil,
> Must give us pause.

Not the dreams that might come, but the fear of what dreams might come, occasioned the pause or hesitation. Respect in the same line may be allowed to pass for consideration; but

> The oppressor's wrong, the proud man's contumely

according to the invariable acceptation of the words wrong and contumely can signify nothing but the wrongs sustained by the oppressor and the contumely or abuse thrown upon the proud man; though it is plain that Shakespeare used them in a different sense; neither is the word spurn a substantive, yet as such he has inserted it in these lines:

> The insolence of office and the spurns
> That patient merit of the unworthy takes.

If we consider the metaphors of the soliloquy, we shall find them jumbled together in a strange confusion.

If the metaphors were reduced to painting, we should find it a very difficult task, if not altogether impracticable, to represent, with any propriety, outrageous fortune using her slings and arrows, between which, indeed, there is no sort of analogy in nature. Neither can any figure be more ridiculously absurd than that of a man taking arms against a sea, exclusive of the incongruous medley of slings, arrows and seas, jostled within the compass of one reflection. What follows is a strange rhapsody of broken images of sleeping, dreaming and shifting off a coil, which last conveys no idea that can be represented on canvas. [310]

A Critical Mousetrap

By W. W. Greg

W. W. Greg, "A Critical Mousetrap,[1] " in *A Book of Homage to Shakespeare,* Israel Gollancz, ed. (London, Oxford University Press, 1916).

THERE IS A POINT in connexion with the players' play in *Hamlet,* which, if significant at all, has certainly not received from commentators the attention it deserves. The orthodox and obvious interpretation of the action is, of course, familiar. King Claudius, who has disposed of his brother and predecessor by the very peculiar device of pouring poison into his ears, is witnessing the performance of a play which Hamlet facetiously calls the "Mousetrap." This reproduces in a remarkably complete manner the circumstances of his own crime, and when the critical moment arrives and he sees the most intimate details of his action represented before the assembled court, his nerve gives way and he rushes terror-stricken from the hall. It should be observed that his alarm must be ascribed solely to the action of the play, for the language is in no way significant.

Now, this interpretation is open to a most serious objection.

---

[1] Before the outbreak of the war made unwonted claims on the activities of so many harmless students, I had drafted a somewhat elaborate study of the problem propounded in the present note. But the criticisms of various friends to whom I submitted it convinced me that my presentation of the case required considerable modification before it could be passed as even moderately satisfactory. Not having found time for the necessary revision, I take this opportunity for a bald statement of the problem, hoping in a happier future to return to the subject at greater length. [For a fuller treatment of "the problem propounded in the present note" see W. W. Greg, "Hamlet's Hallucination," MODERN LANGUAGE REVIEW, XII (October 1917), 393–421.]

For the play itself is preceded by a dumb-show in which the whole action of the piece is minutely set forth. So far as the action is concerned, and it is the action alone that is significant, the play proper adds nothing new whatever. Consequently, on the assumptions usually made, either the King must have betrayed himself over the dumb-show, or there is no conceivable reason why he should betray himself at all. Incidentally, I must point out that there is no getting rid of the dumb-show, for not only is the textual tradition unassailable, but the spectators are actually made to comment upon this unusual feature of the performance.

So far as I can see there are only two possible lines for criticism to take. Either Shakespeare blundered badly in the crucial scene of the play, or else the orthodox interpretation is wrong. If the former, there [179] is no more to be said: but if logic goes for anything in dramatic criticism, then it follows from the action of the scene that it is not the stage poisoning that upsets the King, and consequently that Claudius did not poison his brother in the manner represented. But this immediately leads to a far more important conclusion. If the King did not murder his predecessor by pouring poison into his ears, then the account of the affair given by the Ghost to Hamlet is untrue; in other words, the Ghost's narrative is not a revelation from the dead but a figment of Hamlet's brain.

It will be obvious how important are the implications of this view and what difficulties are involved in its acceptance. I have not yet satisfied myself as to the exact extent of the difficulties, and I therefore put forward this note rather as a suggestion than as a formal proposition. On two cardinal points, however, I think I can indicate the direction in which a solution may be found.

We have for one thing to account for the obvious fact that the King does actually interrupt the performance of the players at the very moment of the murder. To Hamlet this is, of course, proof positive of the truth of his suspicions; but a careful examination of the scene will, I think, show that ample explanation of the King's action is afforded by the wild and menacing behavior of Hamlet himself. Then there is the ghostly interview to be considered. Is this scene, upon the orthodox assumptions, so satisfactory as to make us reject any alternative? Hardly: and to my mind an analysis of the Ghost's narrative supplies the very strongest and strangest confirmation of the theory here proposed. For it can, I believe, be shown that every point in the pretended revelation is but the reflection of something that we either know, or can reasonably infer, to be present in Hamlet's own mind including the minute and surprising details of the murder itself.[180]

The Poetry of Shakespeare's Plays

By F. E. Halliday

F. E. Halliday, from *The Poetry of Shakespeare's Plays* (London, Gerald Duckworth and Company, Ltd., 1954).

SHAKESPEARE WAS STILL a comparatively young man—he was only thirty-seven—when he wrote *Hamlet,* yet he was already the author of more than twenty plays and it is, perhaps, not altogether unprofitable to speculate on the position that he might hold in English literature today had he died in the first year of the seventeenth century. Where should we place the author of *Romeo and Juliet* and *A Midsummer Night's Dream,* of *Henry IV* and *Twelfth Night*—and the *Sonnets?* If we admit, as I think we must, that even without the later tragedies and romances he still remains our greatest poet and dramatist, we get a clearer conception of the immense pre-eminence of the man who was yet to write *Hamlet, Othello, Macbeth, Lear, Antony and Cleopatra* and *The Tempest.*[133]

Hamlet is the great landmark in Shakespeare's progress, standing like a rock, conspicuous and unmistakably defined, exactly in the middle of his career. In sheer bulk it is much the biggest of the plays; the hero is the most famous in all literature, partly because we all tend to identify ourselves with him, partly

because in Hamlet we seem to come closest to Shakespeare himself; the imagery is distinctive both in form and content; it is the
first of the series of great tragedies; and it is the first play in which
Shakespeare's mature style is clearly revealed. All his previous
work was, in a sense, a preparation for *Hamlet;* no other subject
had made such demands, and it is as though Shakespeare, feeling
himself at last equal to the task, decided that the time had come to
show the world what he really could do.

Such a play as he conceived, a tragedy of character in which
the tragic element is thrown into relief by a strain of comedy,
demands every variety of verse and every diversity of speed. In
the writing, therefore, he not only raised the poetry to a new pitch
of tragic intensity, but drew on all the previous styles, modifying
them, however, and subduing them to the theme, incorporating
them in the action and in character, making them, in a word,
completely dramatic, instead of employing them to fashion orna-
mental appendages and dazzling cadenzas.

The staple style, the norm by which all the others may be
judged, is the limpid and open-textured, steady and disciplined
verse of the preceding comedies and histories. This, for example,
might come from *Henry IV :*

> Who, dipping all his faults in their affection,
> Would, like the spring that turneth wood to stone,
> Convert his gyves to graces; so that my arrows,
> Too slightly timbered for so loud a wind,
> Would have reverted to my bow again
> And not where I had aimed them.

Of the slow grace of the early lyrical style there is Horatio's,

> But look, the morn, in russet mantle clad,
> Walks o'er the dew of yon high eastward hill.

Here it is dramatic, not only because the passage is short and [134]
controlled, but it is deliberately inserted to relieve the tension and
to bring to a quiet close the scene of the Ghost's first appearance.
The Queen's description of Ophelia's death, with its elegiac harmony of assonance and rhyme—*willow grows, shows, melodious,*
etc.—is a similar episode, lyrical in treatment, but intensely dramatic in its placing, the verbal music of Belmont applied to a

tragic theme. Even the pedantic lyrical-gnomic becomes dramatic—
and half-humorous—on the lips of Laertes:

> The canker galls the infants of the spring
> Too oft before their buttons be disclosed.

This is the sonnet poetry, but Shakespeare characteristically adds a
parallel in the current idiom:

> And in the morn and liquid dew of youth
> Contagious blastments are most imminent.

Hamlet's words to Horatio are something in the manner of the
detached rhetoric that we associate with the earliest plays:

> for thou hast been
> As one, in suffering all, that suffers nothing;
> A man that fortune's buffets and rewards
> Hast ta'en with equal thanks: and blest are those
> Whose blood and judgment are so well commingled
> That they are not a pipe for fortune's finger
> To sound what stop she please. Give me that man
> That is not passion's slave, and I will wear him
> In my heart's core, ay, in my heart of heart—

Hamlet begins by talking intimately to his friend, but soon appears almost to forget him and to address the audience instead.
But this again is dramatic, for such a process of thought, from the
particular to the general, is of the essence of Hamlet, who suddenly recollects himself and, turning to Horatio, adds, 'As I do
thee. Something too much of this.'

For Hamlet, Horatio is the personification of self-control and
moderation, virtues that he admires as much as he detests any
form of their opposing vices: self-indulgence and excess. Thus, he
loathes his uncle's debauchery and his mother's sensuality, and is
offended to the soul by any [135] intemperance of emotional display or extravagance of language, whether the verbiage of Polonius, the affectation of Osric, the ranting of Laertes, or the mouthing of the players. He exalts reason as much as he deplores passion:
'How noble in reason!' is his first exclamation in his panegyric of
man, 'in apprehension how like a god!' And again:

> Sure, he that made us with such large discourse,
> Looking before and after, gave us not
> That capability and god-like reason
> To fust in us unused.

Yet he himself is passion's slave, and there is tragic irony in his inability to control his emotions, and pathos in his disgust at his own excesses; his fastidious nature is revolted by the way in which he unpacks his heart with words and curses, like a whore, a very drab, a scullion, and when the Ghost interrupts his almost insane onslaught on his mother he knows that it has come to chide him for being 'lapsed in time and passion.'

But Hamlet's rant is very different from the fustian of the braggarts of the early histories; it is not a sustained and monotonous fortissimo, but a controlled intensity of utterance—controlled, that is, by Shakespeare—and it is Hamlet's passionate speech, before it declines into a mere rhapsody of words, that most strikingly evinces the new element in Shakespeare's dramatic poetry. There is nothing in the earlier plays to equal the compression, intensity, and speed of this:

> Rebellious hell,
> If thou canst mutine in a matron's bones,
> To flaming youth let virtue be as wax
> And melt in her own fire: proclaim no shame
> When the compulsive ardour gives the charge,
> Since frost itself as actively doth burn,
> And reason pandars will.

Or the fluid rhythm and melody of this:

> What is he whose grief
> Bears such an emphasis? whose phrase of sorrow
> Conjures the wandering stars and makes them stand
> Like wonder-wounded hearers? [136]

Or, in a quieter vein, there is nothing comparable to the restless imagery of his great soliloquy:

> And thus the native hue of resolution
> Is sicklied o'er with the pale cast of thought,
> And enterprises of great pitch and moment
> With this regard their currents turn awry
> And lose the name of action.

And always this heady poetry is contrasted with a slow lyrical passage. Thus Hamlet stoops from the highest pitch of his assault to,

> Save me, and hover o'er me with your wings,
> You heavenly guards! What would your gracious figure?

and the Queen follows his physical and verbal assault on Laertes
with,

> Anon, as patient as the female dove
> When that her golden couplets are disclosed
> His silence will sit drooping.

For certain effects Shakespeare employs or creates a distinctive
verse. Thus the Ghost speaks a solemn and spacious variety of the
middle style, made strangely stiff and formal by its repetitive
rhetorical structure:

> Thus, was I, sleeping, by a brother's hand
> Of life, of crown, of queen, at once dispatch'd:
> Cut off even in the blossoms of my sin,
> Unhousel'd, disappointed, unaneled. . . .

'The Murder of Gonzago' is in archaic, sententious, and monotonous couplets, but 'Aeneas' tale to Dido' is in the epic manner of
Henry V. This is generally said to be in the antiquated and turgid
style of Marlowe, whose *Dido, Queen of Carthage,* written in
collaboration with Nashe, contains a Virgilian description of the
fall of Troy. It is certainly turgid, but no more so than Henry V's
threat to the citizens of Harfleur, and there is nothing in the verse
of *Dido* that approaches the rhythm of Shakespeare's,

> The rugged Pyrrhus, he whose sable arms,
> Black as his purpose, did the night resemble
> When he lay couched in the ominous horse,
> Hath now this dread and black complexion smear'd
> With heraldry more dismal . . .[137]

The idiom, too, is that of Shakespeare's middle period, and the
whole a fine example of the epic verse in which not only *Henry V*
but much of *Troilus and Cressida* as well is written, and where,
indeed, Hector's sword-play is described in terms almost identical
with those of Pyrrhus's.

The peculiar imagery of *Hamlet*, its compound form and its
dominant figure of disease, is noticed elsewhere, but there is another image which seems generally to escape attention, although
it is curiously insistent and related to the main one—that of a gun
or of a concealed explosive charge. Laertes warns Ophelia to keep
out of the 'shot and danger of desire,' the king compares slan-

der's whisper to the 'poisoned shot' of a cannon, the volley of bad news to that of a 'murdering-piece,' and proposes the second stratagem of the poisoned cup if the first should 'blast in proof.' Then Hamlet talks of lungs that are 'tickle o' the sere,' of 'slings' or culverin, of words 'too light for the bore of the matter,' and one of the most memorable images in the play is his:

> For 'tis the sport to have the enginer
> Hoist with his own petar: and 't shall go hard
> But I will delve one yard below their mines,
> And blow them at the moon.

He has already employed the image of the sapper when he calls his father's ghost 'a worthy pioner,' and Shakespeare's association of disease with mines, primarily military but by extension industrial, is made clear by Hamlet's 'ulcerous place . . . mining all within,' and by the king's,

> But like the owner of a foul disease,
> To keep it from divulging, let it feed
> Even on the pith of life. Where is he gone?

to which the queen—quite falsely—replies,

> To draw apart the body he hath kill'd:
> O'er whom his very madness, like some ore
> Among a mineral [mine] of metals base,
> Shows itself pure.

Again, the king's simile of the murdering-piece follows imme-diately after a double metaphor of infection and [138] pestilence, and his image of the gun blasting in proof is separated from that of the ulcer by only a few lines.

It is dramatically important that Claudius should be a for-midable opponent; we must feel that Hamlet is confronted physi-cally with a difficult task or his delay will make us merely impatient; the smaller the stature of the king the smaller that of Hamlet. That Claudius is an adulterer and a murderer is of the essence of the play, the main premise on which the rest depends; Hamlet calls him 'a mildewed ear,' 'a vice of kings,' a 'bloody, bawdy villain,' but Hamlet is, to put it moderately, prejudiced, and in a less frenzied mood he calls him a 'mighty opposite.' The truth is that Shakespeare is at pains to show us the better qualities

of the king; though he is a deep drinker he can carry his Rhenish
and we never see him drunk; though he seduced Gertrude his love
seems to be more than sensual appetite; and though he murdered
his brother he tries to repent. It is not suggested that Claudius is
not vicious, but he has his virtues too; he is clever, quick-witted,
resolute and brave, and we must do him justice if we are to do
justice to Hamlet. Shakespeare does so, and as he makes tragic
heroes of Macbeth and King John by the poetry that he gives
them to speak, so does he make Claudius a more worthy opponent
of Hamlet:

> In the corrupted currents of this world
> Offence's gilded hand may shove by justice,
> And oft 'tis seen the wicked prize itself
> Buys out the law: but 'tis not so above;
> There is no shuffling . . .

The speech illustrates another quality of the poetry: the pervasive
assonance, a threatening and muttered undertone of short *u*'s that
runs throughout as prologue to the omen coming on. Thus, the
principal assonantal sequence of Claudius—*corrupted currents,
justice, shuffling, shove, above*—remarkably resembles that of
Hamlet's soliloquy, two of the words, indeed, being common to
both: *suffer, troubles, shuffled, undiscovered country, puzzles, currents, rub, grunt.*

As another example there is the king's,[139]

> the people muddied,
> Thick and unwholsome in their thoughts and whispers,
> For good Polonius' death; and we have done but greenly
> In hugger-mugger to inter him: poor Ophelia
> Divided from herself and her fair judgment. . . .

And in prose there is Hamlet's, 'It is such a kind of gain-
giving as would perhaps trouble a woman.'

This subdued and ominous utterance is only one element in
the pervading atmosphere, not so much of revenge and blood, as
of mystery; another is the poetry as a whole. All poetry is mysterious both in its origin and in itself, and the greater the poetry
the more moving and disturbing its remote significances and
strange reverberations of meaning. But Shakespeare was himself
haunted by the mysteries of life and death, and nowhere does he

express this feeling more powerfully and more beautifully than in *Hamlet*, particularly, of course, in the character of Hamlet himself, and this is perhaps the main secret of the almost universal appeal of the tragic hero and his poetry.

Hamlet describes this feeling when he compares himself to a recorder, his 'mystery,' of course, being very much more than his secret knowledge of his father's murder: 'You would play upon me; you would seem to know my stops; you would pluck out the heart of my mystery; you would sound me from my lowest note to the top of my compass: and there is much music in this little organ; yet cannot you make it speak.' Then, in the more powerful medium of verse:

> What may this mean,
> That thou, dead corse, again in complete steel
> Revisit'st thus the glimpses of the moon,
> Making night hideous; and we fools of nature
> So horridly to shake our disposition
> With thoughts beyond the reaches of our souls?

> The dread of something after death,
> The undiscover'd country from whose bourn
> No traveller returns.

Yet Hamlet dies on a note of certitude, his assurance emphasized by the unexpected latinisms so exquisitely set between lines of homely monosyllables: [140]

> If thou didst ever hold me in thy heart,
> Absent thee from felicity awhile,
> And in this harsh world draw thy breath in pain,
> To tell my story.

It is out of this poetry, this synthesis of lyric, epic and elegy, subdued and made dramatic, that the best-loved of Shakespeare's characters is fashioned; for by now it is axiomatic that poetry is character, and this poetry *is* Hamlet.[141]

The Hamlet Controversy
Was Hamlet Mad?

From *The Hamlet Controversy. Was Hamlet Mad?* or, The Lucubra-
tions of Messrs. Smith, Brown, Jones and Robinson (Melbourne,
H. T. Dwight, 1867).

MR. WALTER MONTGOMERY'S "HAMLET"

TO THE EDITOR of the Argus.

Sir—So many queries have been addressed to me, both personally
and by letter, with respect to Mr. Montgomery's *Hamlet,* that I
will venture, with your permission, to reply to them through the
columns of the *Argus.*

Let me premise that every *Hamlet* of note I have ever seen
has been largely affected by, if it has not faithfully reflected, the
temperament of the actor. Mr. Montgomery's *Hamlet* is no exception to the rule. It is essentially lymphatic. The portrait he presents
to us is that of an amiable, affectionate, self-indulgent, plaintive,
and somewhat lachrymose *Prince.* He brings out in strong relief
the vacillating, wayward, irresolute, and half-hearted traits in
Hamlet's character. He shows him to be unstable as water, as
variable as the clouds, as inconstant as the moon. His melancholy
is not so deeply seated as to render him incapable of fugitive
moods of cheerfulness. He can be diverted from his purpose by
trivial incidents, and find a pretext for procrastination in dreamy
reveries. His grief is the indulgence of a weak mind, and not an
influential principle of action operating upon a strong [3] one. It
is content to expend itself in "the windy suspiration of forced
breath." When it should serve as a goad or a spur, it is found to
restrain him like a curb. Were his nature less gracious, his manner
less urbane, and his speech less gentle, we should be provoked to
despise him as a poor shiftless creature, who is always "letting

'I dare not' wait upon 'I would,' like the poor cat i' the adage." He exhibits none of the "stern effects" of which *Hamlet* speaks, and which actors of greater vigour have been accustomed to display; but, on the other hand, he reveals to us—which some of them do not—the deep undercurrent of affection which he supposes the *Prince* to entertain for *Ophelia*, the mental pang which he imagines that *Hamlet* experiences on discovering her prevarication, and the profound reluctance which he conceives the *Prince* must feel in renouncing, from a sense of duty and in disregard of the dictates of his heart, the passion he has cherished for her. Mr. Montgomery's is an eminently agreeable and thoroughly artistic *Hamlet*. It is most effective where other representatives of the character have been least so; and it is comparatively unimpressive in those scenes—the interview with the *Ghost,* and the closet scene, for example—in which previous actors, and Mr. Anderson especially so, have made their strongest points, and produced their most powerful impressions. In both these instances Mr. Montgomery presents us with a striking picture of mental abstraction when, as I think, it should be one of mental absorption. His mood of mind is subjective, when it should be objective. He is occupied with his own meditations when every nerve might be supposed to be strung to the highest tension, and every faculty wholly engrossed by the awful apparition, the hour, the place, and the astounding nature of the revelation made to him by the "dread corse." Thus much is obvious from the text; and it derives additional sanction from the traditions of the stage, handed down to us from the time in which Shakespeare played the *Ghost* in his own tragedy, and is reported to have instructed Burbage in the part of *Hamlet,* and reproved Kemp for his "villanous" gagging. How Garrick bore himself [4] in presence of the spirit we know from Partridge's ingenious remark in *Tom Jones;* and I think we may accept Shakespeare and Garrick as high authorities on this point, and may be justified, in this wise, for disputing the wisdom and propriety of innovations which have nothing to recommend them beyond the fact of their novelty. If the foundations of *Hamlet's* reason are not —as two such experts as Drs. Bucknill and Conolly assert they are —overthrown by the appalling revelation which has been just made to him by the *Ghost;* if he does not join together—as Coleridge, as M. Villemain, and as nearly all the great critics, Eng-

lish, German, and French, declare he does—"the light of reason,
the cunning of intentional error, and the involuntary disorder of
the soul," his mind was unquestionably unsettled; while, physi-
cally, he appears to have been in a state of hysteria. Not otherwise
can we account for the unfilial and scoffing language which he
employs towards his father, which are so significant of *Hamlet's*
state of mind, and which Mr. Montgomery, strange to stay, altogether omits. They are these:

> HAM. Ha, ha, boy! say'st thou so? Art thou there, Truepenny?
> Come on, you hear this fellow in the cellarage.

And again—

> Well said, old mole! Canst work i' the earth so fast?
> A worthy pioneer.

So, too, in the play scene. Mr. Montgomery cuts out whole passages which are not less demonstrative of a disordered intellect,
and not less important aids to the spectator, who is anxious to
divine the true condition of the *Prince's* mind. The lines excised are
these:—

> HAM. Would not this, sir, and a forest of feathers (if the rest of my
> fortunes turn Turk with me), with two Provençal roses on my
> razed shoes, get me a fellowship in a cry of players, sir?
> HOR. Half a share.
> HAM. A whole one, ay.
>> For thou dost know, O Damon dear,
>> This realm dismantled was
>> Of Jove himself, and now reigns here
>> A very, very—peacock.

This extravagance of conduct and language, it will be observed, is exhibited when none but *Horatio* is present, and when
no [5] necessity exists for acting the madman; while the flightiness
of the couplet—

> For if the *King* like not the comedy,
> Why, then, belike—he likes it not, perdy—

resembles that of many of *Madge Wildfire's* crazy speeches.

In the purely colloquial passages of the play Mr. Montgomery is very happy; and while, in the "business" of the piece, he

does not refuse to adopt what has been ingrafted upon it by his predecessors, he gives proof of originality of conception, and endeavors, indeed, to clear up some obscurities of the text by the light which his action projects upon them. Thus, he mitigates the apparent harshness of *Hamlet's* language and conduct to *Ophelia,* in the first scene of the second act, by conveying to the audience, as explicitly as possible, the assurance of the fact that the *King* and his *Chamberlain* are eaves-dropping behind the arras; while he also renders broadly manifest the shock communicated to the *Prince's* moral nature when he discovers *Ophelia* to have paltered with the truth by declaring that her father is at home at the very moment she is aware of his being an ear-witness of all that passes in her interview with her royal lover. Mr. Montgomery represents *Hamlet* as actuated by conflicting emotions throughout the entire scene—grieved and exasperated by *Ophelia's* complicity in the espionage to which he is exposed, but still yearning towards her with a tenderness that transforms wrath into pity, and that converts the injunction, "Get thee to a nunnery," into a loving admonition, springing either from the conviction that there she would find a haven of security and repose, or from the selfishness which would prompt him to debar others from winning that place in her affections which he had held, and had voluntarily, but reluctantly, vacated. Elegant and agreeable, however, as this is, there is nothing either in the text or the stage directions to warrant it; and harsh, violent, and cruel as *Hamlet's* language and demeanor are towards *Ophelia,* they are strictly natural, and are perfectly appropriate to his state of mind. Shakespeare well knew that in cases of mental disease or distemper, the sufferer hates and distrusts, upbraids and abuses, those whom, in mental health, he has [6] loved and esteemed; just as—to digress for a moment— pure-minded women, if they become insane, will indulge in the lewdest conversation. And hence the dramatist, with a rare knowledge of intellectual disorder, puts snatches of coarse ballads into the mouth of the mad *Ophelia.* Therefore any display of tenderness toward her in the particular scene referred to, say softening down of his brutality, must be, as Dr. Conolly justly observes, "an unauthorized departure from the delineation of his character by Shakespeare." I think that experienced physician's criticism of this part of the play is one of the best ever penned; and it derives the utmost weight from his professional experience. *"Hamlet's* expressions," he writes, "from the commencement of his directly addressing *Ophelia,* are all of the tissue of a madman's talk, with no clearly determined applications to immediate circumstances, and addressed by a disturbed mind and heart to the empty air, or to the shadows of images crowding among his troubled thoughts. They contain unconnected allusions to himself, broken reflections unconsciously wounding *Ophelia,* starts of general suspicion, and sudden threats which flash and disappear, but which would have been carefully refrained from if there had been only deception intended to make the path to vengeance clear. If we would unravel all these mingled expressions, we find that it is scarcely of *Ophelia* that *Hamlet* is speaking thus wildly, but of his mother, of her detested marriage, and of his own conscious imperfections; all these things are tinging his discourse, but giving it no true colour."

Furthermore, Mr. Montgomery is wrong, I conceive, in his delivery—graceful and pleasing though it is—of the well-known soliloquy, "To be or not to be"; which is not the philosophical speculation of a Cato or a Seneca, but the passionate utterance of a soul at war with life, but dreading death, and agonised by the struggle between these two sentiments. With these abatements, and with the general objection that Mr. Montgomery does not allow *Hamlet* to exhibit that "exaggerated energy under provocation" of which mild and sensitive natures like his are peculiarly capable, and in which the *Prince* indulges as often as his indignation [7] gets the better of his indecision, the portraiture is graphic, consistent, and harmonious; deficient in power, but careful in finish and delicate in detail. If I were to borrow an illustration from a sister art, I should liken the picture to a clever watercolour drawing, lacking the depth and solidity of an oil-painting, but compensating for the absence of these by the presence of other qualities—by airiness of tone, simplicity of treatment, transparency of colour, lightness of touch, and a certain sobriety of effect —a pleasant twilight, equally removed from the gloom of evening and the garishness of the afternoon.

In brief, Mr. Montgomery tones down the roughness and violence of the poet's *Hamlet,* and presents him to us *en beau.* It is not *Hamlet* the moody, with a wildness that is half false, and a madness that is half real; the misanthropical, the vindictive, with a thin crust of courtly culture overlying the fundamental coarseness of his race, and broken up by fitful eruptions of fiery and ungovernable passion; but *Hamlet,* the lover, *Hamlet* the dawdling dreamy *fainéant, Hamlet* the débonnaire, *Hamlet* with a large infusion of Werther. I am indisposed to disparage it on that account. It is the actor's own conception of the character, and he is to be commended for thinking it out, and for embodying it in a concrete and consistent form. Let us be just to him, and let us be equally just to other actors who offer us the fruits of their genius, their study, their observation, and experience, even although we differ from them in the reading of a passage or the idea of a part.

James Smith [8]

To the Editor of the Argus

Sir—. . . Freely translated, and highly condensed, Mr. Smith's letter appears to me to consist of some such declaration as this:— "Mr. Montgomery is passable, and that is about all; he walks quietly through his part, and reads fairly enough, and—*voila tout.*" If you submit this letter of mine to a similar process of transmutation, it may declare to this effect:—That Mr. Montgomery, being strongly impressed with the prevailing fault of actors in making their characters only pieces of stage-mechanism, more or less skilful or clumsy, has determined on presenting them as living and breathing things, having human passions and prejudices, and so expressing these, not according to arbitrary models, but in obedience to that kind of impulse from which all the greatest works of art result.

Taking Mr. Smith's letter in detail, however, I find that he begins by informing an anxious public that "every *Hamlet* of note has been largely affected by, if it has not faithfully reflected, the temperament of the actor"; and that Mr. Montgomery's temperament is "essentially lymphatic," and I assert, on the contrary, that [9] it is principally of the nervo-sanguineous kind. I assert, further—and in so asserting do but declare what innumerable examples have proved to be an invariable truth—that it would be simply impossible for a man whose temperament was "essentially lymphatic" ever to attain to eminence as an actor in any line of his art, if even the desire for distinction should exist, which is not very likely. So far, therefore, from Mr. Montgomery's *Hamlet* "faithfully reflecting" his temperament, it is an instance of complete subordination of temperament to the necessities of the character. The endeavor, therefore, to explain his acting as consistent with a "lymphatic temperament" needs no reply, as it is nothing else than drawing a conclusion from false data. "But," says Mr. Smith, "Mr. Montgomery's is an eminently agreeable *Hamlet.*" Logically, then, as, according to Mr. Smith, it is vastly different from all other *Hamlets,* I might remind him that this admission leaves us to infer that all preceding *Hamlets* have been eminently disagreeable. But without insisting on this inference, and conceding that this is not precisely what he desires to say, I go on with the letter, and presently find myself in a fog; for one of the reasons adduced to demonstrate this quality of eminent agreeableness is that Mr. Montgomery's *Hamlet* is "comparatively unimpressive in those scenes—the interview with the *Ghost,* and the closet scene, for example—in which previous actors, and Mr. Anderson especially so, have made their strongest points"; and then we are told "Mr. Montgomery presents us with a striking picture of mental abstraction," which we are further informed should have been "mental absorption," and that the state of his mind is "subjective" instead of "objective." I have no doubt that many waverers in opinion about Mr. Montgomery, and Mr. Montgomery's *Hamlet,* wavered no longer when they got to this part of Mr. Smith's letter; because, you see, though this imposing array of the terms "abstraction," "absorption," "subjective," and "objective," may convey no information whatever to a great many of Mr. Smith's readers, they are dictionary words so formidable and important, that they are sure to have created a profound impression. You remember the story of some highly impressible old ladies who always used to weep whenever they [10] heard the Rev. Mr. Whitfield pronounce the word "Mesopotamia." There was no reason in the world why the old ladies should weep at the word Mesopotamia, any more that, let us say, at the word "pickles"; but the fact remains that they did weep; and the fact will also remain that conviction will have followed, with an equal reason for following, the abstraction-absorption-subjective-objective appeal. Then Mr. Smith says, with a triumphant sort of flourish, "Thus much is obvious from the text"; but I confess, with great humiliation at the consciousness of my incapacity, that I do not here see what is obvious, and that I do not know what portion of the text should make it so. But since Mr. Smith follows up the remark by telling us that, as the traditions of the stage have been handed down from the time of Shakespeare, who instructed Burbage and reproved Kemp, and that as *Tom Jones* tells us how Garrick bore himself in the part, we are justified in disputing the wisdom and propriety of certain innovations, his admirers will dispute accordingly.

Next he brings in Drs. Bucknill and Conolly, two most learned physicians and graceful writers, it is true, but who, having been exclusively engaged many years in the treatment of lunatics, manifestly, and perhaps not unnaturally, came at last to consider madness an inevitable condition of humanity, and so found that *Hamlet,* despite his frequent protestation to the contrary, was really mad, the particular proof of his madness consisting in using "unfilial and scoffing language toward his father." I should be afraid to say how many young gentlemen in Victoria are mad, if the use of unfilial and scoffing language towards their fathers is positive proof thereof. But, without staying to inquire how far it might be desirable to make provision for the accommodation of thirty or forty thousand additional lunatics prospectively on the enforcement of this principle, let us see how it applies to *Hamlet,* who, Mr. Smith says, is to be deemed insane because he accosts the subterranean ghost jocularly. It is probably in the experience of every person to have felt an irrepressible desire in certain moments of great solemnity to laugh or utter a jest, or indulge in some grimace or antic, preposterously inconsistent with the time and [11] place. It would seem as the excessive restraint imposed by the circumstances prompted a relief in some shape; and thus it is found sometimes at funerals, that remarks are made strangely at variance with the sombre surroundings. Conformably with this propensity *Hamlet,* who has just experienced a very agony of terror at the sight of his father's spirit, finds much relief in passing, even for a moment, to the extreme state of playful sportiveness. But this feeling Shakespeare very properly makes only a transient one, for, after letting *Hamlet* allude to the ghost as "this fellow in the cellarage," and "an old mole i' the ground," his reverential feelings are allowed again to predominate, and he exclaims, "Rest, rest, perturbed spirit." I do not doubt that Mr. Montgomery's own judgment would incline him to the restoration of these passages of jocularity; and, I dare say, it is only in unavoidable deference to the prejudices of the audience, who have so long been accustomed to a mutilated version, that for a time he consents to follow the beaten track. So again Mr. Smith informs us that the jubilant exclamation beginning with

> For thou dost know, O Damon dear,

is "not less demonstrative of a disordered intellect"; in answer to which I may reply that nothing is more common than for a person suddenly made aware of the successful termination of an experiment, or enterprise, to indulge in a mock-tragic demonstration, a bit of extemporised recitative, a snatch of some song—for *Hamlet* might consistently sing these lines—a quotation from Scripture, however irreverently applied, or any other interjectional mode of testifying satisfaction. For the moment, *Hamlet's* delight at the perfect success of his murder-test overcomes every other feeling, and being, as we know, a humourist as well as a philosopher, he bids *Horatio* congratulate him, and asks him if he does not think he was made an actor? There is certainly nothing inconsistent with sanity in all this; and Mr. Montgomery, I am sure, does not omit these lines because they are inconsistent with *Hamlet's* reason, but because some excisions being necessary, these seem to permit of being excised without material impairment of the rest. Mr. Smith's usually [12] careful attention, however, has been at fault for him not to have observed that Mr. Montgomery does *not* omit the couplet beginning "For if the king," &c. Mr. Smith can only describe Mr. Montgomery's singularly original rendering of the scene with *Ophelia* as "elegant and agreeable," although it throws such a light upon the meaning of the whole passage, and gives such a colour of justification for the rudeness that comes subsequently. He says:—"There is nothing either in the text or the stage directions to warrant it"; *ergo,* I presume, it is unwarrantable. But, on the other hand, there is certainly nothing either in the text or stage directions to forbid it; and I need hardly say how abundant are the examples in the representation of Shakespeare's plays, in which stage business has been introduced admirably auxiliary to the elucidation of the text, but without any basis of warrant in the way of stage directions in the original. If

Shakespeare's own prompter's copy of his plays is ever found, we may haply light upon a good deal of information as to the manner in which they were represented: failing this, it is open to every actor, while keeping strictly within the limits of the approved text, to adopt the best mode his judgment may point out to give it emphasis and intelligibility.

Briefly to sum up my opinions of the condition of *Hamlet's* mind, and *malgré* Dr. Conolly, Dr. Bucknill, Coleridge, Villemain, and—Mr. James Smith, I have to remark that *Hamlet's* own declaration of his motive—namely, that he simulates madness the better to compass his purpose—is by far the most reasonable estimate to entertain of his mental condition. He is eccentric, fitful, vacillating, or, as Mr. Smith would put it, given to the "subjective" rather than the "objective"; but what then? If these qualities be attributes of madness, then is the world a lunatic asylum, and certificates of insanity are but insolent assumptions of power by the majority as against the minority of lunatics. . . .

John Brown [13]

To the Editor of the Argus

Sir—As I have reason to anticipate that a large number of persons are about to inquire of my opinion of Mr. Montgomery's *Hamlet,* I will venture, with your permission, to reply to them through the columns of the *Argus.*

After the elaborate letter from Mr. James Smith which appeared in your issue of yesterday, it is scarcely necessary for me to premise that, were not my convictions materially opposed to those of that practised critic, I should not now address you. However, it so [14] happens that I differ from him almost *in toto,* and cannot conceal my gratification at finding, by to-day's *Argus,* that so excellent an authority as Mr. John Brown has arrived at a conclusion very similar to my own. I dissent from Mr. Smith's *dicta* relative to Mr. Montgomery; I protest against his assumptions regarding the character of *Hamlet.* Mr. Brown has replied to Mr. Smith convincingly upon most of the topics contained in his letter; and I now modestly desire to unfold myself upon one or two points which Mr. Brown has thought proper to treat with indifference.

Mr. Smith's principal cause of complaint against Mr. Montgomery is, that he does not represent *Hamlet* as really mad—that, in short, he takes *Hamlet's* word in preference to that of many of his critics, and believes that he

> essentially is not in madness,
> But mad in craft.

This, which to Mr. Smith is so serious a ground of offence, is to me Mr. Montgomery's surpassing merit. Nothing can be easier than to represent *Hamlet* as an occasional madman. The actor—incapable of comprehending the full scope of *Hamlet's* varied and complex character, disinclined to piece out and supplement the meagre stage directions which accompany the text—falls back upon the ready plea of madness, and in a moment finds an excuse for his wildest extravagances, his densest stupidities. Any meaning, or no meaning, can with ease be covered by it. Does the *Prince* seem to be gratuitously harsh and cruel to *Ophelia*—it is his madness. Is he apparently merry where good Monsieur Critic thinks he should be doleful, and sad where he should be playful—it is his madness. For resourceless actor and soulless critic, this is alike a city of refuge. But it is a Zoar which cannot much longer be tolerated, and, spite of the illustrious names gilding the imposture, it will come to be regarded as a remnant of the system of false criticism of which Nahum Tate is the arch-apostle, which seeks to twist the mighty utterances of Shakespeare into harmony with foregone conclusions, rather than reverently to investigate, by the best light the age can furnish, the true meaning of his grand creations. And in setting about this task, we must not forget that Shakespeare's plays [15] are eminently acting plays; that if we have but capable actors, the enjoyment derivable from the presentation of these dramas on the stage must far surpass that to be obtained from closest study. But, though conceived with an immediate eye to theatrical exhibition, and fitted for the stage as are no other dramatic compositions, they are singularly barren of stage direction. When *Hamlet* requests young *Osric* to "put his bonnet to its right use," we are informed for the first time that the latter has entered bare-headed; and so when *Macduff* is besought not to hide his face with his hat, but to give sorrow vent, the earliest intimation is conveyed of the natural action which marked his reception of the news of his irreparable loss. In these cases

the "business" of the scene is unmistakable; but there are others
of equal importance where it is more obscure. Among these I
rank such scenes as that between *Hamlet* and *Ophelia* in the third
act; and in these it is not only justifiable, but it is the bounden duty
of every actor of mark to study to discover in what way the "business" may be made best conducive to the elucidation of the text.
When Shakespeare was by to explain his own ideal, it mattered
not that the stage directions were few and meagre; but now, when
instead of Shakespeare we have stage tradition, burdened with the
fancies of two and a half centuries, the omission of these finger-
posts becomes an important feature, and every original actor must
seek by study of the text, and perhaps the text alone, to reconstruct
them. It is this which Mr. Montgomery seems to me to have done,
and in this way he has produced a *Hamlet* perfectly sane and consistent with human nature, though not, perhaps, the model, orthodox, methodical character which, if he is not to be mad, some
critics would have him be.

The more closely I look into this character of *Hamlet* the
more revolting does the assumption of semi-madness appear. Was
there ever mind more thoroughly sane? It is so sane that it cannot
take a leap in the dark, though prompted to it by almost ungovernable impulse, but must have

> grounds
> More relative than this.

It is so sane that, when firmly resolved on a course which it
clearly [16] sees to be right, it adheres to it in spite of the most
terrible obstacles, as witness the scene in the *Queen's* chamber,
where, though *Hamlet* has by an unhappy chance killed the father
of her he loves, he yet, with almost ruthless decision, continues
the interview with his mother, and strives to make her

> Repent what's past, avoid what is to come.

If his be madness, it is of a strange nature, which can be pre-
arranged by himself, and put on or off as his purpose serves. The
passages Mr. Smith quotes in token of *Hamlet's* craziness might
well be incorporated in the current acting copy, without in the
slightest degree impairing the conception of the character which
Mr. Montgomery presents to us. Besides, Mr. Smith proves too

much. If *Hamlet* be mad when he asks if the success of his "mouse-trap" scheme might not get him "a fellowship in a cry of players," *Horatio* cannot be sane to reply, "Half a share." And while on this subject, I may remark how strange it is that, if *Hamlet* be really touched, he should be deemed mad by all saving the two who may be supposed best acquainted with his "heart of hearts"— his father's ghost, and his dear friend *Horatio*. Ordinarily, it is those most closely attached to a man who first discern his flightiness.

Another grave fault which Mr. Smith discovers in the *Hamlet* of Mr. Montgomery is that it lacks force, that it has a large infusion of Werther. Strange how minds differ! It is this very absence of mere brute force, this admixture of German dreaminess, which forms in my estimation one of the charms of this conception. *Hamlet* is the realization, the embodiment—if I may use the word in this sense—of mental, not physical greatness. He is no savage hodman, who having found out his wronger goes and punishes him, but a man of genius of "large discourse," a free thinker, who dares to condemn the customs of his country when he conceives them to be at odds with reason. He is irresolute through excess of mental clear-seeing, and his is too highly strung a nervous organization to be forcible.

On this theme one might write by the yard, and still have much to say, but as I cannot hope to induce you to publish a *Hamlet* supplement, I will conclude. Mr. Smith has had his say, happily [17] for mankind; Mr. Brown has had his; and now, by your leave, I have had mine. The world may not be much the wiser by our utterances; for, after all, what can we poor criticlings do in front of such a play as "*Hamlet*," and such a representative of the noble *Prince?* Mainly, to my thinking, be very thankful. As to comparing this *Hamlet* with any of those we have seen before in this colony, it is idle. This is flesh and blood, which they were not; and I should as soon think of comparing the genial Artemus Ward, who died at Southampton, with the figure in Mr. Sohier's window. So far as our stage history extends, I may say of Mr. Montgomery in this character, to a somewhat hackneyed phrase of Macaulay's, "He has distanced all his competitors so decidedly, that it is not worth while to place them. Eclipse is first, and the rest nowhere."

Melbourne, July 31   THOMAS JONES [18]

Some Remarks on
the Tragedy of Hamlet
Prince of Denmark
Written by
William Shakespeare

[*By Thomas Hanmer*]

[Thomas Hanmer],[1] *Some Remarks on the Tragedy of Hamlet, Prince of Denmark, Written by William Shakespeare* (London, 1736).

BEFORE I PROCEED to the particular parts of this tragedy, I must premise, that the great admirers of our poet cannot be offended, if I point out some of his imperfections, since they will find that they are very few in proportion to his beauties. Among the former, we may reckon some anachronisms, and also the inordinate length of time supposed to be employed in several of his pieces; add to all this, that the plots of his plays in general, are charged with some little absurdity or other. But then, how easily may we forgive this, when we reflect upon his many excellencies! The tragedy that is now coming under our examination, is one of the best of his pieces, and strikes us with a certain awe

---

[1] Published anonymously. Authorship for some time attributed to Hanmer. Spelling and capitalization modernized.

and seriousness of mind, far beyond those plays whose whole plot turns upon [4] vehement and uncontrollable love, such as are most of our modern tragedies. These certainly have not the great effect that others have, which turn either upon ambition, the love of one's country, or paternal or filial tenderness. Accordingly we find, that few among the ancients, and hardly any of our author's plays, are built upon the passion of love in a direct manner; by which I mean, that they have not the mutual attachment of a lover and his mistress for their chief basis. Love will always make a great figure in tragedy, if only its chief branches are made use of; as for instance, Jealousy (as in *Othello*) or the beautiul distress of man and wife (as in *Romeo and Juliet*) but never when the whole play is founded upon two lovers desiring to possess each other: and one of the reasons for this seems to be, that this last species of that passion is more commonly met with than the former, and so consequently strikes us less. Add to this, that there may a suspicion arise, that the passion of love in a direct manner may be more sensual than in those branches which I have mentioned; which suspicion is sufficient to take from its dignity, and lessen our veneration for it. Of all Shakespeare's tragedies, none can surpass this, as to the noble passions which it naturally raises in us. That the reader may see what our poet had to work upon, I shall insert the plan of it as abridged from *Saxo Grammaticus's Danish History* by Mr. Theobald.[5] "The historian calls our poet's hero Amlethus, his father Horwendillus, his uncle Fengo, and his mother Gerutha. The old King in single combat, slew Collerus, King of Norway; Fengo makes away with his brother Horwendillus, and marries his widow Gerutha. Amlethus, to avoid being suspected by his uncle of designs, assumes a form of utter madness. A fine woman is planted upon him, to try if he would yield to the impressions of love. Fengo contrives, that Amlethus, in order to wound him, should be closeted by his mother. A man is concealed in the rushes to overhear their discourse; whom Amlethus discovers and kills. When the Queen is frighted at this behaviour of his; he tasks her about her criminal course of life, and incestuous conversation with her former husband's murderer; confesses his madness is but counterfeited, to protect himself, and secure his revenge for his father; to which he enjoins the queen's silence. Fengo sends Amlethus to Britain:

two of the king's servants attend him with letters to the British
King, strictly pressing the death of Amlethus, who, in the night
time, coming at their commission, overreads it, forms a new one,
and turns the destruction designed towards himself on the bearers
of the letters. Amlethus returning home, by a wile surprises and
kills his uncle." I shall have occasion to remark [6] in the sequel,
that in one particular he has followed the plan so closely as to
produce an absurdity in his plot. And I must premise also this,
that in my examination of the whole conduct of the play, the
reader must not be surprised, if I censure any part of it, although
it be entirely in conformity to the plan the author has chosen;
because it is easy to conceive, that a poet's judgment is particularly
shown in choosing the proper circumstances, and rejecting the im-
proper ones of the groundwork which he raises his play upon. In
general we are to take notice, that as history ran very low in his
days, most of his plays are founded upon some old wretched
chronicler, or some empty Italian novelist; but the more base and
mean were his materials, so much more ought we to believe, that
he would have made the greatest use of them? I shall not insist
upon the merit of those who first break through the thick mist of
barbarism in poetry, which was so strong about the time our poet
wrote, because this must easily be sensible to every reader who has
the least tincture of letters; but thus much we must observe, that
before his time there were very few (if any) dramatic performances of any tragic writer, which deserve to be remembered; so
much were all the noble originals of antiquity buried in oblivion.
One would think that the works of Sophocles, Euripides, etc. were
discoveries of the last age only; and not that they had existed for
so many centuries. There is something very astonishing in the
general ignorance and dullness of taste, which for so long a time
over-spread the world, after it had been so gloriously enlightened
by Athens and Rome; especially as so many of their excellent
masterpieces were still remaining, which one would have thought
should have excited even the brutes of those barbarous ages to
have examined them and formed themselves according to such
models. . . .[7]

[The writer of this tract proceeds to write a commentary on
various scenes and passages in the plays. He refers to the pagination of Theobald's edition. Ed.]

As to Hamlet's soliloquy, I shall set down the whole passage, and shall subjoin the remarks of a very prominent author which are in the spirit of true criticism.

Oh that this too, too solid flesh . . .[18]

"The young Prince (says this author in the *Tatler*), was not yet acquainted with all the guilt of his mother; but turns his thoughts on her sudden forgetfulness of his father, and the indecency of her hasty marriage. The several emotions of mind, and breaks of passion in this speech, are admirable. He has touched every circumstance that aggravated the fact, and seemed capable of hurrying the thoughts of a son into distraction. His father's tenderness for his mother, expressed in so delicate a particular; his mother's fondness for his father, no less exquisitely described; the great and amiable figure of his dead parent, drawn by a true filial piety; his disdain of so unworthy a successor to his bed: but above all, the shortness of the time between his father's death, and his mother's second marriage, brought together with so much disorder, make up as noble a part as any in that celebrated tragedy. The circumstances of time I never could enough admire. The widowhood had lasted two months. This is his first reflection: but as his indignation rises, he sinks to scarce two months: afterwards into a month; and at last, into a *little* month. But all this so naturally, that the reader accompanies him [20] in the violence of his passion, and finds the time lessen insensibly, according to the different workings of his disdain. I have not mentioned the incest of her marriage, which is so obvious a provocation; but can't forbear taking notice, that when his fury is at its height, he cries, *Frailty, thy name is woman!* as railing at the sex in general, rather than giving himself leave to think his mother worse than others." [21]

[*On Act I*]

SCENE in Polonius' House.
Enter Laertes and Ophelia, and afterwards Polonius.

It is evident by the whole tenor of Polonius' behavior in the play, that he is intended to represent some buffoonish statesman, not too much fraught with honesty. Whether any particular person's character was herein aimed at, I shall not determine, because it is not to the purpose; for whoever reads our author's plays, will

find that in all of them (even the most serious ones), he has some
regard for the meanest part of his audience, and perhaps too, for
that taste for low jokes and puns, which prevailed in his time
among the better sort. This, I think, was more pardonable in him,
when it was confined to clowns, and such like persons in his plays;
but is by no means excusable in a man, supposed to be in such a
station as Polonius is.

Nay, granting that such ministers of state were common
(which surely they were not), it would even then be a fault in our
Author to introduce them in such pieces as this; for everything that
is natural is not to be made use of improperly: but when it is out of
nature, this certainly much aggravates the poet's mistake. And, to
speak truth, all comic circumstances, all things tending to raise a
laugh, are highly offensive in tragedies. . . .[23]

[On Act II]

Polonius and Reynaldo, and afterwards Ophelia.[32]

To conform to the groundwork of his plot, Shakespeare
makes the young Prince feign himself mad. I cannot but think
this to be injudicious; for so far from securing himself from any
violence which he feared from the usurper, which was his design
in so doing, it seems to have been the most likely way of getting
himself confined, and consequently, debarred from an opportunity of revenging his father's death, which now seemed to be his
only aim; and accordingly it was the occasion of his being sent
away to England. Which design, had it taken effect upon his life,
he never could have revenged his father's murder. To speak
truth, our poet, by keeping too close to the groundwork of his
plot, has fallen into an absurdity; for there appears no reason at
all in nature, why the young Prince did not put the usurper to
death as soon as possible, especially as Hamlet is represented as a
youth so briave, and so careless of his own life.[33]

The case indeed is this: had Hamlet gone naturally to work,
as we could suppose such a Prince to do in parallel circumstances,
there would have been an end of our play. The poet therefore
was obliged to delay his hero's revenge; but then he should have
contrived some good reason for it.

His beginning his scenes of madness by his behaviour to
Ophelia, was judicious, because by this means he might be

thought to be mad for her, and not that his brain was disturbed about state affairs, which would have been dangerous.[34]

[On Act III]

. . . Hamlet's speech upon seeing the King at prayers, has always given me great offence. There is something so unworthy of a hero, that I wish our poet had omitted it. To desire to destroy a man's soul, to make him eternally miserable, by cutting him off from all hopes of repentance; this surely, in a Christian Prince, is such a piece of revenge, as no tenderness for any parent can justify. To put the usurper to death, to deprive him of the fruits of his vile crime, and to rescue the throne of Denmark from pollution, was highly requisite: but there our young Prince's desires should have stopped, nor should he have wished to pursue the criminal in the other world, but rather have hoped for his conversion, before his putting him to death; for even with his repentance, there was at least purgatory for him to pass through, as we find even in a virtuous Prince, the father of Hamlet.[41]

[On Act V]

. . . It does not appear whether Ophelia's madness was chiefly for her father's death, or for the loss of Hamlet. It is not often that young women run mad for the loss of their fathers. It is more natural to suppose, that like Chimene in the *Cid,* her great sorrow proceeded from her father's being killed by the man she loved, and thereby making it indecent for her ever to marry him.[46]

In Hamlet's leaping into Ophelia's grave (which is expressed with great energy and force of passion) we have the first real proof of his love for her, which during this whole piece has been forced to submit to passions of greater weight and force, and here is suffered to break out chiefly, as it is necessary towards the winding up of the piece. It is but an under-passion in the play, and seems to be introduced more to conform to the plan our poet built upon, than for any thing else; though as the whole play is managed, it conduces towards the conclusion, as well as it diversifies, and adds beauties to the whole piece. . . .[47]

As They Liked It
An Essay on Shakespeare
and Morality

By Alfred Harbage

Alfred Harbage, from *As They Liked It: An Essay on Shakespeare and Morality* (New York, The Macmillan Company, 1947).

THE CLASSICAL INSTANCE of the enigma in the plays of Shakespeare is provided by Hamlet. Hamlet's dilemma is so obliquely treated that no two people can see it in precisely the same way, and no agreement will ever be reached on the exact elements of which it is composed. Sometimes our interpretive powers seem challenged directly, as when Hamlet mocks Guildenstern, 'You would play upon me; you would seem to know my stops; you would pluck out the heart of my mystery,' [23] or when immediately after Hamlet's own ambiguities on the value of Fortinbras' [92] expedition against Poland, we are given a description of Ophelia's madness:

> Her speech is nothing,
> Yet the unshaped use of it doth move
> The hearers to collection; they aim at it,
> And botch the words up fit to their own thoughts.[24]

The word *Sphinx* is common in *Hamlet* criticism, and even the word *hoax* is occasionally heard. Some say that the difficulties are imaginary and the meaning perfectly clear—*their* meaning. Others view the play as an accident, resulting from a collision with some

[23] *Hamlet*, III, 2, 381–382.
[24] *Ibid.*, IV, 5, 7–10.

other play, probably by Thomas Kyd. And finally we are treated to
a comedy turn by suave entertainers who soberly assure us that, as
a matter of fact, the play is a failure. But the body of *Hamlet*
criticism is so varied, copious, and fascinating that to deal with it
ever so slightly would be inappropriate in view of our present
modest objectives.

The area of agreement about *Hamlet* includes, one should
suppose, the belief that it tells an absorbing story full of arresting
episodes in magnificent language. Even a meaning, a basic meaning, will probably be agreed upon by most because the story treats
of sin, suffering, and death, and the connection between the three
seems not purely adventitious. Our difficulties have their origin
actually in ourselves. In line with his usual practice, Shakespeare
makes certain that we shall not view his play with passive acceptance, with the drowsy approval we vouchsafe a homily. By
his usual method, he stimulates our moral natures until we see his
tale of adventure and the wages of [93] sin as a projection of all our
sympathies and all our antipathies. Each composes a play as he
reads and a new play on each successive reading. The method
consists of offering us questions rather than statements, doubts
rather than certainties, the heterogeneous rather than the homogeneous, an enigma rather than a demonstration. A multiple crime
is reported by a multiple ghost to a multiple avenger.

First, let us consider the crime. In each of the earlier extant
versions of the story (and it is vain to deal with the non-extant),
there is a single clear version of the crime. In Saxo Grammaticus a
man murders his brother, and his accepted in wedlock by his
brother's widow although she is aware of his guilt.[25] In Belleforest, a man commits adultery with his brother's wife, then slays
him, and weds the widow: the crime is 'double impiete, d'adultere
incestueux, et de felonnie, et parricide.' [26] But what of Shakespeare's play? There are three possibilities in regard to the crime.
In the Ghost's report it is the same crime as related in Belleforest. An 'adulterate beast' won to his lust the 'most seeming-
virtuous' wife of his brother, dispatched him, and wedded her.[27]

[25] Saxo Grammaticus, *Historia Danica,* ed. Gollancz, pp. 100, 114.
[26] Belleforest, *Histoires Tragiques,* ed. Gollancz, p. 188.
[27] *Hamlet,* I, 5, 41–75.

But is this what actually occurred? Claudius admits to fratricide
but never to adultery.

> O, my offence is rank, it smells to heaven;
> It hath the primal eldest curse upon 't,
> A brother's murther! [28]

Gertrude never admits to either adultery or knowledge of murder.
She mentions her 'sin' or 'guilt' in general terms,[29] but it may
consist only of an 'o'er hasty marriage' [30] to a [94] brother-in-law—
a marriage technically incestuous. The version of the crime presented in the mouse-trap playlet [31] is in line with Gertrude's own
admissions rather than the Ghost's charges, and she herself never
speaks or acts like an evil woman. Hamlet himself finally seems
convinced that his mother has not committed adultery or connived
at murder, although he is still filled with disgust at her sexual
offense in marrying hastily in middle age an inferior man.[32] To
inquire about the exact nature of a crime committed before the
action of the play begins may seem like inquiring about the exact
cause of the quarrel between the Montagues and Capulets, but
such is not the case. The sex motif in Hamlet is very prominent,
and part of our excitement is caused by the curiosity and suspicion with which we always regard Gertrude.

There are then three defensible alternatives: that Claudius
and Gertrude are murderers and adulterers, that they are murderers
but not adulterers, that Claudius is a murderer but Gertrude nothing worse than an inconstant woman. If the last is the case, the
Ghost either exaggerates or has, in the nether world, inferior
sources of information. But this is a curious Ghost to begin with.
It is really three ghosts. Santayana describes two: 'It is a Christian
soul in Purgatory, which ought, in theological strictness, to be a
holy and redeemed soul, a phase of penitential and spiritual experience; yet this soul fears to scent the morning air, trembles at
the cock crow, and instigates the revenging of crime by crime.' [33]

[28] *Ibid.*, III, 3, 36–38.
[29] *Ibid.*, IV, 5, 17–20.
[30] *Ibid.*, II, 2, 57.
[31] *Ibid.*, III, 2, 146–157.
[32] *Ibid.*, III, 4, 29–30, 53–101.
[33] Santayana, *Interpretations of Poetry and Religion*, p. 209.

Its third identity is apparent when Hamlet can see it and his mother cannot, suggesting that it may be a mere hallucination. As Professor Campbell [95] says, 'if a papist [who believed ghosts to be Christian spirits] and King James [who believed they were demons] and Timothy Bright [who believed they were figments of the brain] had seen the play, as they probably did, each would have gone home confirmed in his own opinion about ghosts.' [34] Shakespeare is said to have enacted this part himself—an appropriate role for one who has been pictured as divine spirit, sorcerer, and non-existent. There is no ghost in the extant earlier versions of the story, but one seems to have been introduced into it by the author of an earlier Hamlet play. If this author was Kyd, we should judge from the Andrea of his *Spanish Tragedy* that his ghost was a spirit only, and not, like Shakespeare's, a troubler of spirits.

An ambiguous ghost is an unreliable witness, and we have then the first but by no means the only element in Hamlet's dilemma. Hamlet, aside from the extension which each of us gives him, is what he says and does in the play. He is his dilemma. He is a multiple Hamlet because his is a multiple dilemma. Should he slay Claudius or not? And should he do so now or later? All the countless analyses of Hamlet's character are really attempts to answer the question: *Why does not Hamlet slay Claudius now?*

We may dismiss at once as the reason Shakespeare's compulsion to imitate the Ur-Hamlet, his inability to cope with intransigent material, or his nervousness lest prompt action in the Prince would leave him nothing to do with his last two acts. These explanations are psychologically interesting, representing the natural human impulse of analysts [96] to transfer their bafflement to Shakespeare, but they have no other significance. A moment's reflection will determine that the element of compulsion is not a factor. Shakespeare was not forced to write this play or to treat its subject in any prescribed manner. The story was a legend with which he could deal as freely as with the legend of Timon of Athens. He could treat any earlier play upon it as he had treated *King Leir* or *Promos and Cassandra*. Hamlet could have slain Claudius in the second act, as Macbeth slew Duncan, without leaving the playwright at a loss. It would simply have meant that

---

[34] Campbell, *Shakespeare's Tragic Heroes*, p. 128.

he had chosen to write a different play. But the irrefragable fact is that he chose to write *this* play, and the play as it is must be, at least approximately, the play as he wished it to be. The question, *Why does not Hamlet slay Claudius now?* is quite legitimate; and below are the proffered answers:

1

Hamlet is squeamish about blood. We are apt to dismiss this answer with disdain. Goethe's tender prince does not appeal to us; yet we must admit that in our own experience it is difficult enough drowning a litter of kittens, not to mention sticking knives into people. Our standards of endurance are very high—for people in plays.

2

Hamlet is ill. He is suffering from 'melancholy adust,' or the apathy of grief, or hysteria, or mere mental derangement, quite apart from his being 'fat and scant of breath.' [97] This answer is very much in favor in our present age of mental and medical clinics.

3

Hamlet must act with regard for his personal safety. This is never offered as the whole answer. The explanation is too uninteresting and, although the Prince does call himself a 'coward,' it has too little confirmation in the text. Significantly, however, it is practically the whole answer in Saxo Grammaticus and Belleforest.

4

Hamlet does not believe in the righteousness of personal vengeance. This, too, is an unpopular answer although it is the one favored by so distinguished a critic as Santayana.[35] It is rather amusing to observe how many civilized and Christian commentators, Coleridge for instance, have been able to give an easy nod

[35] Santayana, *Interpretations of Poetry and Religion*, pp. 215–216.

of approval to lynch law, or at least to accept its righteousness in
the ethical world of *Hamlet* as if the immorality of personal
vengeance were an unfamiliar notion to Elizabethans. A warning
against vengeance, at least as directed at kings, appears in the
Belleforest version of the Hamlet story itself,[36] and all moralists of
the time fulminated against it. In rejecting it as an expressed
motive for Hamlet's delay, Shakespeare is not revealing a moral
blind spot.

5

Hamlet has an 'Oedipus complex' and unconsciously distrusts
his own reasons for hating Claudius. This is a [98] specialist's contribution, and we cannot greet it with enthusiasm. We must admit,
however, that the Prince, in his conscious mind at least, is tre-
mendously concerned about the sex-life of his mother.

6

Hamlet does not think that vengeance will serve any useful
purpose. It will not restore his dead father or remove from him
personally the soilure of having an adulterous, or at least a sensual, mother. This answer has not figured prominently in Shakespearean criticism, but it expresses a popular attitude toward punishment and could be calculated to suggest itself to some sectors of
any audience.

7

Hamlet resents the call of duty. The role he is destined to
play will separate him from his college companions forever, and
from the soft arms of Ophelia:

> The time is out of joint. O cursed spite
> That ever I was born to set it right.[37]

---

[36] Belleforest, *Histoires Tragiques,* ed. Gollancz, p. 196.
[37] *Hamlet,* I, 5, 189–190.

8

Hamlet must find a way to slay Claudius without exposing the guilt of Gertrude.

9

Hamlet must make certain that the crown of Denmark shall pass to the right head.[99]

10

Hamlet must secure the evidence that will make the justice of slaying Claudius apparent to the world.

There are so many answers, so many reasons for delay that would be cogent indeed if anyone of us were actually placed in Hamlet's position, that any elegant gestures of dismissal (there is really no problem: the facts as they appear fail to warrant all this ado) must, if taken seriously, be evaluated as the bravery of men not under fire. We have yet to list the two most widely accepted answers:

11

Hamlet has the philosophical cast of mind that inhibits practical action.

12

Hamlet must confirm the Ghost's accusations and then find an auspicious moment for his deed.

The first of these favored explanations is the one offered by Coleridge and accepted almost universally during the nineteenth century. It has the valuable endorsement of Hamlet himself—

I

A dull and muddy-mettled rascal, peak
Like John-a-dreams, unpregnant of my cause.[38]

[38] *Ibid.*, II, 2, 593-595.

And again—

> the native hue of resolution
> Is sicklied o'er with the pale cast of thought,[100]
> And enterprises of great pith and moment
> With this regard their currents turn awry
> And lose the name of action.[39]

And again—

> Sure he that made us with such large discourse
> Looking before and after, gave us not
> That capability and godlike reason
> To fust in us unus'd. Now, whether it be
> Bestial oblivion, or some craven scruple
> Of thinking too precisely on th' event,—
> A thought which, quarter'd, hath but one part wisdom
> And ever three parts coward,—I do not know
> Why yet I live to say 'This thing's to do,'
> Since I have cause, and will, and strength, and means
> To do't.[40]

To say that Coleridge had no reason for seeing in Hamlet's character the things he saw is absurd. They are there for all of us to see. But they are not the only things. Moreover, the whole philosophical implication of the reading seems somehow askew. It implies that Hamlet's bad example should spur us to action—any kind of action. We must think of him as culpable, rather than as baffled like ourselves, seeking truth, trying to piece together a puzzle with the essential parts missing. Tired of thought, Hamlet admires Fortinbras' meaningless action in invading Poland, prefers Fortinbras' type of futility to his own; and, tired of thought, Samuel Coleridge concurs, as in some part of our response most of us concur. But does existence offer only a choice between thought without action and action without thought? And if so, is the latter the better choice? [101] Must we assume that the mind is not as good as the stuff it has to work upon? The exaltation of action leads us to some rather somber reflections. Shakespeare spurred John Payne Collier to *action*—literary forgery. And *Hamlet* for a time was read as an indictment by old, unmilitaristic,

---

[39] *Ibid.*, III, 1, 84–88.
[40] *Ibid.*, IV, 4, 36–46.

philosophical Germany. In 1877, after the first of Germany's three modern descents upon France, Horace Howard Furness dedicated his New Variorum edition of *Hamlet*

To the

'GERMAN SHAKESPEARE SOCIETY'

of Weimar

WHOSE RECENT HISTORY

has proved

ONCE FOR ALL

that

'GERMANY IS *NOT* HAMLET'

'True, true,' we must say,—'O would that it were not so!' The second of the favored explanations of Hamlet's delay also finds much authority in the text. Hamlet cannot trust the statement of the Ghost, and is not sure that vengeance is in order until after the performance of the mouse-trap play in the third act. He fails to slay Claudius just afterwards because, as he explains, Claudius is at prayer. Then he is sent out of the country. Hamlet deals actively enough with Polonius behind the arras, and with Rosencrantz and Guildenstern at sea. It is all very reasonable: Hamlet is a man of action. There are only two [102] difficulties with the reading: first, that it renders irrelevant most of the impressions we derive from the play, and second, that Hamlet never does end his delay to take deliberate action. Instead he performs in a fencing-match for Claudius, whom he finally slays almost as an inadvertence.

It is remarkable that the two most plausible single answers to *Why does not Hamlet slay Claudius now?* are mutually contradictory. Our conclusion must be that there is no single answer to the question. There are many answers, or rather many combinations of answers, with each member in each combination susceptible to innumerable degrees of emphasis. The possible range of variation of response is therefore unlimited. It is useless to debate the extent to which all this was a matter of conscious calculation with Shakespeare. No one knows what occurs within the creative mind. It is true that the play contains some purely accidental inconsistencies—on Hamlet's age for instance—and that some of its contradictory elements are traceable to anterior treatments of the story. Much of the old legend remains. Amleth or Amlethus is the folk hero of clever retorts and acute devices, and is harmoniously transfigured into the man of intellectual subtlety: foxiness becomes philosophical aptitude. Shakespeare retained whatever in the traditional story served his purpose, including the contradictions—which do not show as contradictions while we read. The amazing thing is that he could suggest so many explanations for Hamlet's conduct—that is for Hamlet—and commit himself to none of them. He has left this man, who is sad and gay, arrogant and humble,[103] cruel and kind, brutal and tender, who can mock the aged but forbid others from doing so, who can talk bawdry but worship purity, who can kill, 'lug the guts into the neighbour room,' [42] and then 'weep for what is done' [43] as something for us to consider—an enduring moral enigma. It is the most astonishing balancing feat in literature, and the play provides more pleasurable excitement than any other in the world.[104]

The Characters of Shakespeare's Plays

By William Hazlitt

William Hazlitt, from *The Characters of Shakespeare's Plays* (1817) in *Lectures on the Literature of the Age of Elizabeth, and the Characters of Shakespeare's Plays* (London, 1870).

THE CHARACTER OF HAMLET stands quite by itself.[76] It is not a character marked by strength of will or even of passion, but by refinement of thought and sentiment.

---

[42] *Hamlet*, III, 4, 212.
[43] *Ibid.*, IV, 1, 27.

Hamlet is as little of the hero as a man can well be: but he is a young and princely novice, full of high enthusiasm and quick sensibility—the sport of circumstances, questioning with fortune and refining on his own feelings, and forced from the natural bias of his disposition by the strangeness of his situation. He seems incapable of deliberate action, and is only hurried into extremities on the spur of the occasion, when he has no time to reflect, as in the scene where he kills Polonius, and again, where he alters the letters which Rosencrans and Guildenstern are taking with them to England, purporting his death. At other times, when he is most bound to act, he remains puzzled, undecided, and sceptical, dallies with his purposes, till the occasion is lost, and finds out some pretence to relapse into indolence and thoughtfulness again. For this reason he refuses to kill the King when he is at his prayers, and by a refinement in malice, which is in truth only an excuse for his own want of resolution, defers his revenge to a more fatal opportunity, when he shall be engaged in some act "that has no relish of salvation in it."

> Now might I do it pat, now he is praying;
> And now I'll do't—and so he goes to heaven;
> And so am I reveng'd?—that would be scanned:
> A villain kills my father; and for that
> I, his sole son, do this same villain send
> To heaven.[77]
> O, this is hire and salary, not revenge. . . .
> Up sword; and know thou a more horrid bent,
> When he is drunk asleep, or in his rage.
> (Act iii. sc. 3).

He is the prince of philosophical speculators; and because he cannot have his revenge perfect, according to the most refined idea his wish can form, he declines it altogether. So he scruples to trust the suggestions of the ghost, contrives the scene of the play to have surer proof of his uncle's guilt, and then rests satisfied with this confirmation of his suspicions, and the success of his experiment, instead of acting upon it. Yet he is sensible of his own weakness, taxes himself with it, and tries to reason himself out of it. . . .

Still he does nothing; and this very speculation [78] on his own infirmity only affords him another occasion for indulging it. It is not from any want of attachment to his father or of abhorrence of his murder that Hamlet is thus dilatory; but it is more to his taste to indulge his imagination in reflecting upon the enormity of the crime and refining on his schemes of vengeance, than to put them into immediate practice. His ruling passion is to think, not to act: and any vague pretext that flatters this propensity instantly diverts him from his previous purposes.

The moral perfection of his character has been called in question, we think, by those who did not understand it. It is more interesting than according to rules; amiable, though not fault-less. The ethical delineations of "that noble and liberal casuist" (as Shakespear has been well called) do not exhibit the drab-coloured quakerism of morality. His plays are not copies either from the "Whole Duty of Man," or from "The Academy of Compliments!" We confess we are a little shocked at the want of refinement in Hamlet. The neglect of punctilious exactness in his behaviour either partakes of the "licence of the time," or else belongs to the very excess of intellectual refinement in the char-acter,[79] which makes the common rules of life, as well as his own purposes, sit loose upon him. He may be said to be amenable only to the tribunal of his own thoughts, and is too much taken up with the airy world of contemplation to lay as much stress as he ought on the practical consequences of things. His habitual principles of action are unhinged and out of joint with the time. His conduct to Ophelia is quite natural in his circumstances. It is that of assumed severity only. It is the effect of disappointed hope, of bitter regrets, of affection suspended, not obliterated, by the distractions of the scene around him. Amidst the natural and pre-ternatural horrors of his situation, he might be excused in deli-cacy from carrying on a regular courtship. When "his father's spirit was in arms," it was not a time for the son to make love in. He could neither marry Ophelia, nor wound her mind by explain-ing the cause of his alienation, which he durst hardly trust himself to think of. It would have taken him years to have come to a direct explanation on the point. In the harassed state of his mind, he could not have done much otherwise than he did. His conduct does not contradict what he says when he sees her funeral,

> I loved Ophelia: forty thousand brothers
> Could not with all their quality of love
> Make up my sum. (V. i.).

Nothing can be more affecting or beautiful than the Queen's apostrophe to Ophelia on throwing the flowers into the grave.

> Sweets to the sweet, farewell. (Scattering flowers.)
> I hop'd thou should'st have been my Hamlet's wife,
> I thought thy bride-bed to have deck'd, sweet maid,
> And not have strew'd thy grave.

Shakespear was thoroughly a master of the mixed motives of human character, and he here shows us the Queen, who was so criminal in some respects, not without some sensibility and affection in other relations of life,[80]—Ophelia is a character almost too exquisitely touching to be dwelt upon. Oh rose of May, oh flower too soon faded! Her love, her madness, her death, are described with the truest touches of tenderness and pathos. It is a character which nobody but Shakespear could have drawn in the way that he has done, and to the conception of which there is not even the smallest approach, except in some of the old romantic ballads. Her brother, Laertes, is a character we do not like so well: he is too hot and choleric, and somewhat rhodomontade. Polonius is a perfect character in its kind; nor is there any foundation for the objections which have been made to the consistency of this part. It is said that he acts very foolishly and talks very sensibly. There is no inconsistency in that. Again, that he talks wisely at one time and foolishly at another; that his advice to Laertes is very excellent, and his advice to the King and Queen on the subject of Hamlet's madness very ridiculous. But he gives the one as a father, and is sincere in it; he gives the other as a mere courtier, a busy-body, and is accordingly officious, garrulous, and impertinent. In short, Shakespear has been accused of inconsistency in this and other characters, only because he has kept up the distinction which there is in nature, between the understandings and the moral habits of men, between the absurdity of their ideas and the absurdity of their motives. Polonius is not a fool, but he makes himself so. His folly, whether in his actions or speeches, comes under the head of impropriety of intention.

John Gielgud
a Modern and Unusually
Interesting Hamlet

By Elinor Hughes

Elinor Hughes, "John Gielgud a Modern and Unusually Interesting
Hamlet," *Boston Herald* (October 18, 1936).

IT MAY BE TRUE that comparison is not
criticism, but criticism of "Hamlet" is really impossible without
comparison, a fact proven once again by the latest production of
Shakespeare's tragedy at the Empire Theater in New York a few
nights ago. The press was full of comparisons and differences of
opinion, and so marked were these same differences, that we began
to wonder whether all the reviewers had been to the same production. If Leslie Howard's "Hamlet" were not positively opening
here to-morrow night we should have been sure that the press
seats had been mixed and that half the gentlemen of the press
had been to see him and the other half to see John Gielgud.

Before we go any further, we should like to put into the
record our belief that this revival by Guthrie McClintic is about
the most intelligently modern production we have ever seen. Not
in the costumes, praise be, for "Hamlet" does not need modern
dress to make it modern, but in the spirit of its interpretation. An
amazing amount of the text has been left, and for once the tragedy
emerges as a well balanced play, not as a race with only Eclipse
running. In recent years, only Walter Hampden has been willing
to give Shakespeare's play a fair chance, and even he omitted the
short scene introducing Fortinbras and the soliloquy beginning

"How all occasions do inform against me." It is "Hamlet" in generous measure, played rapidly enough to hold the unflagging attention, yet not rushed so that the actors must swallow their lines.

John Gielgud's Hamlet, of which we have heard so much favorable report, is a very striking portrayal; eager, eloquent, vivid and young—above all, young. Until you have seen Hamlet played by an actor who can give you the feeling of an untried youth faced with a heartbreaking duty that he must perform against seemingly insuperable obstacles, you have missed a remarkable experience. "Hamlet," being all things to all men, may be played by a good actor so long as he can walk on the stage, but a mature player must needs give a completely different interpretation from a youthful one.

It is greatly to John Gielgud's credit, young as he is, that he has been able to bring out—and reconcile—so many diverse elements in Hamlet's character. He gives you the passion, the bewilderment, the despair and the quick-flaming lust for vengeance, and at the same time he can suggest the precocious scholar, the disprized lover and the would-be man of action who talks himself out of the completion of his task. Nature has favored him in singularly generous measure: he has a gracious bearing, a princely manner and the imperiousness of a young eagle. His voice, if not rich, is most pleasing to the ear, and his diction is such that not a line is lost even in the most hurried declamation, and he knows the rhythms of poetry even in the stress of emotion.

If something is lacking—and such a thing as the perfect Hamlet is probably unknown—it is the profound and deeply stirring tragedy that a man of different physique and temperament can bring to the role. This Hamlet has pathos but not the true tragic impulse; he is moody, not melancholy, and while he restates Hamlet in terms of our unspacious days, he loses stature in achieving humanity.

The favorite player selected by the New York press to compare with John Gielgud is, of course, John Barrymore. When and if this revival goes on the road, it is more likely to be Walter Hampden and Forbes-Robertson who will be called to the bar of comparisons. Not caring for Mr. Barrymore's Sweet Prince, we could only compare him to Mr. Gielgud in unfavorable terms, citing him for disrespect to the play, wanton misapprehension of the character and speech that dried up the beauty of the lines and made them almost commonplace. Forbes-Robertson we never saw, and to make Walter Hampden our criterion is to contrast such complete opposites that it would only confuse the issue. The stately magnificence, the beautiful cadenced speech of Mr. Hampden's prince is not the same as the electrical sympathetic modernism of Mr. Gielgud, yet both are Hamlet and both have their own place in the scheme of the theater.

Too little comment has been made, we believe, on the restorations and novelties of this new revival. There is, for example, the admirably staged scene when Hamlet overhears the plan of Polonius and Claudius to set Ophelia on him to unravel his mystery. It is but the opening of a door and the noiseless appearance of Hamlet while the others are deep in converse, yet it provides a perfect clue to Hamlet's subsequent harshness to Ophelia. Indeed, it is an admirable rendering of Dover Wilson's suggestion in his interesting commentary, "What Happens in Hamlet." "Hamlet" need not then go through the time-dishonored convention of glimpsing the lawful espials during his interview with Ophelia: he knows they are there and, torn between anger and pity for the submissive girl, he can give the listeners a run for their money.

This is good business, just as is the staging of the play scene, with the players on the level of the stage, acting virtually with their backs to the audience, and Gertrude, Claudius, Hamlet and Horatio on an upper level; effectively grouped. Another of Dover Wilson's suggestions is followed by indicating Hamlet's displeasure with the players for mishandling his plot.

With two innovations, however, we are inclined to disagree. The Barrymore-Hopkins-Jones revival of "Hamlet" turned the Ghost into a spotlight, which made Shakespeare's careful description of the spirit's appearance absurd. Mr. McClintic has chosen to have the Ghost's lines spoken off-stage, by Malcolm Keen while a silent figure maneuvers about the stage, appearing and disappearing in bewildering fashion. It is a clumsy arrangement, not because it departs from tradition but because it is destructive of illusion. The other matter is the terrific speed with which the final scene is played, robbing Hamlet's death of all tragic feeling. Of course, the mass slaughter is melodramatic, but it need not be played with a stop watch in one hand and a starting gun in the other.

Notes on Hamlet

By Samuel Johnson

Samuel Johnson, from "Notes on the Plays" (1765), in *Johnson on Shakespeare; Essays and Notes Selected and Set Forth with an Introduction by Walter Raleigh* (London, Oxford University Press, 1908).

Act II. Scene iv. (II. ii.):

POLONIUS IS A MAN bred in courts, exercised in business, stored with observation, confident of his knowledge, proud of his eloquence, and declining into dotage. His mode of oratory is truly represented as designed to ridicule the practice of those times, of prefaces that made no introduction, and of method that embarrassed rather than explained. This part of his character is accidental, the rest is natural. Such a man is positive and confident, because he knows that his mind was once strong, and knows not that it is become weak. Such a man excels in general principles, but fails in the particular application. He is knowing in retrospect, and ignorant in foresight. While he depends upon his memory, and can draw from his repositories of knowledge, he utters weighty sentences, and gives useful counsel; but as the mind in its enfeebled state cannot be kept long busy and intent, the old man is subject to [190] sudden dereliction of his faculties, he loses the order of his ideas, and entangles himself in his own thoughts, till he recovers the leading principle, and falls again into his former train. This idea of dotage encroaching upon wisdom, will solve all the phænomena of the character of Polonius. . . . [191]

Act III. Scene ii. (III. i. 56 foll.):

To be, or not to be?

Of this celebrated soliloquy, which bursting from a man distracted with contrariety of desires, and overwhelmed with the

magnitude of his own purposes, is connected rather in the speaker's mind, than on his tongue, I shall endeavour to discover the
train, and to show how one sentiment produces another.

Hamlet, knowing himself injured in the most enormous and
atrocious degree, and seeing no means of redress, but such as
must expose him to the extremity of hazard, meditates on his situation in this manner: Before I can form any rational scheme of
action under this pressure of distress, it is necessary to decide,
whether, after our present state, we are to be or not to be. That is
the question, which, as it shall be answered, will determine,
whether 'tis nobler, and more suitable to the dignity of reason, to
suffer the outrages of fortune patiently, or to take arms against
them, and by opposing end them, though perhaps with the loss
of life. If to die, were to sleep, no more, and by a sleep to end the
miseries of our nature, such a sleep were devoutly to be wished;
but if to sleep in death, be to dream, to retain our powers of sensibility, we must pause to consider, in that sleep of death what
dreams may come. This consideration [191] makes calamity so long
endured; for who would bear the vexations of life, which might
be ended by a bare bodkin, but that he is afraid of something an
unknown futurity? This fear it is that gives efficacy to conscience,
which, by turning the mind upon this regard, chills the ardour of
resolution, checks the vigour of enterprise, and makes the current of desire stagnate in inactivity.

We may suppose that he would have applied these general observations to his own case, but that he discovered Ophelia. . . .[192]

Act III. Scene ix. (III. iii. 94-5):

> That his soul may be as damn'd and black,
> As hell, whereto it goes.

This speech, in which Hamlet, represented as a virtuous character, is not content with taking blood for blood, but contrives
damnation for the man that he would punish, is too horrible to be
read or to be uttered. . . .[193]

If the dramas of Shakespeare were to be characterized, each
by the particular excellence which distinguishes it from the rest,
we must allow to the tragedy of *Hamlet* the praise of variety. The
incidents are so numerous, that the argument of the play would

make a long tale. The scenes are interchangeably diversified with merriment and solemnity; with merriment that includes judicious and instructive observations and solemnity, not strained by poetical violence above the natural sentiments of man. New characters appear from time to time in continual succession, exhibiting various forms of life and particular modes of conversation.[195] The pretended madness of Hamlet causes much mirth, the mournful distraction of Ophelia fills the heart with tenderness and every personage produces the effect intended, from the apparition that in the first act chills the blood with horror, to the fop in the last, that exposes affectation to just contempt.

This conduct is perhaps not wholly secure against objections. The action is, indeed, for the most part, in continual progression, but there are some scenes, which neither forward nor retard it. Of the feigned madness of Hamlet there appears no adequate cause, for he does nothing which he might not have done with the reputation of sanity. He plays the madman most, when he treats Ophelia with such rudeness, which seems to be useless and wanton cruelty.

Hamlet is, through the whole play, rather an instrument than an agent. After he has, by the stratagem of the play, convicted the King, he makes no attempt to punish him and his death is at last effected by an instrument which Hamlet has no part in producing.

The catastrophe is not very happily produced; the exchange of weapons is rather an expedient of necessity than a stroke of art. A scheme might easily have been formed to kill Hamlet with the dagger and Laertes with the bowl.

The poet is accused of having shewn little regard to poetical justice and may be charged with equal neglect of poetical probability. The apparition left the regions of the dead to little purpose; the revenge which he demands is not obtained but by the death of him that was required to take it; and the gratification which would arise from the destruction of an usurper and a murderer is abated by the untimely death of Ophelia, the young, the beautiful, the harmless and the pious.[196]

Hamlet and Oedipus

By Ernest Jones

Ernest Jones, from *Hamlet and Oedipus* (New York, Doubleday and Company, Inc., n.d. Originally published by W. W. Norton and Company, Inc., 1949.)

THE PSYCHO-ANALYTICAL SOLUTION

WE ARE COMPELLED then to take the position that there is some cause for Hamlet's vacillation which has not yet been fathomed. If this lies neither in his incapacity for action in general, nor in the inordinate difficulty of the particular task in question, then it must of necessity lie in the third possibility —namely, in some special feature of the task that renders it repugnant to him. This conclusion, that Hamlet at heart does not want to carry out the task, seems so obvious that it is hard to see how any open-minded reader of the play could avoid making it. . . .[1] [51]

. . . he [Hamlet] gave several pretended excuses for his hesitancy, but never once did he hint at any doubt about what his duty was in the matter. He was always clear enough about what he *ought* to do; the conflict in his mind ranged about the question why he couldn't bring himself to do it. If Hamlet had at any time been asked whether it was right for him to kill his uncle, or whether he really intended to do so, no one can seriously doubt what his instant answer would have been. Throughout the play we see his mind irrevocably made up on the desirability of a given course of action, which he fully[54] accepts as being his bounden duty; indeed, he would have resented the mere insinuation of doubt on this point

[1] Anyone who doubts this conclusion is recommended to read Loening's convincing chapter (XII), "Hamlet's Verhalten gegen seine Aufgabe."

as an untrue slur on his filial piety. Ulrici, Baumgart, and Kohler try to meet this difficulty by assuming that the ethical objection to personal revenge was never clearly present to Hamlet's mind; it was a deep and undeveloped feeling which had not fully dawned. I would agree that only in some such way as this can the difficulty be logically met, and further that in recognizing Hamlet's non-consciousness of the cause of his repugnance to his task we are nearing the core of the mystery. In fact Hamlet tells us so himself in so many words (in his bitter cry—Act IV, Sc. 3—*I do not know why*, etc.). But an insurmountable obstacle in the way of accepting any of the causes of repugnance suggested above is that the nature of them is such that a keen and introspective thinker, as Hamlet was, would infallibly have recognized some indication of their presence, and would have openly debated them instead of deceiving himself with a number of false pretexts in the way we shall presently recall. Loening [25] well states this in the sentence: "If it had been a question of a conflict between the duty of revenge imposed from without and an inner *moral* or *juristic* counter-impulse, this discord and its cause *must* have been brought into the region of reflection in a man so capable of thought, and so accustomed to it, as Hamlet was."

In spite of this difficulty the hint of an approaching solution encourages us to pursue more closely the argument at that point. The hypothesis just stated may be correct up to a certain stage and then have failed for lack of special knowledge to guide it further. [55] Thus Hamlet's hesitancy may have been due to an internal conflict between the impulse to fulfil his task on the one hand and some special cause of repugnance to it on the other; further, the explanation of his not disclosing this cause of repugnance may be that he was not conscious of its nature; and yet the cause may be one that doesn't happen to have been considered by any of the upholders of this hypothesis. In other words, the first two stages in the argument may be correct, but not the third. This is the view that will now be developed, but before dealing with the third stage of the argument it is first necessary to establish the probability of the first two—namely that Hamlet's hesitancy was due to some special cause of repugnance for his task and that he was unaware of the nature of this repugnance.

[25] Loening: Die Hamlet-Tragödie Shakespeares, 1893, S. 78.

A preliminary obstruction to this line of thought, based on some common prejudices on the subject of mental dynamics, may first be considered. If Hamlet was not aware of the nature of his inhibition, doubt may be felt concerning the possibility of our penetrating to it. This pessimistic thought was expressed by Baumgart [26] as follows: "What hinders Hamlet in his revenge is for him himself a problem and *therefore* it must remain a problem for us all." Fortunately for our investigation, however, psycho-analytic studies have demonstrated beyond doubt that mental trends hidden from the subject himself may come to external expression in ways that reveal their nature to a trained observer, so that the possibility of success is not to be thus excluded. Loening [27] has further objected to this hypothesis that the poet himself has [56] not disclosed this hidden mental trend, or even given any indication of it. The first part of his objection is certainly true—otherwise there would be no problem to discuss, but we shall presently see that the second is by no means true. It may be asked: why has the poet not put in a clearer light the mental trend we are trying to discover? Strange as it may appear, the answer is probably the same as with Hamlet himself—namely, he could not because he was unaware of its nature. We shall later deal with this question in connection with the relation of the poet to the play.

As Trench well says: [28] "We find it hard, with Shakespeare's help, to understand Hamlet: even Shakespeare, perhaps, found it hard to understand him: Hamlet himself finds it impossible to understand himself. Better able than other men to read the hearts and motives of others, he is yet quite unable to read his own." I know of no more authentic statement than this in the whole literature on the Hamlet problem. But, if the motive of the play is so obscure, to what can we attribute its powerful effect on the audience, since, as Kohler [29] asks, "Who has ever seen Hamlet and not felt the fearful conflict that moves the soul of the hero?" This can only be because the hero's conflict finds its echo in a similar inner conflict in the mind of the hearer, and the more intense is

---

[26] Baumgart: op. cit., S. 48. [Die Hamlet-Tragödie und ihre Kritik]
[27] Loening: op. cit., S. 78, 79.
[28] Trench: op. cit., p. 115. [Shakespeare's Hamlet: A New Commentary]
[29] Kohler: Shakespeare vor dem Forum der Jurisprudenz, 1883, S. 195.

this already present conflict the greater is the effect of the drama.[30] Again, it is certain [57] that the hearer himself does not know the inner cause of the conflict in his own mind, but experiences only the outer manifestations of it. So we reach the apparent paradox that the hero, the poet, and the audience are all profoundly moved by feelings due to a conflict of the source of which they are unaware.

The fact, however, that such a conclusion should appar paradoxical is in itself a censure on popular ignorance of the actual workings of the human mind, and before undertaking to sustain the assertions made in the preceding paragraph it will first be necessary to make a few observations on the prevailing views of motive and conduct in general. The new science of clinical psychology stands nowhere in sharper contrast to the older attitudes towards mental functioning than on this very matter. Whereas the generally accepted view of man's mind, usually implicit and frequently explicit in psychological writings and elsewhere, regards it as an interplay of various processes that are for the most part known to the subject, or are at all events accessible to careful introspection on his part, the analytic methods of clinical psychology have on the contrary decisively proved that a far greater number of these processes than is commonly surmised arises from origins that he never even suspects. Man's belief that he is a self-conscious animal, alive to the desires that impel or inhibit his actions, is the last stronghold of that anthropomorphic and anthropocentric outlook on life which has so long dominated his philosophy, his theology, and, above all, his psychology. In other words, the tendency to take man at his own valuation is rarely resisted, and we assume that the surest way of finding out why a person commits a given act is simply to ask him, relying on the knowledge that he, as we ourselves [58] would in a like circumstance, will feel certain of the answer and will almost infallibly provide a plausible reason for his conduct. Special objective methods of penetrating into the more obscure mental processes, however, disclose the most formidable obstacles in the way of this direct introspective route, and reveal

---

[30] It need hardly be said that the play, like most others, appeals to its audience in a number of different respects. We are here considering only the main appeal, the central conflict in the tragedy.

powers of self-deception in the human mind to which a limit has yet to be found. If I may quote from a former paper: [31] "We are beginning to see man not as the smooth, self-acting agent he pretends to be, but as he really is, a creature only dimly conscious of the various influences that mould his thought and action, and blindly resisting with all the means at his command the forces that are making for a higher and fuller consciousness."

That Hamlet is suffering from an internal conflict the essential nature of which is inaccessible to his introspection is evidenced by the following considerations. Throughout the play we have the clearest picture of a man who sees his duty plain before him, but who shirks it at every opportunity and suffers in consequence the most intense remorse. To paraphrase Sir James Paget's well-known description of hysterical paralysis: Hamlet's advocates say he cannot do his duty, his detractors say he will not, whereas the truth is that he cannot will. Further than this, the deficient will-power is localized to the one question of killing his uncle; it is what may be termed a *specific aboulia*. Now instances of such specific aboulias in real life invariably prove, when analysed, to be due to an unconscious repulsion against the act that cannot be performed (or else against something closely associated with the act, so that the idea of the act becomes [59] also involved in the repulsion). In other words, whenever a person cannot bring himself to do something that every conscious consideration tells him he should do— and which he may have the strongest conscious desire to do—it is always because there is some hidden reason why a part of him doesn't want to do it; this reason he will not own to himself and is only dimly if at all aware of. That is exactly the case with Hamlet. Time and again he works himself up, points out to himself his obvious duty, with the cruellest self-reproaches lashes himself to agonies of remorse—and once more falls away into inaction. He eagerly seizes at every excuse for occupying himself with any other matter than the performance of his duty—even in the last scene of the last act entering on the distraction of a quite irrelevant fencing-match with a man who he must know wants to kill him, an eventuality that would put an end to all hope of ful-

[31] "Rationalization in Every Day Life," *Journal of Abnormal Psychology,* 1908, p. 168.

filling his task: just as on a lesser plane a person faced with a dis-
tasteful task, e.g. writing a difficult letter, will whittle away his
time in arranging, tidying, and fidgeting with any little occupation
that may serve as a pretext for procrastination. Bradley [32] even
goes as far as to make out a case for the view that Hamlet's self-
accusation of "bestial oblivion" is to be taken in a literal sense,
his unconscious detestation of his task being so intense as to enable
him actually to forget it for periods.

Highly significant is the fact that the grounds Hamlet gives
for his hesitancy are grounds none of which will stand any serious
consideration, and which continually change from one time to another. One moment he pretends he is too cowardly to perform [60]
the deed, at another he questions the truthfulness of the ghost, at
another—when the opportunity presents itself in its naked form—
he thinks the time is unsuited, it would be better to wait till the
King was at some evil act and then to kill him, and so on. They
have each of them, it is true, a certain plausibility—so much so
that some writers have accepted them at face value; but surely no
pretext would be of any use if it were not plausible. As Madariaga [33] truly says: "The argument that the reasons given by Hamlet not to kill the king at prayers are cogent is irrelevant. For the
man who wants to procrastinate cogent arguments are more valuable than mere pretexts." Take, for instance, the matter of the
credibility of the ghost. There exists an extensive and very interesting literature concerning Elizabethan beliefs in supernatural
visitation. It was doubtless a burning topic, a focal point of the
controversies about the conflicting theologies of the age, and moreover, affecting the practical question of how to treat witches. But
there is no evidence of Hamlet (or Shakespeare) being specially
interested in theology, and from the moment when the ghost confirms the slumbering suspicion in his mind ("Oh, my prophetic
soul! My uncle!") his intuition must indubitably have convinced
him of the ghost's veridical nature. He never really doubted the
villainy of his uncle.

When a man gives at different times a different reason for his

[32] Bradley: op. cit., pp. 125, 126, 410, 411. [Shakespearean Tragedy, 2nd
Ed., 1905]
[33] Madariaga: op. cit., p. 98. [On Hamlet, 1948]

conduct it is safe to infer that, whether consciously or not, he is concealing the true reason. Wetz,[34] discussing a similar problem in reference to Iago, truly observes: "Nothing proves so well how [61] false are the motives with which Iago tries to persuade himself as *the constant change in these motives.*" We can therefore safely dismiss all the alleged motives that Hamlet propounds, as being more or less successful attempts on his part to blind himself with self-deception. Loening's [35] summing-up of them is not too emphatic when he says: "They are all mutually contradictory; *they are one and all false pretexts.*" The alleged motives excellently illustrate the psychological mechanisms of evasion and rationalization I have elsewhere described.[36] It is not necessary, however, to discuss them here individually, for Loening has with the greatest perspicacity done this in full detail and has effectually demonstrated how utterly untenable they all are.[37]

Still, in his moments of self-reproach Hamlet sees clearly enough the recalcitrancy of his conduct and renews his efforts to achieve action. It is noticeable how his outbursts of remorse are evoked by external happenings which bring back to his mind that which he would so gladly forget, and which, according to Bradley, he does at times forget: particularly effective in this respect are incidents that contrast with his own conduct, as when the player is so moved over the fate of Hecuba (Act II, Sc. 2), or when Fortinbras takes the field and "finds quarrel in a straw when honour's at the stake" (Act IV, Sc. 4). On the former occasion, stung by the monstrous way in which the player pours out his feeling at the thought of Hecuba, he arraigns himself in words which surely [62] should effectually dispose of the view that he has any doubt where his duty lies.

> What's Hecuba to him, or he to Hecuba,
> That he should weep for her? What would he do,
> Had he the motive and the cue for passion
> That I have? He would drown the stage with tears
> And cleave the general ear with horrid speech,

[34] Wetz: Shakespeare vom Standpunkt der vergleichenden Litteraturgeschichte, 1890, Bd. I, S. 186.

[35] Loening: op. cit., S. 245.

[36] Op. cit., p. 161.

[37] See especially his analysis of Hamlet's pretext for non-action in the prayer scene: op. cit., S. 240–2.

Make mad the guilty and appal the free,
Confound the ignorant, and amaze indeed
The very faculties of eyes and ears; yet I,
A dull and muddy-mettled rascal, peak
Like John-a-dreams, unpregnant of my cause,[38]
And can say nothing; no, not for a king,
Upon whose property and most dear life
A damn'd defeat was made: Am I a coward?
Who calls me villain, breaks my pate across,
Plucks off my beard and blows it in my face,
Tweaks me by the nose, gives me the lie i' the throat
As deep as to the lungs? Who does me this?
Ha, 'swounds, I should take it: for it cannot be
But I am pigeon-liver'd, and lack gall
To make oppression bitter, or ere this
I should ha' fatted all the region kites
With this slave's offal. Bloody, bawdy villain!
Remorseless, treacherous, lecherous, kindless villain!
O, vengeance!
Why, what an ass am I! This is most brave,
That I, the son of a dear father murder'd,
Prompted to my revenge by heaven and hell,
Must like a whore unpack my heart with words,
And fall a-cursing like a very drab;
A scullion![39]   [63]

The readiness with which his guilty conscience is stirred into
activity is again evidenced on the second appearance of the Ghost,
when Hamlet cries,

Do you not come your tardy son to chide,
That lapsed in time and passion lets go by
Th'important acting of your dread command?
O, say!

The Ghost at once confirms this misgiving by answering,

Do not forget! this visitation
Is but to whet thy almost blunted purpose.

In short, the whole picture presented by Hamlet, his deep
depression, the hopeless note in his attitude towards the world

---

[38] How the essence of the situation is conveyed in these four words.
[39] Dover Wilson considers this a misprint for "stallion."

and towards the value of life, his dread of death,[40] his repeated reference to bad dreams, his self-accusations, his desperate efforts to get away from the thoughts of his duty, and his vain attempts to find an excuse for his procrastination: all this unequivocally points to a *tortured conscience,* to some hidden ground for shirking his task, a ground which he dare not or cannot avow to himself. We have, therefore, to take up the argument again at this point, and to seek for some evidence that may serve to bring to light the hidden counter-motive.[64]

The extensive experience of the psycho-analytic researches carried out by Freud and his school during the past half-century has amply demonstrated that certain kinds of mental process show a greater tendency to be inaccessible to consciousness (put technically, to be "repressed") than others. In other words, it is harder for a person to realize the existence in his mind of some mental trends than it is of others. In order therefore to gain a proper perspective it is necessary briefly to inquire into the relative frequency with which various sets of mental processes are "repressed." Experience shows that this can be correlated with the degree of compatibility of these various sets with the ideals and standards accepted by the conscious ego; the less compatible they are with these the more likely are they to be "repressed." As the standards acceptable to consciousness are in considerable measure derived from the immediate environment, one may formulate the following generalization: those processes are most likely to be "repressed" by the individual which are most disapproved of by the particular circle of society to whose influence he has chiefly been subjected during the period when his character was being formed. Biologically stated, this law would run: "That which is unacceptable to the herd becomes unacceptable to the individual member," it being understood that the term herd is intended here

---

[40] Tieck (Dramaturgische Blätter, II, 1826) saw in Hamlet's cowardly fear of death a chief reason for his hesitancy in executing his vengeance. How well Shakespeare understood what this fear was like may be inferred from Claudio's words in "Measure for Measure:"

> The weariest and most loathed worldly life
> That age, ache, penury and imprisonment
> Can lay on nature is a paradise
> To what we fear of death.

in the sense of the particular circle defined above, which is by no means necessarily the community at large. It is for this reason that moral, social, ethical, or religious tendencies are seldom "repressed," for, since the individual originally received them from his herd, they can hardly ever come into conflict with the dicta of the latter. This merely says that a man cannot be [65] ashamed of that which he respects; the apparent exceptions to this rule need not be here explained.

The language used in the previous paragraph will have indicated that by the term "repression" we denote an active dynamic process. Thoughts that are "repressed" are actively kept from consciousness by a definite force and with the expenditure of more or less mental effort, though the person concerned is rarely aware of this. Further, what is thus kept from consciousness typically possesses an energy of its own; hence our frequent use of such expressions as "trend," "tendency," etc. A little consideration of the genetic aspects of the matter will make it comprehensible that the trends most likely to be "repressed" are those belonging to what are called the innate impulses, as contrasted with secondarily acquired ones. Loening [41] seems very discerningly to have grasped this, for, in commenting on a remark of Kohler's to the effect that "where a feeling impels us to action or to omission, it is replete with a hundred reasons—with reasons that are as light as soap-bubbles, but which through self-deception appear to us as highly respectable and compelling motives, because they are hugely magnified in the (concave) mirror of our own feeling," he writes: "But this does not hold good, as Kohler and others believe, when we are impelled by *moral* feelings of which reason *approves* (for these we admit to ourselves, they need no excuse), only for feelings that arise from our *natural man,* those the gratification of which is *opposed by our reason."* It only remains to add the obvious corollary that, as the herd unquestionably selects from the "natural" instincts the sexual one on [66] which to lay its heaviest ban, so it is the various psycho-sexual trends that are most often "repressed" by the individual. We have here the explanation of the clinical experience that the more intense and the more obscure is a given case of deep mental conflict the more

[41] Loening: op. cit., S. 245, 246.

certainly will it be found on adequate analysis to centre about a
sexual problem. On the surface, of course, this does not appear
so, for, by means of various psychological defensive mechanisms,
the depression, doubt, despair, and other manifestations of the
conflict are transferred on to more tolerable and permissible topics, such as anxiety about worldly success or failure, about immortality and the salvation of the soul, philosophical considerations
about the value of life, the future of the world, and so on.

Bearing these considerations in mind, let us return to Hamlet. It should now be evident that the conflict hypotheses discussed
above, which see Hamlet's conscious impulse towards revenge
inhibited by an unconscious misgiving of a highly ethical kind,
are based on ignorance of what actually happens in real life, since
misgivings of this order belong in fact to the more conscious
layers of the mind rather than to the deeper, unconscious ones.
Hamlet's intense self-study would speedily have made him aware
of any such misgivings and, although he might subsequently have
ignored them, it would almost certainly have been by the aid of
some process of rationalization which would have enabled him
to deceive himself into believing that they were ill-founded; he
would in any case have remained conscious of the nature of them.
We have therefore to invert these hypotheses and realize—as his
words so often indicate—that the positive striving for vengeance,
the pious [67] task laid on him by his father, was to him the moral
and social one, the one approved of by his consciousness, and that
the "repressed" inhibiting striving against the act of vengeance
arose in some hidden source connected with his more personal,
natural instincts. The former striving has already been considered, and indeed is manifest in every speech in which Hamlet
debates the matter: the second is, from its nature, more obscure
and has next to be investigated.

This is perhaps most easily done by inquiring more intently
into Hamlet's precise attitude towards the object of his vengeance,
Claudius, and towards the crimes that have to be avenged. These
are two: Claudius' incest with the Queen,[42] and his murder of his

---

[42] Had this relationship not counted as incestuous, then Queen Elizabeth
would have had no right to the throne; she would have been a bastard,
Katherine of Aragon being still alive at her birth.

brother. Now it is of great importance to note the profound difference in Hamlet's attitude towards these two crimes. Intellectually of course he abhors both, but there can be no question as to
which arouses in him the deeper loathing. Whereas the murder of
his father evokes in him indignation and a plain recognition of
his obvious duty to avenge it, his mother's guilty conduct awakes
in him the intensest horror. Furnivall [43] remarks, in speaking of
the Queen, "Her disgraceful adultery and incest, and treason to
his noble father's memory, Hamlet has felt in his inmost soul.
Compared to their ingrain die, Claudius' murder of his father
—notwithstanding all his protestations—is only a skin-deep
stain." [68]

Now, in trying to define Hamlet's attitude towards his uncle
we have to guard against assuming off-hand that this is a simple
one of mere execration, for there is a possibility of complexity
arising in the following way: The uncle has not merely committed
each crime, he has committed *both* crimes, a distinction of considerable importance, since the *combination* of crimes allows the
admittance of a new factor, produced by the possible inter-relation
of the two, which may prevent the result from being simply one
of summation. In addition, it has to be borne in mind that the
perpetrator of the crimes is a relative, and an exceedingly near
relative. The possible inter-relationship of the crimes, and the
fact that the author of them is an actual member of the family,
give scope for a confusion in their influence on Hamlet's mind
which may be the cause of the very obscurity we are seeking to
clarify.

Let us first pursue further the effect on Hamlet of his mother's
misconduct. Before he even knows with any certitude, however
much he may suspect it, that his father has been murdered he is in
the deepest depression, and evidently on account of this misconduct. The connection between the two is unmistakable in the
monologue in Act I, Sc. 2, in reference to which Furnivall [44]
writes: "One must insist on this, that before any revelation of his
father's murder is made to Hamlet, before any burden of revenging that murder is laid upon him, he thinks of suicide as a wel-

[43] Furnivall: Introduction to the "Leopold" Shakespeare, p. 72.
[44] Furnivall: op. cit., p. 70.

come means of escape from this fair world of God's, made
abominable to his diseased and weak imagination by his mother's
lust, and the dishonour done by her to his father's memory." [69]

> O that this too too solid [45] flesh would melt,
> Thaw and resolve itself into a dew,
> Or that the Everlasting had not fix'd
> His canon 'gainst self-slaughter, O God, God,
> How weary, stale, flat, and unprofitable
> Seem to me all the uses of this world!
> Fie on 't, O fie, 'tis an unweeded garden
> That grows to seed, things rank and gross in nature
> Possess it merely, that it should come to this,
> But two months dead, nay, not so much, not two,
> So excellent a king; that was to this
> Hyperion to a satyr, so loving to my mother,
> That he might not beteem the winds of heaven
> Visit her face too roughly—heaven and earth
> Must I remember? why, she would hang on him
> As if increase of appetite had grown
> By what it fed on, and yet within a month,
> Let me not think on 't; frailty thy name is woman!
> A little month or ere those shoes were old
> With which she follow'd my poor father's body
> Like Niobe all tears, why she, even she—
> O God, a beast that wants discourse of reason
> Would have mourn'd longer—married with my uncle,
> My father's brother, but no more like my father
> Than I to Hercules, within a month,
> Ere yet the salt of most unrighteous tears
> Had left the flushing in her galled eyes,
> She married. O most wicked speed . . . to post
> With such dexterity to incestuous sheets!
> It is not, nor it cannot come to good,
> But break my heart, for I must hold my tongue.

According to Bradley,[46] Hamlet's melancholic disgust at life
was the cause of his aversion from "any [70] kind of decided action." His explanation of the whole problem of Hamlet is "the

---

[45] Dover Wilson (*Times Literary Supplement*, May 16, 1918) brings forward excellent reasons for thinking that this word is a misprint for "sullied."
I use the Shakespearean punctuation he has restored.

[46] Bradley: op. cit., p. 122.

moral shock of the sudden ghastly disclosure of his mother's true nature," [47] and he regards the effect of this shock, as depicted in the play, as fully comprehensible. He says: [48] "Is it possible to conceive an experience more desolating to a man such as we have seen Hamlet to be; and is its result anything but perfectly natural? It brings bewildered horror, then loathing, then despair of human nature. His whole mind is poisoned . . . A nature morally blunter would have felt even so dreadful a revelation less keenly. A slower and more limited and positive mind might not have extended so widely through the world the disgust and disbelief that have entered it."

But we can rest satisfied with this seemingly adequate explanation of Hamlet's weariness of life only if we accept unquestioningly the conventional standards of the causes of deep emotion. Many years ago Conolly,[49] a well-known psychiatrist, pointed out the disproportion here existing between cause and effect, and gave as his opinion that Hamlet's reaction to his mother's marriage indicated in itself a mental instability, "a predisposition to actual unsoundness"; he writes: "The circumstances are not such as would at once turn a healthy mind to the contemplation of suicide, the last resource of those whose reason has been overwhelmed by calamity and despair." In T. S. Eliot's [50] opinion, also, Hamlet's emotion is in excess of the facts as they appear, and he specially contrasts [71] it with Gertude's negative and insignificant personality. Wihan [51] attributes the exaggerated effect of his misfortunes to Hamlet's "Masslosigkeit" (lack of moderation), which is displayed in every direction. We have unveiled only the exciting cause, not the predisposing cause. The very fact that Hamlet is apparently content with the explanation arouses our misgiving, for, as will presently be expounded, from the very nature of the emotion he cannot be aware of the true cause of it. If we ask, not what ought to produce such soul-paralysing grief and distaste for life, but what in actual fact does produce it, we are compelled to go beyond this explanation and seek for some deeper cause. In

[47] Idem: op. cit., p. 117.
[48] Idem: op. cit., p. 119.
[49] Conolly: A Study of Hamlet, 1863, pp. 22, 23.
[50] T. S. Eliot: loc. cit.
[51] J. Wihan: "Die Hamletfrage," in Leipziger Beiträge zur englischen Philologie, 1921. S. 89.

real life speedy second marriages occur commonly enough without leading to any such result as is here depicted, and when we
see them followed by this result we invariably find, if the opportunity for an analysis of the subject's mind presents itself, that
there is some other and more hidden reason why the event is
followed by this inordinately great effect. The reason always is
that the event has awakened to increased activity mental processes
that have been "repressed" from the subject's consciousness. His
mind has been specially prepared for the catastrophe by previous
mental processes with which those directly resulting from the
event have entered into association. This is perhaps what Furnivall means when he speaks of the world being made abominable
to Hamlet's "diseased imagination." In short, the special nature
of the reaction presupposes some special feature in the mental
predisposition. Bradley himself has to qualify his hyothesis by
inserting [72] the words "to a man such as we have seen Hamlet
to be."

We come at this point to the vexed question of Hamlet's
sanity, about which so many controversies have raged. Dover Wilson [52] authoritatively writes: "I agree with Loening, Bradley and
others that Shakespeare meant us to imagine Hamlet as suffering
from some kind of mental disorder throughout the play." The
question is what kind of mental disorder and what is its significance dramatically and psychologically. The matter is complicated
by Hamlet's frequently displaying simulation (the Antic Disposition), [53] and it has been asked whether this is to conceal his real
mental disturbance or cunningly to conceal his purposes in coping
with the practical problems of this task? This is a topic that
presently will be considered at some length, but there can be few
who regard it as a comprehensive statement of Hamlet's mental
state. As T. S. Eliot [54] has neatly expressed it, "Hamlet's 'madness' is less than madness and more than feigned.". . .[73]

More to the point is the actual account given in the play by
the King, the Queen, Ophelia, and above all, Polonius.[69] In his
description, for example, we note—if the Elizabethan language is

[52] Dover Wilson: What Happens etc., p. 217.
[53] Cp. R. Alexander: "Hamlet, the Classical Malingerer," *Medical Journal
and Record*, Sept. 4, 1929, p. 287.
[54] T. S. Eliot: Selected Essays, 1932, p. 146.
[69] Act 2, Sc. 2. "Fell into a sadness," etc.

translated into modern English—the symptoms of dejection, refusal of food, insomnia, crazy behaviour, fits of delirium, and
finally of raving madness; Hamlet's poignant parting words to
Polonius ("except my life," etc.) cannot mean other than a crav-
ing for death. These are undoubtedly suggestive of certain forms
of melancholia, and the likeness to manic-depressive insanity, of
which melancholia is now known to be but a part, is completed
by the occurrence of attacks of great excitement that would nowa-
days be called "hypomanic," of which Dover Wilson [70] counts no
fewer than eight. This modern diagnosis has indeed been suggested, e.g. by Brock,[71] Somerville,[72] and others. Nevertheless, the
rapid and startling oscillations between intense excitement and
profound depression do not accord with the accepted picture of
this disorder,[75] and if I had to describe such a condition as Hamlet's in clinical terms—which I am not particularly inclined to—it
would have to be as a severe case of hysteria on a cyclothymic
basis.

All this, however, is of academic interest only. What we are
essentially concerned with is the psychological understanding of
the dramatic effect produced by Hamlet's personality and behaviour. That effect would be quite other were the central figure
in the play to represent merely a "case of insanity." When that
happens, as with Ophelia, such a person passes beyond our ken, is
in a sense no more human, whereas Hamlet successfully claims
our interest and sympathy to the very end. Shakespeare certainly
never intended us to regard Hamlet as insane, so that the "mind
o'erthrown" must have some other meaning than its literal one.
Robert Bridges [73] has described the matter with exquisite delicacy:

> Hamlet himself would never have been aught to us, or we
> To Hamlet, wer't not for the artful balance whereby
> Shakespeare so gingerly put his sanity in doubt
> Without the while confounding his Reason.

I would suggest that in this Shakespeare's extraordinary powers of
observation and penetration granted him a degree of insight that it
has taken the world three subsequent centuries to reach. Until our

[70] Dover Wilson: op. cit., p. 213.
[71] J. H. E. Brock: The Dramatic Purpose of Hamlet, 1935.
[72] H. Somerville: Madness in Shakespearean Tragedy, 1929.
[73] Robert Bridges: The Testament of Beauty, I, 577.

generation (and even now in the juristic sphere) a dividing line
separated the sane and responsible from the irresponsible insane.
It is now becoming more and more widely recognized that much
of mankind lives in an intermediate and unhappy state charged
with [76] what Dover Wilson [74] well calls "that sense of frustra-
tion, futility and human inadequacy which is the burden of the
whole symphony" and of which Hamlet is the supreme example
in literature. This intermediate plight, in the toils of which perhaps the greater part of mankind struggles and suffers, is given
the name of psychoneurosis, and long ago the genius of Shakespeare depicted it for us with faultless insight.

Extensive studies of the past half century, inspired by Freud,
have taught us that a psychoneurosis means a state of mind where
the person is unduly, and often painfully, driven or thwarted by
the "unconscious" part of his mind, that buried part that was once
the infant's mind and still lives on side by side with the adult
mentality that has developed out of it and should have taken its
place. It signifies *internal* mental conflict. We have here the reason why it is impossible to discuss intelligently the state of mind
of anyone suffering from a psychoneurosis, whether the description is of a living person or an imagined one, without correlating
the manifestations with what must have operated in his infancy
and is *still operating*. That is what I propose to attempt here.

For some deep-seated reason, which is to him unacceptable,
Hamlet is plunged into anguish at the thought of his father being
replaced in his mother's affections by someone else. It is as if his
devotion to his mother had made him so jealous for her affection
that he had found it hard enough to share this even with his
father and could not endure to share it with still another man.
Against this thought, however, suggestive as it is, may be urged
three objections. First, if it were in itself a full statement of the
matter,[77] Hamlet would have been aware of the jealousy, whereas
we have concluded that the mental process we are seeking is hidden from him. Secondly, we see in it no evidence of the arousing
of an old and forgotten memory. And, thirdly, Hamlet is being
deprived by Claudius of no greater share in the Queen's affection
than he had been by his own father, for the two brothers made
exactly similar claims in this respect—namely, those of a loved

[74] Dover Wilson: op. cit., p. 261.

husband. The last-named objection, however, leads us to the heart of the situation. How if, in fact, Hamlet had in years gone by, as a child, bitterly resented having had to share his mother's affection even with his own father, had regarded him as a rival, and had secretly wished him out of the way so that he might enjoy undisputed and undisturbed the monopoly of that affection? If such thoughts had been present in his mind in childhood days they evidently would have been "repressed," and all traces of them obliterated, by filial piety and other educative influences. The actual realization of his early wish in the death of his father at the hands of a jealous rival would then have stimulated into activity these "repressed" memories, which would have produced, in the form of depression and other suffering, an obscure aftermath of his childhood's conflict. This is at all events the mechanism that is actually found in the real Hamlets who are investigated psychologically.[75]

The explanation, therefore, of the delay and self-frustration exhibited in the endeavour to fulfil his father's demand for vengeance is that to Hamlet the thought of incest and parricide combined is too intolerable to be borne. One part of him tries to carry [78] out the task, the other flinches inexorably from the thought of it. How fain would he blot it out in that "bestial oblivion" which unfortunately for him his conscience contemns. He is torn and tortured in an insoluble inner conflict.[79]

---

[75] See, for instance, Wulf Sachs: Black Hamlet, 1937.

A New Way of
Misunderstanding *Hamlet*

By Thomas M. Kettle

Thomas M. Kettle, "A New Way of Misunderstanding *Hamlet*," (1905), in *The Day's Burden* (New York, Charles Scribner's Sons, 1918).

WHAT ONE FELT most painfully at Mr. Harvey's recent performance of Hamlet was the artistic bankruptcy of the play. Of course no decent citizen confessed his boredom, because Shakespeare is the keystone of the conventions, a "national asset" as is said in England. But if art means freshness, words with raw, vivid sensation behind them, surprise and an element of strangeness? And what else does it mean? Already a hundred years ago the humane Charles Lamb was able to write that all the shining things in the play had been "so handled and pawed by declamatory boys and men" that for him they were "perfect dead members." And since then! The great Law of Ennui has vindicated itself even against Shakespeare. He has been mummified into an orthodoxy. He is a field for antiquarians, a proud heritage, an excuse for sumptuous scenery, but as an artist in the strict sense he hardly exists. Only one thing can restore him, a prolonged bath of oblivion. If he is to be brought to life again he must be redeemed from his immortality, which will be better than to redeem his house from the Americans. Societies must be started to destroy his works, at all events to lose them for a hundred and fifty years, and so make it possible for unborn happier generations to come to him as to a fresh and breathing phenomenon. Failing that he must be excluded from all school and university courses, and forbidden under heavy [62] penalties to any one not having attained his majority.

The pity is that, with the calamity of so long life, he should

not have the happiness to be understood. The inky Dane, in especial, has had as evil fortune in this regard as if he had walked
the actual earth and devoted himself to politics. Critic after critic
has arisen to misrepresent him, and this secular misrepresentation
has so crept into the empire of our imagination that direct vision
of the play is impossible. Tieck's Hamlet we know, and Goethe's
and Coleridge's and Mr. Tree's and Mr. Harvey's, but Shakespeare's Hamlet no man knows. Shakespeare's Hamlet, as a painful matter of fact, no man can ever know. We know how much
sub-meaning and personal colour the same set of words takes on in
different minds, and that these are never exactly what they were in
the creator's mind. And then in Hamlet there is the added barrier
of Elizabethan English, and the fact that Shakespeare is as topical
as a pantomime. What each of us does is to construct a private
understanding of Hamlet (which is certain to be a misunderstanding) out of materials furnished conjointly by ourselves, Shakespeare, a cloud of critics, and the actor who happens to be concrete
before our eyes at the moment; and it is in confession of this, and
not as a poor paradox, that the title of this paper has been devised.

The points I wish modestly to put forward here will be most
intelligible as a comment on the popular reading. That reading
has one merit at least, that of simplicity. According to it the plastic principle of the play, or rather the flaw that suffers it to stream
down its ruinous course, is a vice of character—Hamlet's "inability to act." It is Goethe's "oak planted in a costly vase which
should have only borne pleasant flowers"; it is Coleridge's "man
living in meditation, called upon to act by every motive, human
and divine, but the great object of whose [63] life is defeated by
continually resolving to do, yet doing nothing but resolve." These
are the phrases that have captured the general mind, and flowed
like a mist over the outlines of the play. But consider for a moment. Remembering Goethe's paltry performance—thanks to his
superculture—in the liberation of Germany, and the lamentable
life story of Coleridge, who can doubt that we have here not so
much the poet's imagination as that of his critics? *Quicquid recipi-
tur secundum modum recipientis,* we get out of things what we
bring to them; and I submit that the apocalypse of moral insufficiency discerned by these two eminent minds in Hamlet was
brought with them in the satchels of their conscience. They are
simply making General Confessions at the expense of the unfortu-

nate Prince. Let us analyse this interpretation popularized by them. The kernel of it is this. It demands in the place of Hamlet a crude, gory, gullible, instantaneous savage who not only believes in ghosts but lacks even the elementary savage's knowledge that there are evil as well as good ghosts, and whose will is hung on a hair-trigger dischargeable by the airiest impulse and subject to no restraint, moral or prudential. The commercial blandness with which people talk of Hamlet's "plain duty" makes one wonder if they recognize such a thing as plain morality. The "removal" of an uncle without due process of law and on the unsupported statement of an unsubpoenable ghost; the widowing of a mother and her casting-off as unspeakably vile, are treated as enterprises about which a man has no right to hesitate or even to feel unhappy. Because, meshed about with murder, adultery, usurpation, espionage, hypocrisy, and all other natural horrors, reinforced by the still greater horror of the supernatural, because in these cheerful conditions Hamlet is healthy-minded enough to grow "thought-sick," [64] he is marked down as one "unstable as water." What bewilders most of all is that there lurks in the popular view (and I appeal to the general experience) a vague conviction that if Hamlet had only shown himself morally-fibrous enough, all the blood and tears would somehow have been averted and the curtain would fall on a serene Denmark.

I do not deny that a tragedy derived from superculture and a feeble will would be admirable. Indeed if it be wanted it can be found in the purest essence in Turgéneff's *Rudin*. But I submit that this is not the true ethos of *Hamlet*. I submit that *Hamlet,* so far from being the most "internal" of Shakespeare's plays, is nearly the most "external," and has for plastic principle not character but that veiled force which we call destiny. What, in fine, is it but a tale of justice, bloodily executed through what seem "accidental judgments, casual slaughters?" Such indeed was the reading of the Prince himself:—

> Heaven hath pleased it so
> To punish me with this, and this with me,
> That I must be their scourge and minister.

The problem is set wholly from the outside. It is not a product of Hamlet's superculture, but of the sin of his uncle and the lesser sin of his mother, and it is a problem so overwhelming that, however it be handled and by whatever type of character, it must issue in abundant tears and blood. What is claimed here for Hamlet's solution is, that it is the only one justified by the character of the evidence and the practical means at his command, and that, above all, it is justified by results. The destinies approve and aid him, and when the curtain falls on a terrible harvest of horror we feel, nevertheless, a deep appeasement. The agony of Hamlet is over, the due ransom of sin has been paid with lives guilty [65] and innocent, and with the inearthing of much moral refuse, the world sweeps into pure air again. The roll of Fortinbras' drums is not so much the irony as the recuperative force of life, lingering with praise over the body of him who has made recuperation possible.

This is a point which must not be ignored: the play ends, thanks to Hamlet's course of action, in absolutely the best way in which it could end. The king, of course, was due to the sword. But surely Gertrude also is better out of the world than in it? Had she lived there was nothing but the gnawing of the worm, shame and remorse, or perhaps—and the closet scene shows her capable of it—the triumph of the fouler part of her, and the pursuit of her son with hatred and vengeance. Does anybody drop tears over Laertes, that polished cutter of throats i' the church? There remain Polonius and Ophelia. The comic side of Polonius is always played with such over-emphasis as to hide the dangerous side of him. His complicity in the murder of the elder Hamlet may be disputed, although it is not easy otherwise to explain his overweening influence with Claudius. He certainly conspired with the latter in his usurpation, and we cannot say what is the bound to his falseness. Suppose he had not been slain behind the arras, but had lived to carry his tale to Claudius, what course of action would he have counselled? Like son, like father; his plan would have differed from the poisoned rapier only in being, perhaps, a little more politic. Polonius helps to remind us that we may have comic murderers, just as the Burghleys and other contemporary statesmen show that we may have pious murderers. As for Ophelia, she is one of those who are organized for unhappiness. Hamlet's disgust with life is so violent, just and incurable that the old magic of their love can never return, and his straits are such that, however [66] he acts, enough misery will be produced to dethrone her frail reason.

I have submitted also that the evidence in Hamlet's possession never reaches that daylight certainty which justifies private
vengeance. If Shakespeare had intended to exhibit a mind which
is at once absolutely sure of itself and incapable of action, would
he not have brought the murder to light by the agency of some
courtier who had secretly witnessed it? In fact the ghost is the one
great blot and uncombining ingredient in the play. Had Shakespeare preserved the mental climate of the original story the ghost
might perhaps have been tolerated, but he is quite out of joint
with so thorough a modern as Hamlet. He complicates the whole
action, and steeps it in incongruity. Hamlet's desire to have more
relative grounds than the word of this visitant in whom it is
impossible to believe fully except during his actual presence is in
the highest degree natural. He therefore tries the experiment of the
play, and fails. What he had hoped was to provoke Claudius to
"proclaim his malefaction" in the ear of the court, for the case
that has to be built up is one that will convince not only Hamlet,
but also the public at large. What really is provoked? A temporary indisposition which can be explained away in two sentences
the next day. It may convince Hamlet, but it certainly would not
secure his acquittal before a jury.

But even supposing him to be justifiably certain, has he the
practical means to kill Claudius without, by the same act, sur-
rendering himself to death? Claudius was popular enough to
override Hamlet's claims and have himself chosen king. In that
office he had shown competence, his relations with England and
Norway being most excellent. He had a levy of three thousand
men in the immediate neighbourhood of the court whom he kept
in good humour by [67] frequent carousals. His courtiers were so
loyal that the Court-play apparently awoke not the least suspicion
or hostility in a single one of them, and that, even after Laertes'
confession of his treachery, when Hamlet plunges his rapier into
Claudius, they shriek "Treason! Treason!" and would no doubt
have cut the young prince down were that not plainly superfluous.
As against this, Hamlet is a student, just come home, super-
intelligent and a hater of bores and shams. His opinion of the
masquerade of royalty may be gathered from that one remark of
his: "Let's to the Court! for, by my fay, I cannot reason." He
applies his literary criticism to every-day conversation, and analy-

ses received platitudes with the most ruthless candour. To crown all, he is a Temperance Pioneer! In short, the situation is such that no one would have much chance of organizing support enough to oust Claudius, but that Hamlet, by the sheer force of his superiorities, has no chance at all. Of course it is always possible for him to slay the king and sacrifice his own life to his vengeance. But that would be something worse even than "hire and salary," and he has no enthusiasm for dying. Many people assume that he has, but in fact he is philosopher enough to be afraid of death. True, like every man of high intellect, he has moments of moral nausea, when he almost thinks that the best thing is not to be born, the next best to leave life as quickly as may be. But he recoils from the invisible event; above all, he never caresses the idea of suicide. The great "to be or not to be" monologue, sometimes interpreted in this sense, is really the precise opposite. It is rather an admonition to himself to defy death which he sees to be probably bound up with his revenge, and not to suffer his great enterprise, to be turned away by the fear of death. In short he never is absolutely certain of the facts of the crime, nor in a position to punish it with safety to himself. And,[68] although Shakespeare cannot amend this latter circumstance, he does amend the former, and with exquisite dramatic courtesy allows Hamlet full evidence of the king's guilt of another murder before calling his retributive sword into action.

What counts against Hamlet in popular estimation is his continual self-reproach. But this springs just from his exacting ideal of action, for he would shorten a straight line to reach his end. Religious biography will furnish a parallel; it is not among the actual sinners that we find self-contempt and a consciousness of the unforgiveable sin, but among the Bunyans and the Saint Alphonsus Ligouris. There is another motive behind Hamlet's outbursts. He is not certain enough to act, but his tense and tortured mind must find relief, and words are not irrevocable. But after the emotional debauch of his monologues, the lucid judgment returns, with its questionings and firm grasp of difficulties. Hamlet is compromised also by the speculative embroideries which his mind works over the drab stuff of experience. People think with Horatio that it is "to enquire too curiously" to find the dust of Alexander stopping a beer-barrel. But is it? Is not Hamlet rather

the avid intellect, which must needs think out of things everything
that is to be found in them? "Hamlet's obstacles are internal." He
certainly has internal obstacles. He is hampered by conscience,
natural affection, an exquisite taste and a capacity for metaphysics; very grave obstacles, if what is desired is immediate bloodshed.
Some critics hold that Shakespeare wrote *Hamlet* to purge his
countrymen of these qualities which he perceived spreading, to the
infinite prejudice of Elizabethan jingoism. It may be so, and I am
free to confess that, as far as public policy goes, his countrymen
have reformed them indifferently. But it is just because of these
failings that Hamlet possesses human significance. Without them,
he might be very interesting from the point of view of a tiger,
but [69] he would never have touched and troubled our imagination. As it is, we think of him as the noble and courtly prince
who passes through life, annotating it with a gloss of melancholy
speculation that has been absorbed into the mind of Europe, and
who so confronts it practically that the destinies adopt him for their
minister, and, through him, draw, out of unexampled horrors,
justice and even a certain terrible peace.[1]

As a perhaps tedious supplement, I submit that the character
of Horatio has been as favourably, as that of Hamlet has been
unfavourably, misunderstood. He enjoys the reputation of being
the strong, silent, truly virile man, held up in contrast to the
gusty and barren metaphysician. In support of this there can be
produced just a single speech of Hamlet's: against it there is the
whole of Horatio's words and actions. The eulogy, like so many
other passages, has, however, never been construed in its dramatic
context. It is spoken, be it remembered, immediately before the
play, when Hamlet is tense with the most terrible expectation. He
is about to probe the King's conscience to the quick, and naturally
wants corroboration of his own prejudiced eyes, and perhaps assistance in the scene that may follow. In order to induce the
deplorable Horatio to render even this petty service it is necessary

---

[1] The only sustainable charge that can be made against Hamlet is one of
over-hasty action—with regard, I mean, to Rosencranz and Guildenstern. He
sent them to death without anything like decisive proof of their complicity in
the design to have him executed in England. There is nothing to show that they
knew the contents of the original commission; indeed the contrary is established
by their continuing their journey after losing Hamlet. Most people will, however, accept the latter's justification of himself as satisfactory.

to flatter him, and the exaggerated courtesy, natural to Hamlet—as in the reception of Rosencranz and Guildenstern—combines with his immediate need to produce superlatives. His own fine taste rebels against them, and, as is [70] known, he concludes with "something too much of this!" (Were I a German I would suggest that these words are an amending note of Shakespeare on the MS., which he is known to have been revising, that he meant to recast the lines, and that his private note has been interpolated into Hamlet's speech.) What, as a matter of fact, is Horatio's record in the play? He is at Elsinore two months before he thinks it worth while to call on his old friend Hamlet, although he knows the latter to be in the most grievous trouble. At the first appearance of the ghost he has not wit enough to address it in Latin, although that is what he was brought there for by Marcellus. At the second appearance he is not able even to tell Hamlet the time, and later is guilty of a much grosser ineptitude. Marcellus urges him to come on after the Prince and the ghost. "Oh!" says Horatio, "Heaven will direct it!" and his delegation of his duty to Providence has to be crushed by Marcellus' "Nay, let's follow him." At what stage he comes to know of the King's crime is not clear, but he certainly possesses all Hamlet's knowledge of it after the Court Play. And what does this strong silent man do? Organize a party, as Laertes found friends to organize one, to execute vengeance against Claudius? By no means. He has nothing better to say than that he very well noted the King and that Hamlet ought to rhyme the quatrain in which his frenzy extravagates. Afterwards, when the Prince is sent to England under the most sinister circumstances, does the good Horatio make an attempt either to accompany or to liberate him? As a matter of fact he lies conscientiously low, and cultivates the best relations with Claudius. His next opportunity is at Hamlet's relation of his escape from the death intended for him in England. Horatio has indeed the grace to admire Hamlet's superior firmness of character—"Why, what a king [71] is this!"—but he does his best to cancel this by sympathetic tears over Rosencranz and Guildenstern. Before the duel he administers draughts of discouragement and superstition, and he has not the sense to see that Laertes' rapier is unbated. In fact from beginning to end he is a wandering ineptitude who has never a single suggestion, and whose

speech consists mainly of "Ay, my Lords," "That is most certain,"
"Is it possible," and other helpful phrases. At the last he has one
good impulse to finish the poisoned cup, but the dying Hamlet
intervenes, and Horatio addresses himself to funeral orations
which are certainly much more after his heart. He is prayed
merely to absent himself from felicity awhile, but we may be
sure that he does not construe the last as the emphatic word, but
stands in as an echo to Fortinbras and absents himself as long as
possible. And this is the strong silent man after whom Hamlet
should have modelled himself! In truth he compares poorly with
Osric, who was at any rate a stylist.

I cannot abstain from a word on Hamlet as an art critic. His
theory that the stage should hold the mirror up to nature is of
course absurd, at least as far as gesture and outer expression of
emotion goes. I refer rather to his employment of art as an
oblique moral inquisition—a most remarkable anticipation of
what Browning has to say in the Epilogue of "The Ring and the
Book"; and to his delightful prophetic criticism of the two great
achievements of the modern theatre—the musical comedy and the
problem play. Polonius has grown impatient at the length of the
fine epic passage recited by the players; Hamlet turns on him
with his unforgettable "Oh, he must have a jig or a tale of bawdy,
or he falls asleep." [72]

Form and Meaning in Drama

By H. D. F. Kitto

H. D. F. Kitto, from *Form and Meaning in Drama* (London,
Methuen and Company, Ltd., 1956).

IT SEEMS THAT CRITICISM of the play
has been concerned, in the main, with the character of Hamlet;
the play is something draped around him, something designed to

present his character. For example, the recent film version * carried
as a subtitle: The tragedy of a man who could not make up his
mind. Since this film was as far as possible from being a travesty
made by barbarians for illiterates, but was a distinguished piece of
work, we may assume that this is a representative modern view;
but how far it is from the truth, how little it explains the form
of the play, becomes apparent as soon as we begin to consider
that form constructively. What if *Hamlet* is a play which it would
be reasonable to call 'religious drama,' as we are using the term
here? What if the ingrained individualism of the last two centuries—to say nothing of romanticism—has blinded us to one
aspect of the play without which it cannot possibly appear as a
firm and coherent structure? . . .[248]

In *Hamlet*, eight people are killed, not counting Hamlet's
father; of the two families concerned in the play, those of King
Hamlet and Polonius, both are wiped out. Eight deaths are enough
to attract attention, and to make us wonder if the essential thing
has been said when the play is called 'the tragedy of a man who
could not make up his mind.' And the manner of these deaths is
no less significant than their number. Claudius murders King
Hamlet by poison; thereafter, a metaphorical poison seeps through
the play: rottenness, cankers, 'things rank and gross in nature'
meet us at every turn. Then at the end it once more becomes literal
poison: Gertrude, Claudius, Laertes, Hamlet are all poisoned; and
on Claudius, already dead or dying [249] from the poisoned rapier,
Hamlet forces the poisoned cup. The Ghost had said:

<blockquote>
Nor let thy soul contrive
Against thy mother aught; leave her to Heaven.
</blockquote>

So too Horatio observed:

<blockquote>
Heaven will direct it.
</blockquote>

And what does Heaven do with Gertrude? Of her own accord, and
in spite of a warning, she drinks poison. These are plain and
striking dramatic facts; how far does 'Hamlet's fatal indecision'
explain them? Are they an organic part of a tragedy of character?

---

* [Produced and directed by Sir Laurence Olivier in 1948].

Or did Shakespeare kill so many people merely from force of habit? . . .[250]

This examination of *Hamlet* has been based on the same assumptions as our examination of certain Greek plays: that the dramatist said exactly what he meant, through the medium of his art, and means therefore exactly what he has said. We have tried therefore to observe what in fact he has said, considering every scene and every considerable passage (as one would in [328] analysing a picture, for example, or a piece of music), not passing over this or that because it did not happen to interest us, or illustrate our point; nor being too ready to disregard a passage on the grounds that it was put there for some extraneous reason; remembering too that a dramatist can 'say' things by means other than words. I do not so flatter myself as to suppose that anything new has been brought to light. Nevertheless, if this general account of the play is acceptable, if its structure has been made to appear purposeful, in details big and small, such that the interpretation (blunders excepted) carries some measure of authority, then the critical method and the assumptions on which it is based may be held to be sound. It seems to me that this may be true.

As we said at the outset, the first thing that strikes us, or should strike us, when we contemplate the play is that it ends in the complete destruction of the two houses that are concerned. The character of Hamlet and the inner experience that he undergoes are indeed drawn at length and with great subtlety, and we must not overlook the fact; nevertheless, the architectonic pattern just indicated is so vast as to suggest at once that what we are dealing with is no individual tragedy of character, however profound, but something more like religious drama; and this means that unless we are ready, at every step, to relate the dramatic situation to its religious or philosophical background—in other words, to look at the play from a point of view to which more recent drama has not accustomed us—then we may not see either the structure or the meaning of the play as Shakespeare thought them.

Why do Rosencrantz and Guildenstern die, and Ophelia, and Laertes? Are these disasters casual by-products of 'the tragedy of a man who could not make up his mind?' Or are they necessary parts of a firm structure? Each of these disasters we can refer to something that Hamlet has done or failed to do, and we can say that each reveals something more of Hamlet's character; but if we see no more than this we are short-sighted, and are neglecting Shakespeare's plain directions in favour of our own. We are told much more than this when we hear Horatio, and then Laertes, cry 'Why, what a King is this!', 'The King, the King's to blame'; also when Guildenstern says, with a deep and unconscious irony 'We here give up ourselves . . . ,' [329] and when Laertes talks of 'contagious blastments.' Shakespeare puts before us a group of young people, friends or lovers, none of them wicked, one of them at least entirely virtuous, all surrounded by the poisonous air of Denmark (which also Shakespeare brings frequently and vividly before our minds), all of them brought to death because of its evil influences. Time after time, either in some significant patterning or with some phrase pregnant with irony, he makes us see that these people are partners in disaster, all of them borne down on the 'massy wheel' to 'boisterous ruin.'

In this, the natural working-out of sin, there is nothing mechanical. That is the philosophic reason why character and situation must be drawn vividly. Neither here nor in Greek drama have we anything to do with characters who are puppets in the hands of Fate. In both, we see something of the power of the gods, or the designs of Providence; but these no more override or reduce to unimportance the natural working of individual character than the existence, in the physical world, of universal laws overrides the natural behaviour of natural bodies. It is indeed precisely in the natural behaviour of men, and its natural results, in given circumstances, that the operation of the divine laws can be discerned. In *Hamlet,* Shakespeare draws a complete character, not for the comparatively barren purpose of 'creating' a Hamlet for our admiration, but in order to show how he, like the others, is inevitably engulfed by the evil that has been set in motion, and how he himself becomes the cause of further ruin. The conception which unites these eight persons in one coherent catastrophe may be said to be this: evil, once started on its course, will so work as to attack and overthrow impartially the good and the bad; and if the dramatist makes us feel, as he does, that a Providence is ordinant in all this, that, as with the Greeks, is his way of universalising the particular event.

Claudius, the arch-villain, driven by crime into further crime, meets at last what is manifestly divine justice. 'If his fitness speaks . . .' says Hamlet; the 'fitness' of Claudius has been speaking for a long time. At the opposite pole stands Ophelia, exposed to corruption though uncorrupted, but pitifully destroyed as the chain of evil uncoils itself. Then Gertrude, one of Shakespeare's most tragic characters: she is the first, as Laertes [330] is the last, to be tainted by Claudius; but while he dies in forgiveness and reconciliation, no such gentle influence alleviates her end. In the bedchamber scene Hamlet had pointed out to her the hard road to amendment; has she tried to follow it? On this, Shakespeare is silent; but her last grim experience of life is to find that 'O my dear Hamlet, the drink, the drink! I am poisoned'—poisoned, as she must realise, by the cup that her new husband had prepared for the son whom she loved so tenderly. After her own sin, and as a direct consequence of it, everything that she holds dear is blasted. Her part in this tragedy is indeed a frightening one. She is no Claudius, recklessly given to crime, devoid of any pure or disinterested motive. Her love for her son shines through every line she speaks; this, and her affection for Ophelia, show us the Gertrude that might have been, if a mad passion had not swept her into the arms of Claudius. By this one sin she condemned herself to endure, and, still worse, to understand, all its devastating consequences: her son driven 'mad,' killing Polonius, denouncing herself and her crime in cruel terms that she cannot rebut, Ophelia driven out of her senses and into her grave—nearly a criminal's grave; all her hopes irretrievably ruined. One tragic little detail, just before the end, shows how deeply Shakespeare must have pondered on his Gertrude. We know that she has seen the wild struggle in the graveyard between Laertes and Hamlet. When the Lord enters, to invite Hamlet to the fencing-match, he says: 'The Queen desires you to use some gentle entertainment to Laertes before you fall to play.' 'She well instructs me,' says Hamlet. What can this mean, except that she has vague fears of Laertes' anger, and a pathetic hope that Hamlet might appease it, by talk more courteous than he had used in the graveyard? It recalls her equally pathetic wish that Ophelia's beauty and virtue might 'bring him to his wonted ways again.' The mischief is always much greater than her worst fears. We soon see how Hamlet's gentle entertainment is received by Laertes; and she, in the blinding flash in which she dies, learns how great a treachery had been prepared against her Hamlet.

We cannot think of Gertrude's death, and the manner of it, without recalling what the Ghost had said. Leave her to Heaven. But if we are to see the hand of Providence—whatever that may signify—in her death, can we do other with the death [331] of Polonius? A 'casual slaughter?' A 'rash and bloody deed?' Certainly; and let us by all means blame Hamlet for it, as also for the callousness with which he sends Rosencrantz and Guildenstern to their doom; but if we suppose that Shakespeare contrived these things only to show us what Hamlet was like, we shall be treating as secular drama what Shakespeare designed as something bigger. In fact, Hamlet was *not* like this, any more than he was, by nature, hesitant or dilatory; any more than Ophelia was habitually mad. This is what he has become. The dramatist does indeed direct us to regard the killing of Polonius in two aspects at once: it is a sudden, unpremeditated attack made by Hamlet, 'mad,' on one who he hopes will prove to be Claudius; and at the same time it is the will of Heaven:

> For this same lord
> I do repent; but Heaven hath pleased it so
> To punish me with this and this with me,
> That I must be their scourge and minister.

Surely this is exactly the same dramaturgy that we meet in Sophocles' *Electra*. When Orestes comes out from killing his mother, Electra asks him how things are: 'In the *palace*,' he says, 'all is well—if Apollo's oracle was well.' Perhaps it was a 'rash and bloody deed'; it seems to bring Orestes little joy. We may think of it what we like; Sophocles does not invite us to approve, and if we suppose that he does, we have not understood his play, or his gods. Apollo approves, and Orestes, though he acts for his own reasons, is the gods' 'scourge and minister.' Polonius, no unworthy Counsellor of this King, a mean and crafty man whose soul is mirrored in his language no less than in his acts, meets a violent death while spying; and that such a man should so be killed is, in a large sense, right. Hamlet may 'repent'; Orestes may feel remorse at a dreadful act, but in each case Heaven was ordinant.

The death of Laertes too is a coherent part of this same pattern. To this friend of Hamlet's we can attribute one fault; nor are we taken by surprise when we meet it, for Shakespeare has made his preparations. Laertes is a noble and generous youth, but his sense of honour has no very secure foundations—and [332] Polonius' farewell speech to him makes the fact easy to understand. His natural and unguarded virtue, assailed at once by his anger, his incomplete understanding of the facts, and the evil sugges- tions of Claudius, gives way; he falls into treachery, and through it, as he comes to see, he is 'most justly killed.'

Of Rosencrantz and Guildenstern, two agreeable though un- distinguished young men, flattered and suborned and cruelly de- stroyed, there is no more to be said; but there remains Hamlet, last and greatest of the eight. Why must he be destroyed? It would be true to say that he is destroyed simply because he has failed to destroy Claudius first; but this is 'truth' as it is understood be- tween police-inspectors, on duty. The dramatic truth must be something which, taking this in its stride, goes much deeper; and we are justified in saying 'must be' since this catastrophe too is presented as being directed by Providence, and therefore inevi- table and 'right.' If 'there is a special providence in the fall of a sparrow,' there surely is in the fall of a Hamlet.

Of the eight victims, we have placed Claudius at one pole and Ophelia at the other; Hamlet, plainly, stands near Ophelia. In both Hamlet and Ophelia we can no doubt detect faults: she ought to have been able to see through Polonius, and he should not have hesitated. But to think like this is to behave like a judge, one who must stand outside the drama and sum up from a neu- tral point of view; the critic who tries to do this would be better employed in a police-court than in criticism. We must remain within the play, not try to peer at the characters through a window of our own constructing. If we do remain within the play, we observe that what Shakespeare puts before us, all the time, is not faults that we can attribute to Ophelia and Hamlet, but their vir- tues; and when he does make Hamlet do things deserving of blame, he also makes it evident on whom the blame should be laid. The impression with which he leaves us is not the tragedy that one so fine as Hamlet should be ruined by one fault; it is the tragedy that one so fine should be drawn down into the gulf; and, beyond this, that the poison let loose in Denmark should destroy

indiscriminately the good, the bad and the indifferent. Good and
bad, Hamlet and Claudius, are coupled in the one sentence 'If his
fitness speaks, mine is ready.' That Claudius is 'fit and seasoned
for his passage' is plain enough [333] is it not just as plain that
Hamlet is equally 'ready?' What has he been telling us, throughout
the play, but that life can henceforth have no meaning or value to
him? Confronted by what he sees in Denmark, he, the man of
action, has been reduced to impotence; the man of reason has gone
'mad'; the man of religion has been dragged down to 'knavery,'
and has felt the contagions of Hell. There is room, though not
very much, for subtle and judicious appraisal of his character and
conduct; the core of his tragedy is not here, but in the fact that
such surpassing excellence is, like the beauty and virtue of Ophelia,
brought to nothing by evil. Through all the members of these two
doomed houses the evil goes on working, in a concatenation

> Of carnal, bloody and unnatural acts,
> Of accidental judgments, casual slaughters,
> Of deaths put on by cunning and forced cause,

until none are left, and the slate is wiped clean.

The structure of *Hamlet,* then, suggests that we should treat
it as religious drama, and when we do, it certainly does not lose
either in significance or in artistic integrity. As we have seen
more than once, it has fundamental things in common with Greek
religious drama—yet in other respects it is very different, being
so complex in form and texture. It may be worth while to enquire, briefly, why this should be so.

One naturally compares it with the two Greek revenge-
tragedies, the *Choephori* and Sophocles' *Electra,* but whether we
do this, or extend the comparison to other Greek religious tragedies like the *Agamemnon* or *Oedipus Tyrannus* or *Antigone,* we
find one difference which is obviously pertinent to our enquiry: in
the Greek plays the sin, crime or error which is the mainspring of
the action is specific, while in Hamlet it is something more general, a quality rather than a single act. Thus, although there are
crimes enough in the *Oresteia,* what we are really concerned with,
throughout the trilogy, is the problem of avenging or punishing
crime. The *Agamemnon* is full of hybris, blind folly, blood-lust,
adultery, treachery; but what humanity is suffering from, in the

play, is not these sins in themselves, but a primitive conception
of Justice, one which uses, and can be made to justify, these
crimes, and leads to chaos; and the trilogy ends not in any form
of reconciliation or [334] forgiveness among those who have injured each other, nor in any purging of sin, or acceptance of punishment, but in the resolution of the dilemma.

Hamlet resembles the *Choephori* in this, that the murder of a
King, and adultery, or something like it, are the crimes which
have to be avenged; also that these can be avenged only through
another crime, though perhaps a sinless one; but the differences
are deep and far-reaching. They are not merely that Orestes kills,
and Hamlet shrinks from killing. We may say that both in the
Greek trilogy and in Shakespeare's play the Tragic Hero, ultimately, is humanity itself; and what humanity is suffering from,
in *Hamlet* is not a specific evil, but Evil itself. The murder is
only the chief of many manifestations of it, the particular case
which is the mainspring of the tragic action.

This seems to be typical. In the *Antigone* a whole house is
brought down in ruin, and, again, the cause is quite a specific
one. It is nothing like the comprehensive wickedness of Iago, or
the devouring ambition of Macbeth, or the consuming and all-
excluding love of Antony and Cleopatra. It is, quite precisely,
that Creon makes, and repeats, a certain error of judgment,
ἁμαρτία; and I use the phrase 'error of judgment' meaning not that
it is venial, nor that it is purely intellectual, but that it is specific.
It is not a trivial nor a purely intellectual mistake if a man, in
certain circumstances, rejects the promptings of humanity, and
thinks that the gods will approve; but this is what Creon does,
and the tragedy springs from this and from nothing else. He is
not a wicked man—not lecherous or envious or ambitious or vindictive. All this is irrelevant. He is simply the man to make and
maintain this one specific and disastrous error.

This contrast between the specific and the general obviously
has a close connexion with the contrast between the singleness of
the normal Greek tragic structure and the complexity of *Hamlet*.
In the first place, since Shakespeare's real theme is not the moral
or theological or social problem of crime and vengeance, still less
its effect on a single mind and soul, but the corroding power of
sin, he will present it not as a single 'error of judgment' but as a

hydra with many heads. We have shown, let us hope, how this explains, or helps to explain, such features of the play, so to speak, the simultaneous presentation of three Creons: Claudius, Gertrude and Polonius, each of them, in his [335] own degree, an embodiment of the general evil. Hence too the richer character-drawing. Claudius is a drunkard, and the fact makes its own contribution to the complete structure; if Sophocles had made Creon a drunkard, it would have been an excrescence on the play. Hence too the frequent changes of scene in the first part of the play; also the style of speech invented for Polonius and Osric. The general enemy is the rottenness that pervades Denmark; therefore it is shown in many persons and many guises.

Then, not only are the sources of the corruption diverse, but so are its ramifications too. We are to see how it spreads, whether from Claudius or from Gertrude or from Polonius, and how it involves one after another, destroying as it goes. To be sure, Greek tragedy shows us something similar—but it is not the same. For example, the condemnation of Antigone leads to the death of Haemon, and that to the death of Eurydice; in the *Oresteia* too there is a long succession of crime. In fact, we remarked above that Claudius recalls the *Agamemnon* and its πρώταρχος ἄτη, the crime that sets crime in motion. So he does; but there is a big difference. Both in *Hamlet* and in the Greek plays crime leads to crime, or disaster to disaster, in this linear fashion, but in *Hamlet* it spreads from soul to soul, as a contagion, as when Laertes is tempted by Claudius, or, most notably, when, by his mother's example and Polonius' basely inspired interference, Hamlet's love is corrupted into lewdness, or when he turns against his two compromised friends and pitilessly sends them to death.

Extension of evil in this fashion is, I think, foreign to Greek tragedy. Clearly, it involves a dramatic form which is complexive, not linear and single, like the Greek. Of his successive victims, Sophocles does not even mention Haemon until the middle of the play, and Eurydice not until the end; and the effect is most dramatic. In *Hamlet* there are eight victims, all of whom we have to watch, from time to time, as they become more and more deeply involved.

Further, not only are more people involved at the same time

in this more generalised Tragic Flaw, but they are involved more intimately, which again makes for a richer dramatic texture. We may compare Hamlet with Orestes. Externally,[336] they are in a similar position. But when Aeschylus has shown us that Orestes is an avenger pure in heart, and that his dilemma is from every point of view an intolerable one, it is not far wrong to say that his interest in Orestes, as a character, is exhausted; anything more would be unnecessary. Hamlet exists in a different kind of tragedy, one which requires that we should see how the contagion gradually spreads over his whole spirit and all his conduct.

The same contrast exists between Hamlet and Sophocles' Orestes and Electra. She, one might say, is drawn much more intimately than the Orestes of Aeschylus. True; but still she is drawn, so to speak, all at once: There is the situation, here is Electra, and this is the way in which it makes her act. It is not Sophocles' conception to show how her mother's continuing crime gradually warps her mind, by a stealthy growth of evil. If she is warped, it has all happened already. His dramatic interest in the characters of the avengers is focussed on this, that they, being what they are, and being affected by Clytemnestra's crime in this way, will naturally act as they do.

It is, in short, a general statement which I think will bear examination, that Greek tragedy presents sudden and complete disaster, or one disaster linked to another in linear fashion, while Shakespearean tragedy presents the complexive, menacing spread of ruin; and that at least one explanation of this is that the Greek poets thought of the tragic error as the breaking of a divine law (or sometimes, in Aeschylus, as the breaking down of a temporary divine law), while Shakespeare saw it as an evil quality which, once it has broken loose, will feed on itself and on anything else that it can find until it reaches its natural end. So, for example in *Macbeth:* in 'noble Macbeth,' ambition is stimulated, and is not controlled by reason or religion; it meets with a stronger response from Lady Macbeth, and grows insanely into a monstrous passion that threatens a whole kingdom. It is a tragic conception which is essentially dynamic, and demands the very unhellenic fluidity and expansiveness of expression which the Elizabethan theatre afforded. Whether this is a reflection of some profound difference between Greek and Christian thought is a question which I am not competent to discuss.[337]

The Embassy of Death
An Essay on Hamlet

By G. Wilson Knight

G. Wilson Knight, from "The Embassy of Death: An Essay on
Hamlet," in *The Wheel of Fire* (London, Oxford University
Press, 1930).

IT IS USUAL in Shakespeare's plays for
the main theme to be reflected in subsidiary incidents, persons,
and detailed suggesion throughout. Now the theme of *Hamlet* is
Death. Life that is bound for the disintegration of the grave, love
that does not survive the loved one's life—both, in their insistence
on Death as the primary fact of nature are branded on the mind
of Hamlet, burned into it, searing it with agony. The bereavement of Hamlet and his consequent mental agony bordering on
madness is mirrored in the bereavement of Ophelia and her madness. The death of the Queen's love is reflected in the swift-
passing of the love of the player-queen, in the murder of Gonzago. Death is over the whole play. Polonius and Ophelia die
during the action, and Ophelia is buried before our eyes. Hamlet
arranges the deaths of Rosencrantz and Guildenstern. The plot is
set in motion by the murder of Hamlet's father, and the play
opens with the apparition of the Ghost.

> What may this mean,
> That thou, dead corse, again in complete steel
> Revisit'st thus the glimpses of the moon,
> Making night hideous; and we fools of nature
> So horridly to shake our dispositions
> With thoughts beyond the reaches of our souls?
>   (I. iv. 51)

Those first scenes strike the note of the play—Death. We hear of terrors beyond the grave, from the Ghost (I. v.) and from the meditations of Hamlet (III. i.). We hear of horrors in the grave from Hamlet whose mind is obsessed with hideous thoughts of the body's decay. Hamlet's dialogue with the King about the dead Polonius (IV. iii 17) is painful; and the graveyard meditations,[34] though often beautiful, are remorselessly realistic. Hamlet holds Yorick's skull:

Hamlet   Now, get you to my lady's chamber and tell her, let her paint an inch thick, to this favour she must come; make her laugh at that. Prithee, Horatio, tell me one thing.
Horatio   What's that, my lord?
Hamlet   Dost thou think Alexander looked o' this fashion i' the earth?
Horatio   E'en so.
Hamlet   And smelt so? pah!   (v. i. 212)

The general thought of Death, intimately related to the predominating human theme, the pain in Hamlet's mind, is thus suffused through the whole play. And yet the play, as a whole, scarcely gives us that sense of blackness and the abysms of spiritual Evil which we find in *Macbeth;* nor is there the universal gloom of Lear. This is due partly to the difference in the technique of *Hamlet* from that of *Macbeth* or *Lear*. Macbeth, the protagonist and heroic victim of Evil, rises gigantic from the murk of an evil universe; Lear, the King of Suffering, towers over a universe that itself toils in pain. Thus in *Macbeth* and *Lear* the predominating imaginative atmospheres are used not to contrast with the mental universe of the hero, but to aid and support it, as it were, with similarity, to render realistic the extravagant and daring effects of volcanic passion to which the poet allows his protagonist to give voice. We are forced by the attendant personification, the verbal colour, the symbolism and events of the play as a whole, to feel the hero's suffering, to see with his eyes. Now in *Hamlet* this is not so. We need not see through Hamlet's eyes. Though the idea of death is recurrent through the play, it is not implanted in the minds of the other persons as is the consciousness of evil throughout *Macbeth* and the consciousness of suffering throughout *Lear*. Except for the original murder of Hamlet's father, the Hamlet-universe is one of healthy and robust life, good-nature, humour, romantic strength, and welfare: against this background is the figure of Hamlet pale with [35] the consciousness of death. He is the ambassador of Death, walking amid Life. The effect is at first primarily one of separation. But it is to be noted that the consciousness of death, and consequent bitterness, cruelty, and inaction, in Hamlet not only grows in his own mind disintegrating it as we watch, but also spreads its effects outward among the other persons like a blighting disease, and, as the play progresses, by its very passivity and negation of purpose, insidiously undermines the health of the state, and adds victim to victim until at the end the stage is filled with corpses. It is, as it were, a nihilistic birth in the consciousness of Hamlet that spreads its deadly venom around. That Hamlet is originally blameless, that the King is originally guilty, may well be granted. But, if we refuse to be diverted from a clear vision by questions of praise and blame, responsibility and causality, and watch only the actions and reactions of the persons as they appear, we shall observe a striking reversal of the usual commentary.

Now if we are to attain to a true interpretation of Shakespeare we must work from a centre of consciousness near that of the creative instinct of the poet. We must think less in terms of causality and more in terms of imaginative impact. Now Claudius is not drawn as wholly evil—far from it. We see the government of Denmark working smoothly. Claudius shows every sign of being an excellent diplomatist and king. He is troubled by young Fortinbras, and dispatches ambassadors to the sick King of Norway demanding that he suppress the raids of his nephew. His speech to the ambassadors bears the stamp of clear and exact thought and an efficient and confident control of affairs:

> and we here dispatch
> You, good Cornelius, and you, Voltimand,
> For bearers of this greeting to old Norway;
> Giving to you no further personal power
> To business with the king, more than the scope
> Of these delated articles allow.
> Farewell, and let your haste commend your duty.
>   (I. ii. 33) [36]

The ambassadors soon return successful. Claudius listens to their reply, receives the King of Norway's letter, and hears that young

Fortinbras desires a free pass through Denmark to lead his soldiers against the Poles. Claudius answers:

> It likes us well;
> And at our more consider'd time we'll read,
> Answer, and think upon this business.
> Meantime we thank you for your well-took labour:
> Go to your rest; at night we'll feast together:
> Most welcome home!   (II. ii. 80)

Tact has found an easy settlement where arms and opposition
might have wasted the strength of Denmark. Notice his reservation of detailed attention when once he knows the main issues are
clear; the courteous yet dignified attitude to his subordinates and
the true leader's consideration for their comfort; and the invitation to the feast. The impression given by these speeches is one of
quick efficiency—the efficiency of the man who can dispose of
business without unnecessary circumstance, and so leaves himself
time for enjoying the good things of life: a man kindly, confident,
and fond of pleasure.

   Now throughout the first half of the play Claudius is the
typical kindly uncle, besides being a good king. His advice to
Hamlet about his exaggerated mourning for his father's death is
admirable common sense:

> Fie! 'Tis a fault to heaven,
> A fault against the dead, a fault to nature,
> To reason most absurd; whose common theme
> Is death of fathers, and who still hath cried,
> From the first corse, till he that died to-day,
> 'This must be so.'   (I. ii. 101)

It is the advice of worldly common sense opposed to the extreme
misery of a sensitive nature paralysed by the facts of death and
unfaithfulness. This contrast points the relative significance of the
King and his court to Hamlet. They are of the world—with their
crimes, their follies, their shallowness, their pomp and glitter;
they are of [37] humanity, with all its failings, it is true, but yet of
humanity. They assert the importance of human life, they believe
in it, in themselves. Whereas Hamlet is inhuman, since he has
seen through the tinsel of life and love, he believes in nothing, not
even himself, except the memory of a ghost, and his black-robed

presence is a reminder to every one of the fact of Death. There is
no question but that Hamlet is right. The King's smiles hide
murder, his mother's love for her new consort is unfaithfulness to
Hamlet's father, Ophelia has deserted Hamlet at the hour of his
need. Hamlet's philosophy may be inevitable, blameless, and ir-
refutable. But it is the negation of life. It is death. Hence Hamlet
is a continual fear to Claudius, a reminder of his crime. It is a
mistake to consider Claudius as a hardened criminal. When Polonius remarks on the hypocrisy of mankind, he murmurs to himself:

> O, 'tis too true!
> How smart a lash that speech doth give my conscience!
> The harlot's cheek, beautied with plastering art,
> Is not more ugly to the thing that helps it
> Than is my deed to my most painted word:
> O heavy burthen!   (III. i. 48)

Again, Hamlet's play wrenches his soul with remorse—primarily
not fear of Hamlet, as one might expect, but a genuine remorse—
and gives us that most beautiful prayer of a stricken soul beginning, 'O, my offence is rank, it smells to heaven' (III. iii. 36):

> What if this cursed hand
> Were thicker than itself with brother's blood,
> Is there not rain enough in the sweet heavens
> To wash it white as snow? Whereto serves mercy
> But to confront the visage of offence?

He fears that his prayer is worthless. He is still trammelled by
the enjoyment of the fruits of his crime. 'My fault is past,' he
cries. But what does that avail, since he has his crown and his
queen still, the prizes of murder? His dilemma is profound and
raises the problem I am pointing in this essay. Claudius, as he
appears in the play,[38] is not a criminal. He is—strange as it may
seem—a good and gentle king, enmeshed by the chain of causality linking him with his crime. And this chain he might, perhaps, have broken except for Hamlet, and all would have been
well. But, granted the presence of Hamlet—which Claudius at first
genuinely desired, persuading him not to return to Wittenberg as
he wished—and granted the fact of his original crime which
cannot now be altered, Claudius can hardly be blamed for his

later actions. They are forced on him. As King, he could scarcely
be expected to do otherwise. Hamlet is a danger to the state, even
apart from his knowledge of Claudius' guilt. He is an inhuman—
or superhuman—presence, whose consciousness—somewhat like
Dostoievsky's Stavrogin—is centred on death. Like Stavrogin, he
is feared by those around him. They are always trying in vain to
find out what is wrong with him. They cannot understand him. He
is a creature of another world. As King of Denmark he would
have been a thousand times more dangerous than Claudius. The
end of Claudius' prayer is pathetic:

> What then? What rests?
> Try what repentance can: what can it not?
> Yet what can it when one can not repent?
> O wretched state! O bosom black as death!
> O limed soul, that, struggling to be free,
> Art more engaged! Help, angels; make assay!
> Bow, stubborn knees; and, heart with strings of steel,
> Be soft as sinews of the new-born babe!
> All may be well.   (III. iii. 64)

Set against this lovely prayer—the fine flower of a human soul in
anguish—is the entrance of Hamlet, the late joy of torturing the
King's conscience still written on his face, his eye a-glitter with
the intoxication of conquest, vengeance in his mind; his purpose
altered only by the devilish hope of finding a more damning
moment in which to slaughter the King, next hastening to his
mother to wring her soul too. Which then, at this moment in the
play, is nearer the Kingdom of Heaven? Whose words would
be [39] more acceptable of Jesus' God? Which is the embodiment
of spiritual good, which of evil? The question of the relative
morality of Hamlet and Claudius reflects the ultimate problem of
this play.

Other eminently pleasant traits can be found in Claudius. He
hears of Hamlet's murder of Polonius:

> O Gertrude, come away!
> The sun no sooner shall the mountains touch,
> But we will ship him hence: and this vile deed
> We must, with all our majesty and skill,
> Both countenance and excuse.   (IV. i. 28)

Though a murderer himself, he has a genuine horror of murder.
This does not ring hypocritical. He takes the only possible course.
Hamlet is a danger.

> His liberty is full of threats to all.   (IV. i. 14)

To hurry him from Denmark is indeed necessary: it is the only
way of saving himself, and, incidentally, the best line of action in
the interests of the state. During the scene of Ophelia's madness
(IV. v.) Claudius shows a true and sensitive concern, exclaiming,
'How do you, pretty lady?' and 'Pretty Ophelia!' and after he has
told Horatio to look after her, he speaks in all sincerity to his
Queen:

> O, this is the poison of deep grief; it springs
> All from her father's death. O Gertrude, Gertrude,
> When sorrows come, they come not single spies,
> But in battalions. First, her father slain:
> Next, your son gone; and he most violent author
> Of his most just remove . . .   (IV. v. 76)

He continues the catalogue of ills. The people are dissatisfied,
Laertes has returned. The problems are indeed overwhelming.
When Laertes enters, Claudius rouses our admiration by his cool
reception of him:

> What is the cause, Laertes,
> That thy rebellion looks so giant-like?
> Let him go, Gertrude; do not fear our person:
> There's such divinity doth hedge a king,
> That treason can but peep to what it would,[40]
> Acts little of its will. Tell me, Laertes,
> Why thou art thus incensed. Let him go, Gertrude.
> Speak, man.   (IV. v. 120)

When he hears of Hamlet's return he plots treachery with Laertes.
Everything considered, one can hardly blame him. He has, it is
true, committed a dastardly murder, but in the play he gives us
the impression of genuine penitence and a host of good qualities.
After the murder of Polonius we certainly feel that both the King
and the Queen are sane and doing their level best to restrain the
activities of a madman. That is the impression given by the play
at this point, as we read. If we think in terms of logic, we remem-

ber at once that we must side with Hamlet. And we perhaps remember the continual and sudden emergences of a different
Hamlet: a Hamlet loving and noble and sane. But intermittent
madness is more dangerous by far than obvious insanity. At the
best we only prove that Hamlet's madness is justifiable, a statement which makes nonsense. For Hamlet's behaviour, so utterly
out of harmony with his environment of eminently likeable people, in that relation may well be called a kind of madness. Whatever it is, it is extremely dangerous and powerful.

Now I have concentrated on Claudius' virtues. They are
manifest. So are his faults—his original crime, his skill in the less
admirable kind of policy, treachery, and intrigue. But I would
point clearly that, in the movement of the play, his faults are
forced on him, and he is distinguished by creative and wise action,
a sense of purpose, benevolence, a faith in himself and those
around him, by love of his Queen:

> and for myself—
> My virtue or my plague, be it either which—
> She's so conjunctive to my life and soul,
> That as the star moves not but in his sphere,
> I could not but by her.   (IV. vii 12)

In short, he is very human. Now these are the very qualities Hamlet lacks. Hamlet is inhuman. He has seen [41] through humanity.
And this inhuman cynicism, however justifiable in this case, on the
plane of causality and individual responsibility, is a deadly and
venomous thing. Instinctively the creatures of earth—Laertes, Polonius, Ophelia, Rosencrantz and Guildenstern, league themselves
with Claudius: they are of his kind. They sever themselves from
Hamlet. Laertes sternly warns Ophelia against her intimacy with
Hamlet, so does Polonius. They are, in fact, all leagued against
him, they are puzzled by him or fear him: he has no friend except
Horatio, and Horatio, after the ghost scenes, becomes a queer
shadowy character who rarely gets beyond 'E'en so, my lord,' 'My
lord—,' and such-like phrases. The other persons are firmly
drawn, in the round, creatures of flesh and blood. But Hamlet is
not of flesh and blood, he is a spirit of penetrating intellect and
cynicism and misery, without faith in himself or any one else,
murdering his love of Ophelia, on the brink of insanity, taking

delight in cruelty, torturing Claudius, wringing his mother's heart, a poison in the midst of the healthy bustle of the court. He is a superman among men. And he is a superman because he has walked and held converse with Death, and his consciousness works in terms of Death and the Negation of Cynicism. He has seen the truth, not alone of Denmark, but of humanity, of the universe: and the truth is evil. Thus Hamlet is an element of evil in the state of Denmark. The poison of his mental existence spreads outwards among things of flesh and blood, like acid eating into metal. They are helpless before his very inactivity and fall one after the other, like victims of an infectious disease. They are strong with the strength of health—but the demon of Hamlet's mind is a stronger thing than they. Futilely they try to get him out of their country; anything to get rid of him, he is not safe. But he goes with a cynical smile, and is no sooner gone than he is back again in their midst, meditating in graveyards, at home with Death. Not till it has slain all, is the demon that grips Hamlet satisfied. And last it slays Hamlet himself: [42]

> The spirit that I have seen
> May be the devil . . .   (II. ii. 627)

It was.

It was the devil of the knowledge of death, which possesses Hamlet and drives him from misery and pain to increasing bitterness, cynicism, murder, and madness. He has indeed bought converse with his father's spirit at the price of enduring and spreading hell on Earth. But however much we may sympathize with Ophelia, with Polonius, Rosencrantz, Guildenstern, the Queen, and Claudius, there is one reservation to be made. It is Hamlet who is right. What he says and thinks of them is true, and there is no fault in his logic. His own mother is indeed faithless, and the prettiness of Ophelia does in truth enclose a spirit as fragile and untrustworthy as her earthly beauty; Polonius is 'a foolish prating knave.' Rosencrantz and Guildenstern are timeservers and flatterers; Claudius, whose benevolence hides the guilt of murder, is, by virtue of that fact, 'a damned smiling villain.' In the same way the demon of cynicism which is in the mind of the poet and expresses itself in the figures of this play, has always this characteristic: it is right. One cannot argue with the cynic. It is unwise to offer him battle. For in the warfare of logic it will be found that he has all the guns.

Now in this play we are confronted by a curious problem of technique. I pointed out early in my essay that the effects are gained by contrast, and it will be seen from my analysis that this contrast has its powerful imaginative effects. But it is also disconcerting. Though we instinctively tend at first to adopt the view-point of Hamlet himself, we are not forced to do so throughout. My analysis has shown that other methods of approach are possible; and, if they are possible, they are, in objective drama, legitimate. It is, indeed, necessary that we should be equally prepared to adopt the point of view of either side, otherwise we are offering a biassed interpretation. And though the Hamlet-theme preponderates over that of any one other individual in the play, it will be clear that [43] Hamlet has set in contrast to him all the other persons: they are massed against him. In the universe of this play—whatever may have happened in the past—he is the only discordant element, the only hindrance to happiness, health, and prosperity: a living death in the midst of life. Therefore a balanced judgement is forced to pronounce ultimately in favour of life as contrasted with death, for optimism and the healthily second-rate, rather than the nihilism of the superman: for he is not, as the plot shows, safe; and he is not safe, primarily because he is right—otherwise Claudius could soon have swept him from his path. If we think primarily of the state of Denmark during the action of the play, we are bound to applaud Claudius, as he appears before us: he acts throughout with a fine steadiness of purpose. By creating normal and healthy and lovable persons around his protagonist, whose chief peculiarity is the abnormality of extreme melancholia, the poet divides our sympathies. The villain has become a kindly uncle, the princely hero is the incarnation of cynicism. It is true that if Hamlet had promptly avenged his father, taken the throne, forgotten his troubles, resumed a healthy outlook on life, he would have all our acclamations. Laertes entering in wrath at the death of his father, daring 'damnation' (IV. V. 133) and threatening Claudius, comes on us like a blast of fresh air, after the stifling, poisonous atmosphere of Hamlet's mind: Laertes and Hamlet struggling at Ophelia's grave are like symbols of Life and Death contending for the prize of Love. Laertes is brave in his course of loyalty. But to expect such a course from Hamlet is to misunderstand him quite and his place in the play. The time is out of joint, he is thrown out of any significant relation with his world. He cannot bridge the gulf by rational action. Nor can he understand the rest any more than they understand him. His 'ideals'—which include an insistent memory of death—are worth nothing to them, and, most maddening fact of all, they get on perfectly well as they are—or would do if Hamlet were out of the way. Thus, through no fault of his own,[44] Hamlet has been forced into a state of evil: Claudius, whose crime originally placed him there, is in a state of healthy and robust spiritual life. Hamlet, and we too, are perplexed. Thus Hamlet spends a great part of his time watching, analysing, and probing others. He unhesitatingly lances each in turn in his weakest spot. He is usually quite merciless. But all he actually accomplishes is to torment them all, terrorize them. They are dreadfully afraid of him. Hamlet is so powerful—he is, as it were, the channel of a mysterious force: which force derives largely from his having seen through them all. In contact with him they know their own faults: neither they nor we should know them otherwise. He exposes faults everywhere. But he is not tragic in the usual Shakespearian sense; there is no surge and swell of passion pressing onward through the play to leave us, as in *Lear,* with the mighty crash and backwash of a tragic peace. There is not this direct rhythm in Hamlet—there is no straight course. Instead of being dynamic, the force of Hamlet is, paradoxically, static. Its poison is the poison of negation, nothingness, threatening a world of positive assertion. But even this element is not the whole of Hamlet. He can speak lovingly to his mother at one moment, and the next, in an excess of revulsion, torment her with a withering and brutal sarcasm. One moment he can cry:

> I loved Ophelia: forty thousand brothers
> Could not, with all their quantity of love,
> Make up my sum.   (v. i. 292)

Shortly after he scorns himself for his outbreak. His mind reflects swift changes. He may for a moment or two see with the eyes of humour, gentleness, love—then suddenly the whole universe is blackened, goes out, leaves utter vacancy. This is, indeed, the secret of the play's fascination and its lack of unified and concise poetic statement. Hamlet is a dualized personality, wavering, oscillating between grace and the hell of cynicism. The plot reflects this see-saw motion; it lacks direction, pivoting on [45] Hamlet's incertitude, and analysis holds the fascination of giddiness. Nor can Hamlet feel anything passionately for long, since passion implies purpose, and he has no one purpose for any length of time. One element in Hamlet, and that a very important one, is the negation of any passion whatsoever. His disease—or vision— is primarily one of negation, of death. Hamlet is a living Death in the midst of Life; that is why the play sounds the note of death so strong and sombre at the start. The Ghost was conceived throughout as a portent not kind but sinister. That sepulchral cataclysm at the beginning is the key to the whole play. *Hamlet* begins with an explosion in the first act; the rest of the play is the reverberation thereof. From the first act onwards Hamlet is, as it were, blackened, scorched by that shattering revelation. The usual process is reversed and the climax is at the start. Hamlet, already in despair, converses early with Death: through the remaining acts he lives within that death, remembering the Ghost, spreading destruction wherever he goes, adding crime to crime, like Macbeth, and becoming more and more callous, until his detestable act of sending his former friends to unmerited death 'not shriving-time allow'd' (v. ii. 47). Finally 'that fell sergeant, death' (v. ii. 347) arrests him too. This is his mysterious strength, ghost-begotten, before which the rest succumb. That is why this play is so rich in Death—why its meaning is analysed by Hamlet in soliloquy, why Hamlet is so fascinated by the skulls the grave-digger unearths; why so many 'casual slaughters' and 'deaths put on by cunning and forced cause' (v. ii. 393) disrupt the action, till we are propelled to the last holocaust of mortality and Fortinbras's comment:

> This quarry cries on havoc. O proud death,
> What feast is toward in thine eternal cell,
> That thou so many princes at a shot
> So bloodily hast struck?   (v. ii. 375)

The Ghost may or may not have been a 'goblin damned'; it certainly was no 'spirit of health' (I. IV. 40). The play ends with a

dead march. The action grows out of eternity,[46] closes in it. The
ominous discharge of ordnance thus reverberates three times: once,
before Hamlet sees the Ghost, and twice in Act v. The eternity of
death falls as an abyss at either end, and Hamlet crosses the stage
of life aureoled in its ghostly luminance. . . .[47]

But we properly know Hamlet himself only when he is alone
with Death: then he is lovable and gentle, then he is beautiful
and noble, and, there being no trivial things of life to blur our
mortal vision, our minds are tuned to the exquisite music of his
soul. We know the real Hamlet only in his address to the Ghost,
in his 'To be or not to be . . .' soliloquy, in the lyric prose of the
graveyard scene:

> Here hung those lips that I have kissed I know not how oft . . .
>   (v. i. 207)

These touch a melody that holds no bitterness. Here, and when he
is dying, we glimpse, perhaps, a thought wherein death, not life,
holds the deeper assurance for humanity. Then we will understand why Hamlet knows death to be felicity:

> Absent thee from felicity awhile,
> And in this harsh world draw thy breath in pain
> To tell my story . . .   (v. ii. 358)

The story of a 'sweet prince' (v. ii. 370) wrenched from Life and
dedicate alone to Death.[50]

Hamlet
The Prince or the Poem?

By C. S. Lewis

C. S. Lewis, "Hamlet: The Prince or the Poem?" Annual Shakespeare Lecture of the British Academy, in *Proceedings of the
British Academy* XXXVIII (London, Oxford University Press,
1942).

$\mathcal{A}$ CRITIC who makes no claim to be a
true Shakespearian scholar and who has been honoured by an invitation to speak about Shakespeare to such an audience as this, feels
rather like a child brought in at dessert to recite his piece before
the grown-ups. I have a temptation to furbish up all my meagre
Shakespearian scholarship and to plunge into some textual or
chronological problem in the hope of seeming, for this one hour,
more of an expert than I am. But it really wouldn't do. I should
not deceive you: I should not even deceive myself. I have therefore decided to bestow all my childishness upon you.

And first, a reassurance. I am not going to advance a new
interpretation of the character of Hamlet. Where great critics
have failed I could not hope to succeed; it is rather my ambition (a
more moderate one, I trust) to understand their failure. The problem I want to consider to-day arises in fact not directly out of the
Prince's character nor even directly out of the play, but out of the
state of criticism about the play.

To give anything like a full history of this criticism would
be beyond my powers and beyond the scope of a lecture; but, for
my present purpose, I think we can very roughly divide it into
three main schools or tendencies. The first is that which maintains
simply that the actions of Hamlet have not been given adequate

motives and that the play is so far bad. Hanmer is perhaps the
earliest exponent of this view. According to him Hamlet is made
to procrastinate because 'had he gone naturally to work, there
would have been an end to our play.' But then, as Hanmer points
out, Shakespeare ought to have 'contrived some good reason' for
the procrastination. Johnson, while praising the tragedy for its
'variety,' substantially agrees with Hanmer: 'of the feigned madness of Hamlet there appears no adequate cause.' Rümelin thinks
that the 'wisdom' which Shakespeare has chosen to hide under 'the
wild utterances of insanity' is a 'foreign and disturbing element'
as a result of which the piece 'presents the greatest discrepancies.'
In our own time Mr. Eliot has taken the same view: *Hamlet* is
rather like a film on which two photographs have been taken—an
unhappy superposition [3] of Shakespeare's work 'upon much cruder material.' The play 'is most certainly an artistic failure.' If this
school of critics is right, we shall be wasting our time in attempting to understand why Hamlet delayed. The second school, on the
other hand, thinks that he did not delay at all but went to work as
quickly as the circumstances permitted. This was Ritson's view.
The word of a ghost, at second hand, 'would scarcely in the eye of
the people have justified his killing their king.' That is why he
'counterfeits madness and . . . puts the usurper's guilt to the test of
a play.' Klein, after a very fierce attack on critics who want to make
the Prince of Denmark 'a German half-professor, all tongue and
no hand,' comes to the same conclusion. So does Werder, and so
does Macdonald; and the position has been brilliantly defended in
modern times. In the third school or group I include all those
critics who admit that Hamlet procrastinates and who explain the
procrastination by his psychology. Within this general agreement
there are, no doubt, very great diversities. Some critics, such as
Hallam, Sievers, Raleigh, and Clutton Brock, trace the weakness
to the shock inflicted upon Hamlet by the events which precede,
and immediately follow, the opening of the play; others regard it
as a more permanent condition; some extend it to actual insanity,
others reduce it to an almost amiable flaw in a noble nature. This
third group, which boasts the names of Richardson, Goethe, Coleridge, Schlegel, and Hazlitt, can still, I take it, claim to represent
the central and, as it were, orthodox line of *Hamlet* criticism.

Such is the state of affairs; and we are all so accustomed to it

that we are inclined to ignore its oddity. In order to remove the
veil of familiarity I am going to ask you to make the imaginative
effort of looking at this mass of criticism as if you had no independent knowledge of the thing criticized. Let us suppose that a
picture which you have not seen is being talked about. The first
thing you gather from the vast majority of the speakers—and a
majority which includes the best art critics—is that this picture is
undoubtedly a very great work. The next thing you discover is that
hardly any two people in the room agree as to what it is a picture
of. Most of them find something curious about the pose, and perhaps even the anatomy, of the central figure. One explains it by
saying that it is a picture of the raising of Lazarus, and that the
painter has cleverly managed to represent the uncertain gait of a
body just recovering from the stiffness of death. Another, taking
the central figure to be [4] Bacchus returning from the conquest of
India, says that it reels because it is drunk. A third, to whom it is
self-evident that he has seen a picture of the death of Nelson, asks
with some temper whether you expect a man to look quite normal
just after he has been mortally wounded. A fourth maintains that
such crudely representational canons of criticism will never penetrate so profound a work, and that the peculiarities of the central
figure really reflect the content of the painter's subconsciousness.
Hardly have you had time to digest these opinions when you run
into another group of critics who denounce as a pseudo-problem
what the first group has been discussing. According to this second
group there is nothing odd about the central figure. A more natural and self-explanatory pose they never saw and they cannot
imagine what all the pother is about. At long last you discover—
isolated in a corner of the room, somewhat frowned upon by the
rest of the company, and including few reputable *connoisseurs* in
its ranks—a little knot of men who are whispering that the picture
is a villainous daub and that the mystery of the central figure
merely results from the fact that it is out of drawing.

Now if all this had really happened to any one of us, I believe that our first reaction would be to accept, at least provision-
ally, the third view. Certainly I think we should consider it much
more seriously than we usually consider those critics who solve the
whole *Hamlet* problem by calling *Hamlet* a bad play. At the very
least we should at once perceive that they have a very strong case

against the critics who admire. 'Here is a picture,' they might say, 'on whose meaning no two of you are in agreement. Communication between the artist and the spectator has almost completely broken down, for each of you admits that it has broken down as regards every spectator except himself. There are only two possible explanations. Either the artist was a very bad artist, or you are very bad critics. In deference to your number and your reputation, we choose the first alternative; though, as you will observe, it would work out to the same result if we chose the second.' As to the next group—those who denied that there was anything odd about the central figure—I believe that in the circumstances I have imagined we should hardly attend to them. A natural and self-explanatory pose in the central figure would be rejected as wholly inconsistent with its observed effect on all the other critics, both those who thought the picture good and those who thought it bad.

If we now return to the real situation, the same reactions [5] appear reasonable. There is, indeed, this difference, that the critics who admit no delay and no indecision in Hamlet have an opponent with whom the corresponding critics of the picture were not embarrassed. The picture did not answer back. But Hamlet does. He pronounces himself a procrastinator, an undecided man, even a coward: and the ghost in part agrees with him. This, coupled with the more general difficulties of their position, appears to me to be fatal to their view. If so, we are left with those who think the play bad and those who agree in thinking it good and in placing its goodness almost wholly in the character of the hero, while disagreeing as to what that character is. Surely the devil's advocates are in a very strong position. Here is a play so dominated by one character that 'Hamlet without the Prince' is a byword. Here are critics justly famed, all of them for their sensibility, many of them for their skill in catching the finest shades of human passion and pursuing motives to their last hiding-places. Is it really credible that the greatest of dramatists, the most powerful painter of men, offering to such an audience his consummate portrait of a man should produce something which, if any one of them is right, all the rest have in some degree failed to recognize? Is this the sort of thing that happens? Does the meeting of supremely creative with supremely receptive imagination usually produce such results? Or is it not far easier to say that Homer nods,

and Alexander's shoulder drooped, and Achilles' heel was vulner-
able, and that Shakespeare, for once, either in haste, or over-
reaching himself in unhappy ingenuity, has brought forth an
abortion?

Yes. Of course it is far easier. 'Most certainly,' says Mr. Eliot,
'an artistic failure.' But is it 'most certain?' Let me return for a
moment to my analogy of the picture. In that dream there was one
experiment we did not make. We didn't walk into the next room
and look at it for ourselves. Supposing we had done so. Suppose
that at the first glance all the cogent arguments of the unfavourable
critics had died on our lips, or echoed in our ears as idle babble.
Suppose that looking on the picture we had found ourselves caught
up into an unforgettable intensity of life and had come back from
the room where it hung haunted for ever with the sense of vast
dignities and strange sorrows and teased 'with thoughts beyond
the reaches of our souls'—would not this have reversed our judgment and compelled us, in the teeth of *a priori* probability, to
maintain that on one point at least the orthodox critics were in the
right? 'Most certainly an artistic failure.' All argument is for that
conclusion—until you [6] read or see *Hamlet* again. And when you
do, you are left saying that if this is failure, then failure is better
than success. We want more of these 'bad' plays. From our first
childish reading of the ghost scenes down to those golden minutes
which we stole from marking examination papers on *Hamlet* to
read a few pages of *Hamlet* itself, have we ever know the day or
the hour when its enchantment failed? That castle is part of our
own world. The affection we feel for the Prince, and, through him,
for Horatio, is like a friendship in real life. The very turns of expression—half-lines and odd connecting links—of this play are
worked into the language. It appears, said Shaftesbury in 1710,
'most to have affected English hearts and has perhaps been oftenest
acted.' It has a taste of its own, an all-pervading relish which we
recognize even in its smallest fragments, and which, once tasted,
we recur to. When we want that taste, no other book will do instead. It may turn out in the end that the thing is not a complete
success. This compelling quality in it may coexist with some radical defect. But I doubt if we shall ever be able to say, sad brow
and true maid, that it is 'most certainly' a failure. Even if the
proposition that it has failed were at last admitted for true, I can

think of few critical truths which most of us would utter with less certainty, and with a more divided mind.

It seems, then, that we cannot escape from our problem by pronouncing the play bad. On the other hand, the critics, mostly agreeing to place the excellence of it in the delineation of the hero's character, describe that character in a dozen different ways. If they differ so much as to the kind of man whom Shakespeare meant to portray, how can we explain their unanimous praise of the portrayal? I can imagine a sketch so bad that one man thought it was an attempt at a horse and another thought it was an attempt at a donkey. But what kind of sketch would it have to be which looked like a *very good* horse to some, and like a *very good* donkey to others? The only solution which occurs to me is that the critics' delight in the play is not in fact due to the delineation of Hamlet's character but to something else. If the picture which you take for a horse and I for a donkey, delights us both, it is probable that what we are both enjoying is the pure line, or the colouring, not the delineation of an animal. If two men who have both been talking to the same woman agree in proclaiming her conversation delightful, though one praises it for its ingenuous innocence and the other for its clever sophistication, I should be inclined to conclude [7] that her conversation had played very little part in the pleasure of either. I should suspect that the lady was nice to look at.

I am quite aware that such a suggestion about what has always been thought a 'one man play' will sound rather like a paradox. But I am not aiming at singularity. In so far as my own ideas about Shakespeare are worth classifying at all, I confess myself a member of that school which has lately been withdrawing our attention from the characters to fix it on the plays. Dr. Stoll and Professor Wilson Knight, though in very different fashions, have led me in this direction; and Aristotle has long seemed to me simply right when he says that tragedy is an imitation not of men but of action and life and happiness and misery. By action he means, no doubt, not what a modern producer would call action but rather 'situation.'

What has attached me to this way of thinking is the fact that it explains my own experience. When I tried to read Shakespeare in my teens the character criticism of the nineteenth century stood between me and my enjoyment. There were all sorts of things in the plays which I could have enjoyed; but I had got it into my head that the only proper and grown-up way of appreciating Shakespeare was to be very interested in the truth and subtlety of his character drawing. A play opened with thunder and lightning and witches on a heath. This was very much in my line: but oh the disenchantment when I was told—or thought I was told—that what really ought to concern me was the effect of these witches on Macbeth's character! An Illyrian Duke spoke, in an air which had just ceased vibrating to the sound of music, words that seemed to come out of the very heart of some golden world of dreamlike passion: but all this was spoiled because the meddlers had told me it was the portrait of a self-deceiving or unrealistic man and given me the impression that it was my business to diagnose like a straightener from Erewhon or Vienna instead of submitting to the charm. Shakespeare offered me a King who could not even sentence a man to banishment without saying

> The sly slow hours shall not determinate
> The dateless limit of thy dear exile.

Left to myself I would simply have drunk it in and been thankful. That is just how beautiful, wilful, passionate, unfortunate kings killed long ago ought to talk. But then again the critic was at my elbow instilling the pestilential notion that I ought to prize such words chiefly as illustrations of what he called [8] Richard's weakness, and (worse still) inviting me to admire the vulgar, bustling efficiency of Bolingbroke. I am probably being very unjust to the critics in this account. I am not even sure who they were. But somehow or other this was the sort of idea they gave me. I believe they have given it to thousands. As far as I am concerned it meant that Shakespeare became to me for many years a closed book. Read him in *that* way I could not; and it was some time before I had the courage to read him in any other. Only much later, reinforced with a wider knowledge of literature, and able now to rate at its true value the humble little outfit of prudential maxims which really underlay much of the talk about Shakespeare's characters, did I return and read him with enjoyment. To one in my position the opposite movement in criticism came as a kind of Magna Carta. With that help I have come to one very definite conclusion. I do not say that the characters—especially the comic characters—count for nothing. But the first thing is to surrender oneself to the poetry and the situation. It is only through them that you can reach the characters, and it is for their sake that the characters exist. All conceptions of the characters arrived at, so to speak, in cold blood, by working out what sort of man it would have to be who in real life would act or speak as they do, are in my opinion chimerical. The wiseacres who proceed in that way only substitute our own ideas of character and life, which are not often either profound or delectable, for the bright shapes which the poet is actually using. Orsino and Richard II are test cases. Interpretations which compel you to read their speeches with a certain superiority, to lend them a note of 'insincerity,' to strive in any way against their beauty, are self-condemned. Poets do not make beautiful verse in order to have it 'guyed.' Both these characters speak golden syllables, wearing rich clothes, and standing in the centre of the stage. After that, they may be wicked, but it can only be with a passionate and poetic wickedness; they may be foolish, but only with follies noble and heroical. For the poetry, the clothes, and the stance are the substance; the character 'as it would have to be in real life' is only a shadow. It is often a very distorted shadow. Some of my pupils talk to me about Shakespeare as if the object of his life had been to render into verse the philosophy of Samuel Smiles or Henry Ford.

A good example of the kind of play which can be twisted out of recognition by character criticism is the *Merchant of Venice*. Nothing is easier than to disengage and condemn the mercenary [9] element in Bassanio's original suit to Portia, to point out that Jessica was a bad daughter, and by dwelling on Shylock's wrongs to turn him into a tragic figure. The hero thus becomes a scamp, the heroine's love for him a disaster, the villain a hero, the last act an irrelevance, and the casket story a monstrosity. What is not explained is why anyone should enjoy such a depressing and confused piece of work. It seems to me that what we actually enjoy is something quite different. The real play is not so much about men as about metals. The horror of usury lay in the fact that it treated metal in a way contrary to nature. If you have cattle they will breed. To make money—the mere medium of exchange—breed as if it were alive is a sort of black magic. The speech about Laban and Jacob is put into Shylock's mouth to show that he cannot grasp

this distinction; and the Christians point out that friendship does
not take 'a breed of barren metal.' The important thing about
Bassanio is that he can say, 'Only my blood speaks to you in my
veins,' and again, 'All the wealth I had ran in my veins.' Sir
Walter Raleigh most unhappily, to my mind, speaks of Bassanio as
a 'pale shadow.' *Pale* is precisely the wrong word. The whole contrast is between the crimson and organic wealth in his veins, the
medium of nobility and fecundity, and the cold, mineral wealth in
Shylock's counting-house. The charge that he is a mercenary
wooer is a product of prosaic analysis. The play is much nearer the
Märchen level than that. When the hero marries the princess we
are not expected to ask whether her wealth, her beauty, or her rank
was the determining factor. They are all blended together in the
simple man's conception of Princess. Of course great ladies are
beautiful: of course they are rich. Bassanio compares Portia to the
Golden Fleece. That strikes the proper note. And when once we
approach the play with our senses and imaginations it becomes
obvious that the presence of the casket story is no accident. For it
also is a story about metals, and the rejection of the commercial
metals by Bassanio is a kind of counterpoint to the conquest of
Shylock's metallic power by the lady of the beautiful mountain.
The very terms in which they are rejected proclaim it. Silver is the
'pale and common drudge 'twixt man and man.' Gold is 'hard
food for Midas'—Midas who, like Shylock, tried to use as the fuel
of life what is in its own nature dead. And the last act, so far
from being an irrelevant *coda,* is almost the thing for which the
play exists. The 'naughty world' of finance exists in the play chiefly
that we may perceive the light of the 'good deed,' or rather of the
good state, which is [10] called Belmont. I know that some will call
this 'far-fetched'; but I must ask them to take my word for it that
even if I am wrong, 'far-fetched' is the last epithet that should
be applied to my error. I have not fetched it from far. This, or
something like it, is my immediate and spontaneous reaction. A
wicked ogre of a Jew is ten thousand miles nearer to that reaction
than any of the sad, subtle, realistic figures produced by critics. If
I err, I err in childishness, not in sophistication.

   Now *Hamlet* is a play as nearly opposite to the *Merchant* as
possible. A good way of introducing you to my experience of it
will be to tell you the exact point at which anyone else's criticism
of it begins to lose my allegiance. It is a fairly definite point. As

soon as I find anyone treating the ghost merely as the means whereby Hamlet learns of his father's murder—as soon as a critic leaves us with the impression that some other method of disclosure (the finding of a letter or a conversation with a servant) would have done very nearly as well—I part company with that critic. After that, he may be as learned and sensitive as you please; but his outlook on literature is so remote from mine that he can teach me nothing. Hamlet for me is no more separable from his ghost than Macbeth from his witches, Una from her lion, or Dick Whittington from his cat. The Hamlet formula, so to speak, is not 'a man who has to avenge his father' but 'a man who has been given a task by a ghost.' Everything else about him is less important than that. If the play did not begin with the cold and darkness and sickening suspense of the ghost scenes it would be a radically different play. If, on the other hand, only the first act had survived, we should have a very tolerable notion of the play's peculiar quality. I put it to you that everyone's imagination here confirms mine. What is against me is the abstract pattern of motives and characters which we build up as critics when the actual flavour or tint of the poetry is already fading from our minds.

This ghost is different from any other ghost in Elizabethan drama—for, to tell the truth, the Elizabethans in general do their ghosts very vilely. It is permanently ambiguous. Indeed the very word 'ghost,' by putting it into the same class with the 'ghosts' of Kyd and Chapman, nay by classifying it at all, puts us on the wrong track. It is 'this thing,' 'this dreaded sight,' an 'illusion,' a 'spirit of health or goblin dam'nd,' liable at any moment to assume 'some other horrible form' which reason could not survive the vision of. Critics have disputed whether Hamlet is sincere when he doubts whether the apparition is his [11] father's ghost or not. I take him to be perfectly sincere. He believes while the thing is present: he doubts when it is away. Doubt, uncertainty, bewilderment to almost any degree, is what the ghost creates not only in Hamlet's mind but in the minds of the other characters. Shakespeare does not take the concept of 'ghost' for granted, as other dramatists had done. In his play the appearance of the spectre means a breaking down of the walls of the world and the germination of thoughts that cannot really be thought: chaos is come again.

This does not mean that I am going to make the ghost the

hero, or the play a ghost story—though I might add that a very good ghost story would be, to me, a more interesting thing than a maze of motives. I have started with the ghost because the ghost appears at the beginning of the play not only to give Hamlet necessary information but also, and even more, to strike the note. From the platform we pass to the court scene and so to Hamlet's first long speech. There are ten lines of it before we reach what is necessary to the plot: lines about the melting of flesh into a dew and the divine prohibition of self-slaughter. We have a second ghost scene after which the play itself, rather than the hero, goes mad for some minutes. We have a second soliloquy on the theme 'to die . . . to sleep'; and a third on 'the witching time of night, when churchyards yawn.' We have the King's effort to pray and Hamlet's comment on it. We have the ghost's third appearance. Ophelia goes mad and is drowned. Then comes the comic relief, surely the strangest comic relief ever written—comic relief beside an open grave, with a further discussion of suicide, a detailed inquiry into the rate of decomposition, a few clutches of skulls, and then 'Alas, poor Yorick!' On top of this, the hideous fighting in the grave; and then, soon, the catastrophe.

I said just now that the subject of the *Merchant* was metals. In the same sense, the subject of *Hamlet* is death. I do not mean by this that most of the characters die, or even that life and death are the stakes they play for; that is true of all tragedies. I do not mean that we rise from the reading of the play with the feeling that we have been in cold, empty places, places 'outside,' *nocte tacentia late,* though that is true. Before I go on to explain myself let me say that here, and throughout my lecture, I am most deeply indebted to my friend Mr. Owen Barfield. I have to make these acknowledgements both to him and to other of my friends so often that I am afraid of their being taken for an affectation. But they are not. The next best thing to being wise [12] oneself is to live in a circle of those who are: that good fortune I have enjoyed for nearly twenty years.

The sense in which death is the subject of *Hamlet* will become apparent if we compare it with other plays. Macbeth has commerce with Hell, but at the very outset of his career dismisses all thought of the life to come. For Brutus and Othello, suicide in the high tragic manner is escape and climax. For Lear death is deliverance. For Romeo and Antony, poignant loss. For all these, as for their author while he writes and the audience while they watch, death is the end: it is almost the frame of the picture. They think of dying: no one thinks, in these plays, of *being dead*. In *Hamlet* we are kept thinking about it all the time, whether in terms of the soul's destiny or of the body's. Purgatory, Hell, Heaven, the wounded name, the rights—or wrongs—of Ophelia's burial, and the staying-power of a tanner's corpse: and beyond this, beyond all Christian and all Pagan maps of the hereafter, comes a curious groping and tapping of thoughts, about what dreams may come.' It is this that gives to the whole play its quality of darkness and of misgiving. Of course there is much else in the play: but nearly always, the same groping. The characters are all watching one another, forming theories about one another, listening, contriving, full of anxiety. The world of *Hamlet* is a world where one has lost one's way. The Prince also has no doubt lost his, and we can tell the precise moment at which he finds it again. 'Not a whit. We defy augury. There's a special providence in the fall of a sparrow. If it be now, 'tis not to come: if it be not to come, it will be now: if it be not now, yet it will come: the readiness is all: since no man has aught of what he leaves, what is't to leave betimes?' [1]

If I wanted to make one more addition to the gallery of Hamlet's portraits I should trace his hesitation to the fear of death; not to a physical fear of dying, but a fear of being dead. And I think I should get on quite comfortably. Any serious attention to the state of being dead, unless it is limited by some definite religious or anti-religious doctrine, must, I suppose, paralyse the will by introducing infinite uncertainties and rendering all motives inadequate. Being dead is the unknown *x* in our sum. Unless you ignore it or else give it a value, you can get no answer. But this is not what I am going to do. Shakespeare has not left in the text clear lines of causation which would enable us [13] to connect Hamlet's hesitations with this source. I do not believe he has given us data for any portrait of the kind critics have tried to draw. To that extent I agree with Hanmer, Rümelin, and Mr. Eliot. But I differ from them in thinking that it is a fault.

For what, after all, is happening to us when we read any of

---

[1] I think the last clause is best explained by the assumption that Shakespeare had come across Seneca's *Nihil perdis ex tuo tempore, nam quod relinquis alienum est* (Epist. lxix).

Hamlet's great speeches? We see visions of the flesh dissolving
into a dew, of the world like an unweeded garden. We think of
memory reeling in its 'distracted globe.' We watch him scampering
hither and thither like a maniac to avoid the voices wherewith he
is haunted. Someone says 'Walk out of the air,' and we hear the
words 'Into my grave' spontaneously respond to it. We think of
being bounded in a nut-shell and king of infinite space: but for
bad dreams. There's the trouble, for 'I am most dreadfully attended.' We see the picture of a dull and muddy-mettled rascal, a
John-a-dreams, somehow unable to move while ultimate dishonour
is done him. We listen to his fear lest the whole thing may be an
illusion due to melancholy. We get the sense of sweet relief at the
words 'shuffled off this mortal coil' but mixed with the bottomless
doubt about what may follow then. We think of bones and skulls,
of women breeding sinners, and of how some, to whom all this
experience is a sealed book, can yet dare death and danger 'for an
egg-shell.' But do we really enjoy these things, do we go back to
them, because they show us Hamlet's character? Are they, from
that point of view, so very interesting? Does the mere fact that a
young man, literally haunted, dispossessed, and lacking friends,
should feel thus, tell us anything remarkable? Let me put my question in another way. If instead of the speeches he actually utters
about the firmament and man in his scene with Rosencrantz and
Guildenstern Hamlet had merely said, 'I don't seem to enjoy
things the way I used to,' and talked in that fashion throughout,
should we find him interesting? I think the answer is 'Not very.' It
may be replied that if he talked commonplace prose he would
reveal his character less vividly. I am not so sure. He would certainly have revealed *something* less vividly; but would that something be himself? It seems to me that 'this majestical roof' and
'What a piece of work is a man' give me primarily an impression
not of the sort of person he must be to lose the estimation of
things but of the things themselves and their great value; and that
I should be able to discern, though with very faint interest, the
same condition of loss in a personage who was quite unable so to
put before me what he was losing. And I do not think it true to
reply that he would be a different [14] character if he spoke less
poetically. This point is often misunderstood. We sometimes speak
as if the characters in whose mouths Shakespeare puts great poetry

were poets: in the sense that Shakespeare was depicting men of poetical genius. But surely this is like thinking that Wagner's Wotan is the dramatic portrait of a baritone? In opera song is the medium by which the representation is made and not part of the thing represented. The actors sing; the dramatic personages are feigned to be speaking. The only character who sings dramatically in *Figaro* is Cherubino. Similarly in poetical drama poetry is the medium, not part of the delineated characters. While the actors speak poetry written for them by the poet, the dramatic personages are supposed to be merely talking. If ever there is occasion to *represent* poetry (as in the play scene from *Hamlet*), it is put into a different metre and strongly stylized so as to prevent confusion.

I trust that my conception is now becoming clear. I believe that we read Hamlet's speeches with interest chiefly because they describe so well a certain spiritual region through which most of us have passed and anyone in his circumstances might be expected to pass, rather than because of our concern to understand how and why this particular man entered it. I foresee an objection on the ground that I am thus really admitting his 'character' in the only sense that matters and that all characters whatever could be equally well talked away by the method I have adopted. But I do really find a distinction. When I read about Mrs. Proudie I am not in the least interested in seeing the world from her point of view, for her point of view is not interesting; what does interest me is precisely the sort of person she was. In *Middlemarch* no reader wants to see Casaubon through Dorothea's eyes; the pathos, the comedy, the value of the whole thing is to understand Dorothea and see how such an illusion was inevitable for her. In Shakespeare himself I find Beatrice to be a character who could not be thus dissolved. We are interested not in some vision seen through her eyes, but precisely in the wonder of her being the girl she is. A comparison of the sayings we remember from her part with those we remember from Hamlet's brings out the contrast. On the one hand, 'I wonder that you will still be talking, Signior Benedick,' 'There was a star danced and under that I was born,' 'Kill Claudio'; on the other, 'The undiscovered country from whose bourne no traveller returns,' 'Use every man after his desert, and who should 'scape whipping?', 'The rest is silence.' [15] Particularly noticeable is the passage where Hamlet professes to be describing his own character. 'I am myself indifferent honest: but yet I could accuse me of such things that it were better my mother had not borne me. I am very proud, revengeful, ambitious.' It is, of course, possible to devise some theory which explains these self-accusations in terms of character. But long before we have done so the real significance of the lines has taken possession of our imagination for ever. 'Such fellows as I' does not mean 'such fellows as Goethe's Hamlet, or Coleridge's Hamlet, or any Hamlet': it means *men*—creatures shapen in sin and conceived in iniquity—and the vast, empty vision of them 'crawling between earth and heaven' is what really counts and really carries the burden of the play.

It is often cast in the teeth of the great critics that each in painting *Hamlet* has drawn a portrait of himself. How if they were right? I would go a long way to meet Beatrice or Falstaff or Mr. Jonathan Oldbuck or Disraeli's Lord Monmouth. I would not cross the room to meet Hamlet. It would never be necessary. He is always where I am. The method of the whole play is much nearer to Mr. Eliot's own method in poetry than Mr. Eliot suspects. Its true hero is man—haunted man—man with his mind on the frontier of two worlds, man unable either quite to reject or quite to admit the supernatural, man struggling to get something done as man has struggled from the beginning, yet incapable of achievement because of his inability to understand either himself or his fellows or the real quality of the universe which has produced him. To be sure, some hints of more particular motives for Hamlet's delay are every now and then fadged up to silence our questions, just as some show of motives is offered for the Duke's temporary abdication in *Measure for Measure*. In both cases it is only scaffolding or machinery. To mistake these mere *succedanea* for the real play and to try to work them up into a coherent psychology is the great error. I once had a whole batch of School Certificate answers on the Nun's Priest's Tale by boys whose form-master was apparently a breeder of poultry. Every thing that Chaucer had said in describing Chauntecleer and Pertelote was treated by them simply and solely as evidence about the precise breed of these two birds. And, I must admit, the result was very interesting. They proved beyond doubt that Chauntecleer was very different from our modern specialized strains and much closer to the Old English 'barn-door fowl.' But I couldn't help feeling that they had missed something.[16] I believe our attention to Hamlet's 'character' in the usual sense misses almost as much.

Perhaps I should rather say that it *would* miss as much if our behaviour when we are actually reading were not wiser than our criticism in cold blood. The critics, or most of them, have at any rate kept constantly before us the knowledge that in this play there is greatness and mystery. They were never entirely wrong. Their error, in my view, was to put the mystery in the wrong place—in Hamlet's motives rather than in that darkness which enwraps Hamlet and the whole tragedy and all who read or watch it. It is a mysterious play in the sense of being a play about mystery. Mr. Eliot suggests that 'more people have thought *Hamlet* a work of art because they found it interesting, than have found it interesting because it is a work of art.' When he wrote that sentence he must have been very near to what I believe to be the truth. This play is, above all else, *interesting*. But artistic failure is not in itself interesting, nor often interesting in any way: artistic success always is. To interest is the first duty of art; no other excellences will even begin to compensate for failure in this, and very serious faults will be covered by this, as by charity. The hypothesis that this play interests by being good and not by being bad had therefore the first claim on our consideration. The burden of proof rests on the other side. Is not the fascinated interest of the critics most naturally explained by supposing that this is the precise effect the play was written to produce? They may be finding the mystery in the wrong place; but the fact that they can never leave *Hamlet* alone, the continual groping, the sense, unextinguished by over a century of failures, that we have here something of inestimable importance, is surely the best evidence that the real and lasting mystery of our human situation has been greatly depicted.

The kind of criticism which I have attempted is always at a disadvantage against either historical criticism or character criticism. Their vocabulary has been perfected by long practice, and the truths with which they are concerned are those which we are accustomed to handle in the everyday business of life. But the things

I want to talk about have no vocabulary and criticism has for centuries kept almost complete silence on them. I make no claim to be a pioneer. Professor Wilson Knight (though I disagree with nearly everything he says in detail), Miss Spurgeon, Miss Bodkin, and Mr. Barfield are my leaders. But those who do not enjoy the honours of a pioneer may yet [17] share his discomforts. One of them I feel acutely at the moment. I feel certain that to many of you the things I have been saying about *Hamlet* will appear intolerably sophisticated, abstract, and modern. And so they sound when we have to put them into words. But I shall have failed completely if I cannot persuade you that my view, for good or ill, has just the opposite characteristics—is naïve and concrete and archaic. I am trying to recall attention from the things an intellectual adult notices to the things a child or a peasant notices—night, ghosts, a castle, a lobby where a man can walk four hours together, a willow-fringed brook and a sad lady drowned, a graveyard and a terrible cliff above the sea, and amidst all these a pale man in black clothes (would that our producers would ever let him appear!) with his stockings coming down, a dishevelled man whose words make us at once think of loneliness and doubt and dread, of waste and dust and emptiness, and from whose hands, or from our own, we feel the richness of heaven and earth and the comfort of human affection slipping away. In a sense I have kept my promise of bestowing all my childishness upon you. A child is always thinking about those details in a story which a grown-up regards as indifferent. If when you first told the tale your hero was warned by three little men appearing on the left of the road, and when you tell it again you introduce one little man on the right of the road, the child protests. And the child is right. You think it makes no difference because you are not living the story at all. If you were, you would know better. *Motifs,* machines, and the like are abstractions of literary history and therefore interchangeable: but concrete imagination knows nothing of them.

You must not think I am setting up as a sort of literary Peter Pan who does not grow up. On the contrary, I claim that only those adults who have retained, with whatever additions and enrichments, their first childish response to poetry unimpaired, can be said to have grown up at all. Mere change is not growth.

Growth is the synthesis of change and continuity, and where there is no continuity there is no growth. To hear some critics, one would suppose that man had to lose his nursery appreciation of *Gulliver* before he acquired his mature appreciation of it. It is not so. If it were, the whole concept of maturity, of ripening, would be out of place: and also, I believe we should very seldom read more than three pages of *Gulliver* at a sitting.[18]

Shakespeare Once More

By James Russell Lowell

James Russell Lowell, from "Shakespeare Once More," (1870) in *The English Poets* (London, Walter Scott, 1888).

THAT THE UNCONSCIOUS Hamlet should stumble on *this* grave of all others, that it should be *here* that he should pause to muse humorously on death and decay,—all this prepares us for the revulsion of passion in the next scene, and for the frantic confession,—

> I loved Ophelia; forty thousand brothers
> Could not with all *their* quantity of love
> Make up my sum!

And it is only here that such an asseveration would be true even to the feeling of the moment; for it is plain from all we know of Hamlet that he could not so have loved Ophelia, that he was incapable of the self-abandonment of a true passion, that he would have analyzed this emotion as he does all others, would have peeped and botanized upon it till it became to him a mere [133] matter of scientific interest. All this force of contrast and this horror of surprise were necessary so to intensify his remorseful regret that he should believe himself for once in earnest. The

speech of the King, "O, he is mad, Laertes," recalls him to himself, and he at once begins to rave:—

> Zounds! show what thou 'lt do!
> Woul't weep? woul't fight? woul't fast? woul't tear thyself?
> Woul't drink up eysil? eat a crocodile?

It is easy to see that the whole plot hinges upon the character of Hamlet, that Shakespeare's conception of this was the ovum
out of which the whole organism was hatched. And here let me
remark, that there is a kind of genealogical necessity in the character,—a thing not altogether strange to the attentive reader of
Shakespeare. Hamlet seems the natural result of the mixture of
father and mother in his temperament, the resolution and per-
sistence of the one, like sound timber wormholed and made shaky,
as it were, by the other's infirmity of will and discontinuity of purpose. In natures so imperfectly mixed it is not uncommon to find
vehemence of intention the prelude and counterpoise of weak performance, the conscious nature striving to keep up its self-respect
by a triumph in words all the more resolute that it feels assured
beforehand of inevitable defeat in action. As in such slipshod
housekeeping men are their own largest creditors, they find it easy
to stave off utter bankruptcy of conscience by taking up one unpaid
promise with another larger, and at heavier interest, till such self-
swindling becomes habitual and by degrees almost painless. How
did Coleridge discount his own notes of this kind with less and
less specie as the figures lengthened on the paper! As with Hamlet, so it is with Ophelia and Laertes. The father's feebleness comes
up again in the wasting heartbreak and gentle lunacy of the daughter, while the son shows it in a rashness of impulse and act, a kind
of crankiness, of whose essential feebleness we are all the more
sensible as contrasted with a nature so steady on its keel, and drawing so much water, as that of Horatio,—the foil at once, in different ways, both to him and Hamlet. It was [134] natural, also, that
the daughter of self-conceited old Polonius should have her soft-
ness stiffened with a fibre of obstinacy; for there are two kinds of
weakness, that which breaks, and that which bends. Ophelia's is of
the former kind; Hero is her counterpart, giving way before calamity, and rising again so soon as the pressure is removed. . . .[135]

I do not believe that Horatio ever thought he "was not a pipe for Fortune's finger to play what stop she please," till Hamlet told him so. That was Fortune's affair, not his; let her try it, if she liked. He is unconscious of his own peculiar qualities, as men of decision commonly are, or they would not be men of decision. When there is a thing to be done, they go straight at it, and for the time there is nothing for them in the whole universe but themselves and their object. Hamlet, on the other hand, is always studying himself. This world and the other, too, are always present to his mind, and there in the corner is the little black kobold of a doubt making mouths at him. He breaks down the bridges before him, not behind him, as a man of action would do; but there is something more than this. He is an ingrained sceptic; though his is the scepticism, not of reason, but of feeling, whose root is want of faith in himself. In him it is passive, a malady rather than a function of the mind. We might call him insincere: not that he was in any sense a hypocrite, but only that he never was and never could be in earnest. Never could be, because no man without intense faith in something ever can. Even if he only believed in himself, that were better than nothing; for it will carry a man a great way in the outward successes of life, nay, will even sometimes give him the Archimedean fulcrum for moving the world. But Hamlet doubts everything. He doubts the immortality of the soul, just after seeing his father's spirit, and hearing from its mouth the secrets of the other world. He doubts Horatio even, and swears him to secrecy on the cross of his sword, though probably he himself has no assured belief in [139] the sacredness of the symbol. He doubts Ophelia, and asks her, "Are you honest?" He doubts the ghost, after he has had a little time to think about it, and so gets up the play to test the guilt of the king. And how coherent the whole character is! With what perfect tact and judgment Shakespeare, in the advice to the players, makes him an exquisite critic! For just here that part of his character which would be weak in dealing with affairs is strong. A wise scepticism is the first attribute of a good critic. He must not believe that the fire-insurance offices will raise their rates of premium on the Charles, because the new volume of poems is printing at Riverside or the University Press. He must not believe so profoundly in the ancients as to think it wholly out of the question that the world has still vigor enough in its loins to beget some one who will one of these days be as good an ancient as any of them.

Another striking quality in Hamlet's nature is his perpetual inclination to irony. I think this has been generally passed over too lightly, as if it were something external and accidental, rather assumed as a mask than part of the real nature of the man. It seems to me to go deeper, to be something innate, and not merely factitious. It is nothing like the grave irony of Socrates, which was the weapon of a man thoroughly in earnest,—the *boomerang* of argument, which one throws in the opposite direction of what he means to hit, and which seems to be flying away from the adversary, who will presently find himself knocked down by it. It is not like the irony of Timon, which is but the wilful refraction of a clear mind twisting awry whatever enters it,—or of Iago, which is the slime that a nature essentially evil loves to trail over all beauty and goodness to taint them with distrust: it is the half-jest, half-earnest of an inactive temperament that has not quite made up its mind whether life is a reality or no, whether men were not made in jest, and which amuses itself equally with finding a deep meaning in trivial things and a trifling one in the profoundest mysteries of being, because the want of earnestness in its own essence infects everything else with its own [140] indifference. If there be now and then an unmannerly rudeness and bitterness in it, as in the scenes with Polonius and Osrick, we must remember that Hamlet was just in the condition which spurs men to sallies of this kind: dissatisfied, at one neither with the world nor with himself, and accordingly casting about for something out of himself to vent his spleen upon. But even in these passages there is no hint of earnestness, of any purpose beyond the moment; they are mere cat's-paws of vexation, and not the deep-raking ground-swell of passion, as we see it in the sarcasm of Lear.

The question of Hamlet's madness has been much discussed and variously decided. High medical authority has pronounced, as usual, on both sides of the question. But the induction has been drawn from too narrow premises, being based on a mere diagnosis of the *case,* and not on an appreciation of the character in its completeness. We have a case of pretended madness in the Edgar of *King Lear;* and it is certainly true that that is a charcoal sketch, coarsely outlined, compared with the delicate drawing, the lights, shades, and half-tints of the portraiture in Hamlet. But does this tend to prove that the madness of the latter, because truer to the recorded observation of experts, is real, and meant to be real, as the other to be fictitious? Not in the least, as it appears to me. Hamlet, among all the characters of Shakespeare, is the most eminently a metaphysician and psychologist. He is a close observer, continually analyzing his own nature and that of others, letting fall his little drops of acid irony on all who come near him, to make them show what they are made of. Even Ophelia is not too sacred, Osrick not too contemptible for experiment. If such a man assumed madness, he would play his part perfectly. If Shakespeare himself, without going mad, could so observe and remember all the abnormal symptoms as to be able to reproduce them in Hamlet, why should it be beyond the power of Hamlet to reproduce them in himself? If you deprive Hamlet of reason, there is no truly tragic motive left. He would be a fit subject for Bedlam, but not for the stage. We might have pathology enough, but no [141] pathos. Ajax first becomes tragic when he recovers his wits. If Hamlet is irresponsible, the whole play is a chaos. That he is not so might be proved by evidence enough, were it not labor thrown away.

This feigned madness of Hamlet's is one of the few points in which Shakespeare has kept close to the old story on which he founded his play; and as he never decided without deliberation, so he never acted without unerring judgment. Hamlet *drifts* through the whole tragedy. He never keeps on one tack long enough to get steerage-way, even if, in a nature like his, with those electric streamers of whim and fancy forever wavering across the vault of his brain, the needle of judgment would point in one direction long enough to strike a course by. The scheme of simulated insanity is precisely the one he would have been likely to hit upon, because it enabled him to follow his own bent, and to drift with an apparent purpose, postponing decisive action by the very means he adopts to arrive at its accomplishment, and satisfying himself with the show of doing something that he may escape so much the longer the dreaded necessity of really doing anything at all. It enables him to *play* with life and duty, instead of taking them by the rougher side, where alone any firm grip is possible,—to feel

that he is on the way towards accomplishing somewhat, when he
is really paltering with his own irresolution. Nothing, I think,
could be more finely imagined than this. Voltaire complains that
he goes mad without any sufficient object or result. Perfectly true,
and precisely what was most natural for him to do, and, accordingly, precisely what Shakespeare meant that he should do. It was
delightful to him to indulge his imagination and humor, to prove
his capacity for something by playing a part: the one thing he
could not do was to bring himself to *act,* unless when surprised by
a sudden impulse of suspicion,—as where he kills Polonius, and
there he could not see his victim. He discourses admirably of suicide, but does not kill himself; he talks daggers, but uses none. He
puts by his chance to kill the king with the excuse that he will not
do it while he is praying, lest his soul be saved thereby, though it
be [142] more than doubtful whether he believed himself that, if
there were a soul to be saved, it could be saved by that expedient.
He allows himself to be packed off to England, without any
motive except that it would for the time take him farther from a
present duty, the more disagreeable to a nature like his because it
was present, and not a mere matter for speculative consideration.
When Goethe made his famous comparison of the acorn planted
in a vase which it bursts with its growth, and says that in like
manner Hamlet is a nature which breaks down under the weight of
a duty too great for it to bear, he seems to have considered the
character too much from one side. Had Hamlet actually killed
himself to escape his too onerous commission, Goethe's conception
of him would have been satisfactory enough. But Hamlet was
hardly a sentimentalist, like Werther; on the contrary, he saw
things only too clearly in the dry north-light of the intellect. It is
chance that at last brings him to his end. It would appear rather
that Shakespeare intended to show us an imaginative temperament
brought face to face with actualities, into any clear relation of
sympathy with which it cannot bring itself. The very means that
Shakespeare makes use of to lay upon him the obligation of acting
—the ghost—really seems to make it all the harder for him to
act; for the spectre but gives an additional excitement to his
imagination and a fresh topic for his scepticism.

I shall not attempt to evolve any high moral significance from
the play, even if I thought it possible; for that would be aside

from the present purpose. The scope of the higher drama is to represent life, not every-day life, it is true, but life lifted above the plane of bread-and-butter associations, by nobler reaches of language, by the influence at once inspiring and modulating of verse, by an intenser play of passion condensing that misty mixture of feeling and reflection which makes the ordinary atmosphere of existence into flashes of thought and phrase whose brief, but terrible, illumination prints the outworn landscape of every-day upon our brains, with its little motives and mean results, in lines of telltale fire. The moral office of tragedy is to show us our own weaknesses idealized in grander [143] figures and more awful results,—to teach us that what we pardon in ourselves as venial faults, if they seem to have but slight influence on our immediate fortunes, have arms as long as those of kings, and reach forward to the catastrophe of our lives; that they are dry-rotting the very fibre of will and conscience, so that, if we should be brought to the test of a great temptation or a stringent emergency, we must be involved in a ruin as sudden and complete as that we shudder at in the unreal scene of the theatre. But the primary *object* of a tragedy is not to inculcate a formal moral. Representing life, it teaches, like life, by indirection, by those nods and winks that are thrown away on us blind horses in such profusion. We may learn, to be sure, plenty of lessons from Shakespeare. We are not likely to have kingdoms to divide, crowns foretold us by weird sisters, a father's death to avenge, or to kill our wives from jealousy; but Lear may teach us to draw the line more clearly between a wise generosity and a loose-handed weakness of giving; Macbeth, how one sin involves another, and forever another, by a fatal parthenogenesis, and that the key which unlocks forbidden doors to our will or passion leaves a stain on the hand, that may not be so dark as blood, but that will not out; Hamlet, that all the noblest gifts of person, temperament, and mind slip like sand through the grasp of an infirm purpose; Othello, that the perpetual silt of some one weakness, the eddies of a suspicious temper depositing their own impalpable layer after another, may build up a shoal on which an heroic life and an otherwise magnanimous nature may bilge and go to pieces. All this we may learn, and much more, and Shakespeare was no doubt well aware of all this and more; but I do not believe that he wrote his plays with any such didactic purpose. He

knew human nature too well not to know that one thorn of experience is worth a whole wilderness of warning,—that, where
one man shapes his life by precept and example, there are a thousand who have it shaped for them by impulse and by circumstances. He did not mean his great tragedies for scarecrows, as if
the nailing of one hawk to the barn-door would prevent the next
from coming down souse into the hen-yard. No, it is not the [144]
poor bleaching victim hung up to moult its draggled feathers in
the rain that he wishes to show us. He loves the hawk-nature as
well as the hen-nature; and if he is unequalled in anything, it is in
that sunny breadth of view, that impregnability of reason, that
looks down on all ranks and conditions of men, all fortune and
misfortune, with the equal eye of the pure artist.[145]

Hamlet:
The Film and the Play

By Sir Laurence Olivier

Sir Laurence Olivier, from Foreword to *Hamlet: The Film and the
Play.* Alan Dent, ed. (London, World Film Publications Ltd.,
1948), unpaged.

IT WAS—as may well be imagined—with
feelings of some trepidation, a kind of fearful awe, that I ap-
proached the idea of a Hamlet film. Indeed, it will be noticed,
and doubtless commented upon, that I took the precaution of being
in Australia when the film opened in London! But more seriously, the snares and pitfalls that await anybody who touches so
world-famous a masterpiece were only too obvious to me. . . .

First, Hamlet is probably the best known of all the great
plays. We are only too well aware of that, and of the certainty
that say what we will, we shall receive dozens of letters, mainly

abusive, telling us what we already know, namely, that this or that famous passage has been omitted. Here, the mere fact that the play is so well-known helps to put this matter in clearer perspective. For one thing it means that we have had to do all our work, as it were, in the open, because we knew that no careless emendation or sleight-of-hand would pass unnoticed or be tolerated.

It should always be borne in mind when discussing the question of what has been cut, that Hamlet is very seldom played in its entirety even on the stage. And it makes a very long evening of over four hours when it is played whole—a running time that is difficult enough in the theatre, and obviously out of the question in the cinema. And it may, too, be noted in passing that we, in this film, have allowed ourselves considerably less licence in the matter of cutting than did that fine English-American actor, Maurice Evans, when he took a version of his superb "Hamlet" to army camps during the war. That Hamlet took a stand on the fact that some of the finer shades of the play, that are caught by a select New York audience, would pass over the heads of greater and less instructed masses, who would be bored and demand a swifter action in the plot. We would not, of course, go so far as to say that those who know their Hamlet must take into account what has been left out, and that those who do not will never miss it! But think for a moment of the audience reached by the films who never go to a theatre, and you will appreciate a basic difficulty that determined many of the decisions we made in this matter. And whilst, as I have made clear, we took infinite care and nothing but the best advice, it is possible to be so pernickety in the way of retaining the original that one can follow a process that ends in grieving over the loss of so much Belleforest amongst the encircling Shakespeare (who borrowed the bare bones of his plot from Belleforest!).

. . . Suffice it to say that, allowing for the distinction between the two media [stage and film], the same basic problems remain, of reducing the length, elucidating the plot, unravelling irrelevancies, and relating the result to the type of audience. . . .

Bear in mind, all the time, that the cinema is even more insistent on the visual aspect of art than theatre, that the camera can, and must, nose into corners and magnify details that escape notice or pass muster on the stage. On the screen, too, the essential consideration is for what is seen, and characters or passages of poetry that may be kept in the theatre, on account of their intrinsic interest or beauty respectively, cannot be reconciled with the more closely-knit demands of a two-hour film.

. . . my whole aim and purpose has been to make a film of "Hamlet" as Shakespeare himself, were he living now, might make it. It is easy to retort, "But Shakespeare is not living now, therefore you should not do this." Every Shakespeare film must, by its very nature, be a re-creation of a Shakespeare play in a quite different art-medium than that for which it was primarily intended. But does that make it impermissible? If you think it does, you must agree to forbid the performance of Verdi's operas of "Otello" and "Falstaff."

If I did not consider the translation of "Hamlet" to the film to be a legitimate experiment, I would never have attempted it. You may be assured of that.

The Mystery of Hamlet Notes Toward an Archetypal Solution

By Robert Ornstein

Robert Ornstein, "The Mystery of Hamlet: Notes Toward an Archetypal Solution," *College English*, XXI (October, 1959).

WILL THE PROBLEM of *Hamlet* ever be solved? As the years pass, the solutions multiply and the issue grows more doubtful. What a bizarre variety of suspects has already [30] appeared in the scholarly line-up: some gay and debonair as only an Elizabethan courtier can be—others curled in the foetal position on Ophelia's lap. Hamlet [30] the malcontent, Hamlet the lunatic, Hamlet the ideal Prince, and Hamlet the neurotic make interesting academic conversation, but they are not, as Renaissance scholars would have it, the "whole man." They do not embrace the primordial mythic darkness that lies at the heart of Shakespearean tragedy; they do not project the eternal anguish of the human situation. Our most brilliant critics have already realized that Hamlet is a ritual scapegoat, but they have not yet grasped the artistic particularity of his archetypal role. They do not yet see that he is Dying God *as* Juvenile Delinquent.

Almost as soon as Hamlet appears we learn that he is a truant from school and the victim of an unsatisfactory home environment. His stepfather is a tippling criminal; his mother is a shallow, good-natured creature too easy with her affections. (In more sentimental embodiments of the delinquency myth, the stepfather becomes a genial but indigent Irish uncle who is forever cadging whiskies. The mother becomes a haggard charwoman who does not understand her boy but who is convinced like Gertrude that he is not really bad.) Unable to communicate with his parents, Hamlet seeks affection outside the home through close association with a childhood companion. He is maladjusted and emotionally unstable: he has bad dreams. He is moody, hostile, withdrawn, cynically contemptuous of authority. He has homicidal and suicidal tendencies—he carries a knife and knows how to use it. He is abnormally preoccupied with sex and yet incapable of returning the love of the girl he sadistically maltreats. He is an exhibitionist in speech and clothing: he dresses completely in black (how true to the type!) and affects a casual slovenliness (he appears to Ophelia "unbraced"). Deprived of status in his society, he seeks attention through acts of violence. But after creating a scene in the theater and killing Polonius, he is sent away for radical therapy—or what is vulgarly called a head-shrinking. In sum he is, as T. S. Eliot brilliantly observed, a rebel without a cause, consumed with an unfathomable hatred of a world in which he never had a chance.

Once we grasp the mythic design of *Hamlet,* the lesser figures fall quickly in place. Polonius, archetypal "informer," suffers the classic fate of the stool-pigeon—murdered while trying to call the authorities. Ophelia in modern dress becomes the blond-haired kid from the next tenement who is shattered when her lover kills her dearest relative (cf. *On the Waterfront*). Laertes is her hot-tempered, mixed-up younger brother who seeks his initiation into adult society by matching knives with the hero. (In American folk-lore the attributes of the hero and the younger brother often curiously intermingle, i.e., the younger brother, not the hero, dresses in black and labors under the mortal delusion that he is the fastest gun west of the Pecos.) Rosencrantz and Guildenstern, need I say, are crooked social workers who try unsuccessfully to gain the delinquent's confidence. When they betray the gang ethos, they are framed by the hero. In the inevitable denouement Fortinbras, a reformed delinquent, delivers the valedictory over the hero's corpse and makes Denmark safe for the Police Athletic League.

It is hardly accidental then that images of disease predominate in *Hamlet,* for they embody the profound mythic intuition that juvenile delinquency is a symptom of social malaise—the ulcer of a sick society. In his soliloquies Hamlet realizes that he is an intrinsic part of the corruption he loathes. And he senses too that his criminal protests against the social conditions which shape his personality are ultimately suicidal. He delays his revenge because he knows that he cannot destroy Claudius without destroying himself. For when harmony is restored in family and state, the juvenile delinquent ceases to exist.

Other authors give memorable expression to the delinquency archetype. One thinks of Achilles sulking in his tent, Tom Jones, Huck Finn, and Lt. Henry. But no author has created so rich a gallery of delinquents as Shakespeare. Place beside Hamlet, Laertes, and Fortinbras, the figures of Hal the tavern-brawler, Cassio drunk on duty, and the "boy" Coriolanus itching for a street-fight. Was it merely an accident that Marlon Brando was cast not long ago as Mark Antony? Or that modern playwrights have transferred the gang wars of *Romeo and Juliet* to New York's West Side? Or must we not conclude that the [35] delinquency of Shakespeare's youth—the deer-poaching, the sexual license that precipitated his marriage and is again recorded in the sonnets, and the intimate acquaintance with Cheapside taverns and brothels—was a seminal influence on his creative imagination?

Consider finally the vexing problem of the Ghost. Surely

Shakespeare could have invented a more plausible way of communicating vital information. Dead men tell no tales, but drunkards brag in their cups, poison comes from apothecaries, and grave-diggers are notoriously loose-tongued. It is striking, is it not, that Shakespeare sophisticates his tale of primitive passion by staging it in Renaissance dress and yet retains in the Ghost a vestige of primeval superstition. Through deliberate inconsistency, I suggest, he alerts us to the mythic symbolism of a force that in the dark of the night brings to present consciousness the hidden memory of the past. In short, does not the ancestral "Ghost" whisper to us that the mystery of Shakespeare's play is the "dark backward and abysm" of the Racial Unconscious? [36]

Review of "The Characters of Shakespeare," by William Hazlitt

By Edgar Allan Poe

Edgar Allan Poe, [from Review of William Hazlitt, *The Characters of Shakespeare,* Wiley and Putnam's Library of Choice Reading, No. XVII], in *Broadway Journal* (August 16, 1845), in *The Complete Works of Edgar Allan Poe,* Vol. XII, James A. Harrison, ed. (New York, George D. Sproul, 1902).

IN ALL COMMENTATING upon Shakspeare, there has been a radical error, never yet mentioned. It is the error of attempting to expound his characters—to [226] account for their actions—to reconcile his inconsistencies—not as if they were the coinage of a human brain, but as if they had been actual existences upon earth. We talk of Hamlet the man, instead of

Hamlet the *dramatis persona*—of Hamlet that God, in place of Hamlet that Shakspeare created. If Hamlet had really lived, and if the tragedy were an accurate record of his deeds, from this record with some trouble) we might, it is true, reconcile his inconsistencies and settle to our satisfaction his true character. But the task becomes the purest absurdity when we deal only with a phantom. It is not (then) the inconsistencies of the acting man which we have as a subject of discussion—(although we proceed as if it were, and thus *inevitably* err) but the whims and vacillations—the conflicting energies and indolences of the poet. It seems to us little less than a miracle, that this obvious point should have been overlooked.

While on this topic we may as well offer an ill-considered opinion of our own as to the *intention of the poet* in the delineation of the Dane. It must have been well known to Shakspeare, that a leading feature in certain more intense classes of intoxication, (from whatever cause,) is an almost irresistible impulse to counterfeit a farther degree of excitement than actually exists. Analogy would lead any thoughtful person to suspect the same impulse in madness—where beyond doubt it is manifest. This, Shakspeare *felt*—not thought. He felt it through his marvellous power of *identification* with humanity at large—the ultimate source of his magical influence upon mankind. He wrote of Hamlet as if Hamlet he were; and having, in the first instance, imagined his hero excited to partial insanity by the disclosures of the ghost—he (the [227] poet) *felt* that it was natural he should be impelled to exaggerate the insanity.[228]

Shakespeare's Self

By W. Teignmouth Shore

W. Teignmouth Shore, from *Shakespeare's Self* (London, Philip
Allan and Company, 1920).

ONCE, WHEN READING in the Library
of the British Museum, the notion occurred to me that perhaps
the dead were allotted ghostly Reader's Tickets by deceased Li-
brarians, and it amused me to conjecture what Shakespeare would
think if he were to turn to the Catalogue. Surely he would laugh
hugely when he found over twenty columns occupied with the
titles of copies of the text and of commentaries upon "Hamlet!"
But there is a tragic side to this.

"Hamlet," as should all Shakespeare's plays, ought to be
judged as an acting play, written for an Elizabethan audience,
which revelled in horrors, jeered at madmen, loved ghostly thrills,
believing in the appearance on earth of the spirits of the dead,
and which delighted in watching fine sword-play.[142]

Being a business man, Shakespeare would choose, or would
accept, "Hamlet" for adaptation because it was a popular tale and
sure to please. He was always anxious to provide his company with
a box-office success. Being more a poet than a playwright, he often
muddles his effects.

The story of Hamlet was very familiar to Elizabethan play-
goers, and his new tragedy may be taken as equivalent to the
adaptation of a well-known novel set before a present-time audience. Sir Sidney Lee dates "Hamlet" 1602, but whatever there is
as evidence to the date of production there is none as to how long
Shakespeare was engaged in writing the play. Probably he was not
long about it; in many ways it seems to be hasty work; this was

customary with him, a play being provided because a new one was
due or desirable.

The documentary evidence as to date is as follows. The entry
at Stationers' Hall is 1602. Actual publication in 1603, in quarto;
and this is on the title-page: "The Tragicall Historie of Hamlet
Prince of Denmarke. By William Shake-speare. As it hath beene
diverse times acted by his Highnesse servants in the Cittie of
London: as also in the two Universities of Cambridge and Oxford, and elsewhere." A Second Quarto came forth in 1604, with
this additional information on the title-page: "Newly imprinted
and enlarged to almost as much againe as it was, according to the
true and perfect Coppie." Evidently the First Quarto was not considered a true and perfect text. Two other Quarto editions appeared before the Folio of 1623.

The texts in the First Quarto and the other editions vary
amazingly, affording an opportunity too good to be missed by the
Conjecturists; they have let themselves "go," and are still at it. But
whatever theory is based on *this* evidence can be upset by *that*.
Madness lies both ways, and little else. The question of the two
first Quartos is an unsolved riddle, and not really of any grave
import. What is important is the play as Shakespeare finally left it
to us.[143]

Dowden gives this queer mixture of sense and nonsense; he
likes to think "of Shakespeare as setting to work with the intention
of rehandling the subject of an old play, so as to give it fresh
interest on the stage; as following the subject given to him, and as
following the instinctive leading of his genius. The traditional
Hamlet was distinguished by intellectual subtlety, by riddling
speech, by a power of ingeniously baffling his pursuers, and, at the
same time, by a love of truth."

But from what we know of Shakespeare's methods, what he
really did was no more than this. He took up the old play, and
rewrote it; but did not remodel the plot to any great extent. If he
did do so, then he must have been an exceedingly poor playwright.
But he must not be judged by the standard of modern methods of
play-construction, but by those of his times and contemporaries.
The Elizabethan playgoer wanted and demanded melodrama
decked out with poetics, as far as serious drama was concerned. He
did not worry about the careful working out of the plot, or care

much for subtlety in the character drawing. So Shakespeare naturally took, or was given, melodramatic plots for the majority of his
tragedies, and, as he wrote, his muse of fire would catch alight,
blaze up, and poetry would pour out like lava from a volcano. It is
only in a few of his tragedies that he makes us feel that the fate of
his characters is inevitable; in "Hamlet" and "Lear" he does not
achieve this result; and it is no use trying to explain away our dis-
satisfaction by taking the blame on ourselves for limited compre-
hension, saying that Shakespeare could do no wrong. That is to do
a wrong to Shakespeare.

If we strip "Hamlet" of its poetic trappings, what have we
left? Crude melodrama, which is quite exciting when it is acted as
melodrama, as it was by Sarah Bernhardt.

Consider the plot. Hamlet comes home to find that his mother
has married her brother-in-law very shortly after her husband's
death. The ghost of Hamlet's father appears and accuses his
brother of having murdered him.[144] Hamlet swears "Revenge!"
But then it occurs to him that the ghost may be an evil spirit and a
liar, so he puts the King to the test in the play-scene. The King
very naturally grows suspicious and unsuccessfully plots Hamlet's
death. Then, in the last scene, all the principal characters who are
left alive are killed off by poison and the sword. Such a plot is no
advance on "Titus Andronicus." The poetry, however, in "Hamlet" is vastly superior, some of it the best that Shakespeare ever
wrote, and the characters, with the exception of Hamlet, are drawn
with a hand far more skilled, and with matured knowledge of
human nature and increased experience of life. The greatness of
"Hamlet" lies first in the poetry; second, in the characters of the
King and Queen, Polonius, Ophelia and a few of the minor folk.*

* NOTE.—I have found the following among my notes. "During a recent
re-reading of "Hamlet" I made note of some of the dramatically superfluous
passages, which should be 'cut' in order to secure swift action and to retain
the purely acting values:—Act I., scene 2, Hamlet's speech about inky cloaks,
etc., omit from ' 'Tis not alone' down to the end of the speech. Act I., scene 5.
the Ghost's *talk,* from after 'I am thy father's spirit' down to 'flesh and blood;'
a lot more of the Ghost's verbosity should go by the board, such as 'Oh,
Hamlet, what a falling off,' down to 'prey on garbage.' The Ghost pretends to
be in a hurry, yet talks, talks, talks! Almost all the talk with the players is
irrelevant to the action; very interesting but bad playwriting; all the 'rugged
Pyrrhus' business should be cut. Act III., scene 1, Ophelia's description of
Hamlet, 'The courtiers, soldiers, etc.' stops the action and is of no assistance

Hamlet's character is a puzzle. Why? For two reasons. It is partly our own fault, because we will absurdly probe Hamlet as if he had actually lived, whereas he is only an imaginary character. It is partly [145] Shakespeare's fault, the character being badly drawn, Hamlet, as far as the skeleton is concerned, is an *actor's* part, probably taken unaltered from the old piece. For the rest, he is an outlet for Shakespeare's unconquerable impulse to pour out poetry on the slightest provocation. Hamlet is a poor piece of material too richly embroidered. To make him out to be a wonderful psychological study is absurd. What Dowden said is a fair sample of that kind of thing: "Hamlet's intellectual subtlety sees every side of every question, thinks too precisely on the event, considers all things too curiously, studies anew every conviction, doubts of the past, interrogates the future; . . . Hamlet the subtle is pre-eminently a critic—a critic of art, a critic of character, a critic of society, a critic of life, a critic of himself." All this to explain away the fact that Shakespeare had no clear idea himself of what he meant Hamlet to be.

Again and again Hamlet is made to talk because Shakespeare could not resist the temptation to write poetry. What doubt can there be in such blatant cases as when Hamlet gives the players a lecture (in prose) on the art of acting, referring at length to Elizabethan theatrical events, of which *he,* Hamlet, could not have known anything? It is the same with many of Hamlet's discourses on philosophical matters. What we learn from these poetical and other interludes is not anything of the character of Hamlet, but that Shakespeare was a typical Elizabethan in his views of life and

---

to the play except the last line and a half of the speech, which are dramatic and pathetic. Act III., scene 2, Hamlet's long talk to long-suffering Horatio. In the play within the play cut the player king's speech from 'Purpose is' down to the end of the speech. Act III., scene 3, cut out Rosencrantz's speech 'The single and peculiar life.' A good deal of Hamlet's profuse talk in the bedroom scene should go; poor woman, no wonder the Queen worried about her son's sanity. Act IV., scene 4, 'How all occasions,' this is not in the Folio; perhaps it *was* cut? Act IV., scene 7, cut the King's speech, 'Not that I think' down to 'quick o' the ulcer,' also a good lot of the Queen's account of the death of Ophelia. Personally I should like to see the grave-diggers go wholesale; at any rate all the first part of their chatter should be excised. Act V., scene 2, Hamlet is very wordy in his recounting his voyage . . . The play ends with Hamlet's death; all the Fortinbras affair is doubtless the old play, which Shakespeare did not bother to omit."

in his criticism of it. It was only as an emotional poet that he soared to heaven's gate. In short, Hamlet *does* what he did in the tale or play that was adapted; he *talks* Shakespeare.

The Ghost is, for the most part, a dreadful bore, because he will babble so much and to so little purpose; a weakness that his son inherited from him! His message to Hamlet could have been conveyed in a dozen or so dramatic lines. But we must not forget that Shakespeare may have been swayed by the desire to give some declamatory actor a chance of distinction. Perhaps himself? [146]

Ophelia is one of the most pathetic of Shakespeare's girls; the poet possessed a wonderful sympathy with, and insight into, the mind of budding womanhood. This kind of knowledge does not come by intuition; nor does any kind of knowledge. He must have gained it by personal experience and observation. Why not at home, at Stratford, with his own daughters?

Hamlet's speech to Ophelia is akin to Sonnet LXX.:—

> Be thou as chaste as ice, as pure as snow,
> Thou shalt not escape calumny.

It may just be the poetic treatment of a common thought; it may possibly be a reference to some incident of which he was aware.

Yes; it is the poetry in "Hamlet" that gives the play its fascination. Many of the speeches are like the *arias* that give charm to the old-fashioned operas. One almost expects "To be, or not to be" to win an encore when finely delivered. It is noteworthy that famous performers of Hamlet are remembered not so much for their general reading of the part and their endeavours to make the character true to life as for their famous "solos" and usually too ingenious "business."

As an example of how a word was sufficient to set a light to Shakespeare's muse, making the play-writer succumb to the poet, take this:—

Act I., Scene 2. The Queen says:—

> Why seems it so particular with thee?

Off goes Shakespeare, not Hamlet, with "Seems, madam!" etc. Which is a typical way of working with most imaginative poets. Immediately following is the King's long speech, upbraiding Hamlet for mourning unduly for the death of his father. This may, or may not, be a characteristic argument for the King to use; but it feels to me singularly like Shakespeare unburdening himself anent his own father's death.[147]

Act. I., Scene 5. Hamlet, agitated, says to the Ghost:—

> Haste me to know't, that I, with wings as swift
> As meditation or the thoughts of love,
> May sweep to my revenge.

Are not these two similes undramatic and mere poetics?

When the Ghost vanishes, Hamlet breaks out into this:—

> O all you host of heaven! O earth! what else?
> And shall I couple hell? Od, fie! Hold, hold, my heart;
> And you, my sinews, grow not instant old,
> But bear me stiffly up. Remember thee?
> Ay, thou poor ghost, while memory holds a seat
> In this distracted globe. Remember thee?
> Yea, from the table of my memory
> I'll wipe away all trivial fond records,
> All saws of books, all forms, all pressures past,
> That youth and observation copied there;
> And thy commandment all alone shall live
> Within the book and volume of my brain,
> Unmixed with baser matter; yes, by heaven!
> O most pernicious woman!
> O villain, villain, smiling damned villain!
> My tables,—meet it is I set it down,
> That one may smile, and smile, and be a villain;
> At least I'm sure it may be so in Denmark.—
>   (Writing.)
> So, uncle, there you are—Now to my word;
> It is "Adieu, adieu! remember me."
> I have sworn't.

Is that really the kind of thoughts that would have been seething through the brain of a man who had just seen a visitor from the other world and who had been given such astounding news? In fact, I cannot believe that Shakespeare was able to conjure up in his own mind any horror at this wooden ghost, and so could not catch fire and show to us the horror that was in Hamlet's mind, the amazed stupefaction that Hamlet must have felt. The [148] speech is laboured, and, in places, very stagey. Effective in the mouth of a clever actor, who, indeed, would scarcely need any words to convey the horror of the situation. It is all expression, not emotion. In such terrific moments as this is meant to be, a man is almost speechless, and certainly would neither think nor express himself in the wordy speech just quoted.

Then there follows the "Illo, ho, hoing" business; falconry terms. Scarcely what would have been used by a man shaken to his soul by an appalling apparition. And the "Truepenny," "old mole," and the absurdities of the swearing business. We are told that this is Hamlet's agitation showing itself in buffoonery; but it does not ring to me as either tragic or true. I cannot imagine Aeschylus giving us such talk in such a situation.

The "tag" at the close of the scene, "Oh, cursed spite," etc., is just what an *actor* would write who is seeking an effective exit.

In Act II., Scene 2, the *actor*-writer shows again; Polonius has to read a ridiculous set of verses, purporting to have been written by the scholarly prince to his lady-love! This is merely a stage trap to catch a laugh. I suppose the commentators see in it a wonderful piece of psychological insight, and prove that it is meant to show the incipient madness in Hamlet!

Hamlet's talk with the players is very interesting to students of Shakespeare's self, but has not anything to do with the play, stopping the march of events, save only the necessary directions for the production of the trap-play. We have in these speeches Shakespeare's own views and criticisms of contemporary acting, and references to happenings in his theatrical world. Whatever may have been his abilities as a player, he must have been a *thoughtful* actor, knowing what he *should* do.

Are not Hamlet's directions to the players as to how to deliver a speech one of the finest specimens of Elizabethan or any other prose? Curiously, near the end of this speech, Hamlet, that is, Shakespeare, says: [149] "though in the mean time some necessary question of the play be then to be considered." This applies, or should apply, not only to clowning and gagging, but also and as truly to unnecessary outbursts of poetry. Not that anyone could wish that Shakespeare had been able to restrain himself, but he is the less great for not being able to smother his muse of fire when, as a dramatist, he should have done so.

Later in this scene, Hamlet says of the "mouse-trap" play,

"Marry, how? Tropically?" I do not want to pose as a commentator; but may this not be "topically"? I do not remember, though, if topical were used in the modern sense in Elizabethan days.*

What is the finest speech in the play? Both dramatically and poetically is it not the King's speech, "Oh, my offence is rank"? It is all splendid, but especially these lines:—

> But, oh, what form of prayer
> Can serve *my* turn? "Forgive me my foul murder?"
> That cannot be, since I am still possess'd
> Of these effects for which I *did* the murder,
> My crown, mine own ambition, and my queen.
> May one be pardon'd and retain the offence?
> In the corrupted currents of the world
> Offence's gilded hand may shove by justice,
> And oft 'tis seen the wicked prize itself
> Buys out the law; but 'tis *not* so *above;*
> *There,* is no shuffling; *there,* the action lies
> In his *true* nature, and we ourselves compell'd
> Even to the teeth and forehead of our faults
> To give in evidence.[150]

The words italicised are those which should be emphasised by the actor.

Is not the plot of the play well summed up by Fortinbras's lines in the second scene of the last Act?

> so shall you hear
> Of carnal, bloody, and unnatural acts,
> Of accidental judgments, casual slaughters,
> Of deaths put on by cunning and forced cause.

Yet we must thank heaven that Shakespeare *was* more of a poet than a dramatist.[151]

---

* But here are some small shot:—

In Act I., Scene 1, Horatio speaks of Fortinbras's "unimproved mettle"; should not this be "*un*proved"?

In Act II., Scene 2, Hamlet says of the King:—
> I'll tent him to the quick; if he but blench. . . .

Surely "tent" does not mean "probe," as Dowden says it does, but is a reference to the tenter hooks used for straining cloth. These are shown, by the way, in Aggas's map of London.

Shakespeare's Imagery
And What It Tells Us

By Caroline Spurgeon

Caroline Spurgeon, from *Shakespeare's Imagery and What It Tells Us* (Cambridge, The University Press, 1935).

IN HAMLET, NATURALLY, we find ourselves in an entirely different atmosphere. If we look closely we see this is partly due to the number of images of sickness, disease or blemish of the body, in the play . . . and we discover that the idea of an ulcer or tumour, as descriptive of the unwholesome condition of Denmark morally, is, on the whole, the dominating one.

HAMLET

Hamlet speaks of his mother's sin as a blister on the 'fair forehead of an innocent love,' she speaks of her 'sick soul,' and as in *King Lear* the emotion is so strong and the picture so vivid, that the metaphor overflows into the verbs and adjectives: heaven's face, he tells her, is *thought-sick* at the act; her husband is a *mildew'd ear, blasting* his *wholesome* brother; to have married him, her sense must be not only *sickly,* but *apoplex'd.* Finally, at the end of that terrific scene (3.4), he implores her not to soothe herself with the belief that his father's apparition is due to her son's madness, and not to her own guilt, for that

Ham. 3. 4. 43

4. 5. 17

3. 4. 51
3. 4. 64–5

3. 4. 73, 80

3. 4. 147   will but skin and film the ulcerous place,
Whiles rank corruption, mining all within,
Infects unseen.

So also, later, he compares the unnecessary
fighting between Norway and Poland to a kind of
4. 4. 27   tumour which grows out of too much prosperity.
He sees the country and the people in it alike in
terms of a sick body needing medicine or the
surgeon's knife. When he surprises Claudius at
his prayers, he exclaims,

3. 3. 96   This physic but prolongs thy sickly days;

and he describes the action of conscience in the
3. 1. 84   unforgettable picture of the healthy, ruddy coun-
Ham. 1. 1. 112 tenance [316] turning pale with sickness. A mote in
1. 4. 24; 5. 1. the eye, a 'vicious mole,' a galled chilblain, a
148; 2. 2. 622; probed wound and purgation, are also among
3. 2. 312   Hamlet's images; and the mind of Claudius runs
equally on the same theme.
When he hears of the murder of Polonius,
he declares that his weakness in not sooner having had Hamlet shut up was comparable to the
cowardly action of a man with a 'foul disease'
who

4. 1. 21   To keep it from divulging, let it feed
Even on the pith of life;

and later, when arranging to send Hamlet to
England and to his death, he justifies it by the
proverbial tag:

4. 3. 9   diseases desperate grown
By desperate appliance are relieved,
Or not at all;

and adjures the English king to carry out his
behest, in the words of a fever patient seeking a
sedative:

4. 3. 68   For like the hectic in my blood he rages,
And thou must cure me.

When working on Laertes, so that he will easily fall in with the design for the fencing match, his speech is full of the same underlying thought of a body sick, or ill at ease:

> goodness, growing to a plurisy,   4. 7. *118*
> Dies in his own too much;

and finally, he sums up the essence of the position and its urgency with lightning vividness in a short medical phrase:

> But, to the quick o' the ulcer: 4. 7. *124*
> Hamlet comes back.

In marked contrast to *King Lear,* though bodily disease is emphasised, bodily action and strain are little [317] drawn upon; indeed, only in *Ham. 3. 1. 56–88* Hamlet's great speech are they brought before us at all (*to be shot at* with slings and arrows, *to take arms against* troubles and *oppose* them, *to suffer* shocks, *to bear* the lash of whips, and *endure* pangs, to *grunt* and *sweat* under burdens, and so on), and here, as in *King Lear,* they serve to intensify the feeling of mental anguish. In *Hamlet,* however, anguish is not the dominating thought, but *rottenness,* disease, corruption, the result of *dirt;* the people are 'muddied,'

> Thick and unwholesome in their thoughts and   4. 5. *82*
> whispers;

and this corruption is, in the words of Claudius, 'rank' and 'smells to heaven,' so that the state of things in Denmark which shocks, paralyses and finally overwhelms Hamlet, is as the foul tumour breaking inwardly and poisoning the whole body, while showing

> no cause without   4. 4. *28*
> Why the man dies.

This image pictures and reflects not only the outward condition which causes Hamlet's spiritual illness, but also his own state. Indeed, the shock of the discovery of his father's murder and the sight of his mother's conduct have been such that when the play opens Hamlet has already begun to die, to die internally; because all the springs of life—love, laughter, joy, hope, belief in others—are becoming frozen at their source, are being gradually infected by the disease of the spirit which is—unknown to him—killing him.

To Shakespeare's pictorial imagination, therefore, the problem in *Hamlet* is not predominantly that of will and reason, of a mind too philosophic or a nature temperamentally unfitted to act quickly; he sees it [318] pictorially *not as the problem of an individual at all*, but as something greater and even more mysterious, as a *condition* for which the individual himself is apparently not responsible, any more than the sick man is to blame for the infection which strikes and devours him, but which, nevertheless, in its course and development, impartially and relentlessly, annihilates him and others, innocent and guilty alike. That is the tragedy of *Hamlet,* as it is perhaps the chief tragic mystery of life.

It is hardly necessary to point out, in a play so well known, and of such rich imaginative quality, how the ugliness of the dominating image (disease, ulcer) is counteracted, and the whole lighted up by flashes of sheer beauty in the imagery; beauty of picture, of sound and association, more particularly in the classical group and in the personifications. Thus, the tragic, murky atmosphere of Hamlet's interview with his mother, with its ever-repeated insistence on physical sickness and revolting disease, is illumined by the glow of his description of his father's portrait, the associations of beauty called up by Hyperion, Jove and Mars, or the exquisite picture evoked by the contemplation of the grace of his father's poise:

> like the herald Mercury   *Ham.* 3. 4. 58
> New-lighted on a heaven-kissing hill.

These beauties are specially noticeable in the many
personifications, as when, with Horatio, we see   *1. 1. 166*
'the morn, in russet mantle clad,' as she 'walks
o'er the dew of yon high eastward hill,' or, with
Hamlet, watch Laertes leaping into Ophelia's
grave, and ask,

> Whose phrase of sorrow   *5. 1. 267*
> Conjures the wandering stars and makes them stand
> Like wonder-wounded hearers? [319]

Peace, with her wheaten garland, Niobe all tears,   *Ham.* 5. 2. 41;
Ophelia's garments 'heavy with their drink,'   *1. 2. 149*
which pull her from her 'melodious lay' to muddy   *4. 7. 182*
death, or the magnificent picture of the two sides
of the queen's nature at war, as seen by the elder
Hamlet:

> But look, amazement on thy mother sits:
> O, step between her and her fighting soul;   *3. 4. 112*

these, and many more, are the unforgettable and
radiant touches of beauty in a play which has, as
images, much that is sombre and unpleasant.[320]

A Study of Shakespeare

By A. C. Swinburne

A. C. Swinburne, from *A Study of Shakespeare* (London, Chatto
and Windus, 1880).

IN HAMLET, as it seems to me, we set
foot as it were on the bridge between the middle and the [160]
final period of Shakespeare. That priceless waif of piratical sal-

vage which we owe to the happy rapacity of a hungry publisher
is of course more accurately definable as the first play of *Hamlet*
than as the first edition of the play. And this first *Hamlet,* on the
whole, belongs altogether to the middle period. The deeper com-
plexities of the subject are merely indicated. Simple and trenchant
outlines of character are yet to be supplanted by features of subtler
suggestion and infinite interfusion. Hamlet himself is almost more
of a satirist than a philosopher: Asper and Macilente, Felice and
Malevole, the grim studies after Hamlet unconsciously or consciously taken by Jonson and Marston, may pass as wellnigh
passable imitations, with an inevitable streak of caricature in
them, of the first Hamlet; they would have been at once puerile
and ghastly travesties of the second. The Queen, whose finished
figure is now something of a riddle, stands out simply enough in
the first sketch as confidant of Horatio if not as accomplice of
Hamlet. There is not more difference between the sweet quiet flow
of those plain verses which open the original play within the play
and the stiff sonorous tramp of their substitutes, full-charged with
heavy classic artillery of [161] Phoebus and Neptune and Tellus and
Hymen, than there is between the straightforward agents of their
own destiny whom we meet in the first *Hamlet* and the obliquely
moving patients who veer sideways to their doom in the second.

This minor transformation of style in the inner play, made
solely with the evident view of marking the distinction between
its duly artificial forms of speech and the duly natural forms of
speech passing between the spectators, is but one among innumerable indications which only a purblind perversity of prepossession
can overlook of the especial store set by Shakespeare himself on
this favourite work, and the exceptional pains taken by him to
preserve it for aftertime in such fullness of finished form as might
make it worthiest of profound and perpetual study by the light of
far other lamps than illuminate the stage. Of all vulgar errors the
most wanton, the most wilful, and the most resolutely tenacious
of life, is that belief bequeathed from the days of Pope, in which
it was pardonable, to the days of Mr. Carlyle, in which it is not
excusable, to the effect that Shakespeare threw off Hamlet as an
eagle may moult a feather or a fool may break a jest; that he
dropped his work as a bird may drop an egg [162] or a sophist a
fallacy; that he wrote 'for gain, not glory,' or that having written

Hamlet he thought it nothing very wonderful to have written. For himself to have written, he possibly, nay probably, did not think it anything miraculous; but that he was in the fullest degree conscious of its wonderful positive worth to all men for all time, we have the best evidence possible—his own; and that not by mere word of mouth but by actual stroke of hand. Ben Jonson might shout aloud over his own work on a public stage, 'By God, 'tis good,' and so for all its real goodness and his real greatness make sure that both the workman and his work should be less unnaturally than unreasonably laughed at; Shakespeare knew a better way of showing confidence in himself, but he showed not a whit less confidence. Scene by scene, line for line, stroke upon stroke and touch after touch, he went over all the old laboured ground again; and not to ensure success in his own day and fill his pockets with contemporary pence, but merely and wholly with a purpose to make it worthy of himself and his future students. Pence and praise enough it had evidently brought him in from the first. No more palpable proof of this can be desired than the instantaneous attacks on it, the jeers,[163] howls, hoots and hisses of which a careful ear may catch some far faint echo even yet; the fearful and furtive yelp from beneath of the masked and writing poeticule, the shrill reverberation all around it of plagiarism and parody. Not one single alteration in the whole play can possibly have been made with a view to stage effect or to present popularity and profit; or we must suppose that Shakespeare, however great as a man, was naturally even greater as a fool. There is a class of mortals to whom this inference is always grateful—to whom the fond belief that every great man must needs be a great fool would seem always to afford real comfort and support: happy, in Prior's phrase, could their inverted rule prove every great fool to be a great man. Every change in the text of *Hamlet* has impaired its fitness for the stage and increased its value for the closet in exact and perfect proportion. Now, this is not a matter of opinion—of Mr. Pope's opinion or Mr. Carlyle's; it is a matter of fact and evidence. Even in Shakespeare's time the actors threw out his additions; they throw out these very same additions in our own. The one especial speech, if any one such especial speech there be, in which the personal genius of Shakespeare soars up to the [164] very highest of its height and strikes down to the very deepest of its depth, is passed over by modern actors; it was cut away by Hemings and Condell. We may almost assume it as certain that no boards have ever echoed—at least, more than once or twice—to the supreme soliloquy of Hamlet. Those words which combine the noblest pleading ever proffered for the rights of human reason with the loftiest vindication ever uttered of those rights, no mortal ear within our knowledge has ever heard spoken on the stage. A convocation even of all priests could not have been more unhesitatingly unanimous in its rejection than seems to have been the hereditary verdict of all actors. It could hardly have been found worthier of theological than it has been found of theatrical condemnation. Yet, beyond all question, magnificent as is that monologue on suicide and doubt which has passed from a proverb into a byword, it is actually eclipsed and distanced at once on philosophic and on poetical grounds by the later soliloquy on reason and resolution.

That Shakespeare was in the genuine sense—that is, in the best and highest and widest meaning of the term—a free thinker, this otherwise practically and avowedly superfluous effusion of all inmost [165] thought appears to me to supply full and sufficient evidence for the conviction of every candid and rational man. To that loftiest and most righteous title which any just and reasoning soul can ever deserve to claim, the greatest save one of all poetic thinkers has thus made good his right for ever.

I trust it will be taken as no breach of my past pledge to abstain from all intrusion on the sacred ground of Gigadibs and the Germans, if I venture to indicate a touch inserted by Shakespeare for no other perceptible or conceivable purpose than to obviate by anticipation the indomitable and ineradicable fallacy of criticism which would find the keynote of Hamlet's character in the quality of irresolution. I may observe at once that the misconception involved in such a reading of the riddle ought to have been evident even without this episodical stroke of illustration. In any case it should be plain to any reader that the signal characteristic of Hamlet's inmost nature is by no means irresolution or hesitation or any form of weakness, but rather the strong conflux of contending forces. That during four whole acts Hamlet cannot or does not make up his mind to any direct and deliberate action against his uncle is true enough; true, also, we may say, that Hamlet had somewhat [166] more of mind than another man to make up, and might properly want somewhat more time than might another man to do it in; but not, I venture to say in spite of Goethe, through innate inadequacy to his task and unconquerable weakness of the will; not, I venture to think in spite of Hugo, through immedicable scepticism of the spirit and irremediable propensity to nebulous intellectual refinement. One practical point in the action of the play precludes us from accepting so ready a solution of the riddle as is suggested either by the simple theory of half-heartedness or by the simple hypothesis of doubt. There is absolutely no other reason, we might say there was no other excuse, for the introduction or intrusion of an else superfluous episode into a play which was already, and which remains even after all possible excisions, one of the longest plays on record. The compulsory expedition of Hamlet to England, his discovery by the way of the plot laid against his life, his interception of the King's letter and his forgery of a substitute for it against the lives of the King's agents, the ensuing adventure of the sea-fight, with Hamlet's daring act of hot-headed personal intrepidity, his capture and subsequent release on terms giving no less patent proof of his cool-headed and [167] ready-witted courage and resource than the attack had afforded of his physically impulsive and even impetuous hardihood—all this serves no purpose whatever but that of exhibiting the instant and almost unscrupulous resolution of Hamlet's character in time of practical need. But for all that he or Hamlet has got by it, Shakespeare might too evidently have spared his pains; and for all this voice as of one crying in a wilderness, Hamlet will too surely remain to the majority of students, not less than to all actors and all editors and all critics, the standing type and embodied emblem of irresolution, half-heartedness, and doubt.

That Hamlet should seem at times to accept for himself, and even to enforce by reiteration of argument upon his conscience and his reason, some such conviction or suspicion as to his own character, tells much rather in disfavour than in favour of its truth. A man whose natural temptation was to swerve, whose inborn inclination was to shrink and skulk aside from duty and from action, would hardly be the first and last person to suspect his own weakness, the one only unbiassed judge and witness of sufficiently sharp-sighted candour and accuracy to estimate aright his poverty of nature and the malformation of his mind. But the high-hearted [168]

and tender-conscienced Hamlet, with his native bias towards introspection intensified and inflamed and directed and dilated at once
by one imperative pressure and oppression of unavoidable and
unalterable circumstance, was assuredly and exactly the one only
man to be troubled by any momentary fear that such might indeed
be the solution of his riddle, and to feel or to fancy for the
moment some kind of ease and relief in the sense of that very
trouble. A born doubter would have doubted even of Horatio;
hardly can all positive and almost palpable evidence of underhand
instigation and inspired good intentions induce Hamlet for some
time to doubt even of Ophelia.[169]

Hamlet: A Study in Critical Method

By A. J. A. Waldock

A. J. A. Waldock, from *Hamlet: A Study in Critical Method* (Cambridge, The University Press, 1931).

*P*ROFESSOR *C. M. LEWIS*, writing in
1907, made a revolutionary suggestion about the problem of *Hamlet*. He suggested that the problem, in the form in which, since
Goethe and Coleridge, it had always been understood, might not
exist. That is to say, it might be that there is *no* psychological
cause for the delay. Suppose (and it is interesting to note how, in
such a suggestion, we return to the neighbourhood of our starting-
point, in the comments of Hanmer: the critical wheel comes full
circle), suppose that it amounted to this: that Shakespeare had a
"delay" on his hands that in his freshly conceived plot was rather
awkward to account for; suppose that he took the easiest way out
of the difficulty and, instead of supplying new motivation, induced
us by clever subterfuge, disguises and makeshifts to overlook the

absence of motivation; suppose, in short, that instead of re-explaining the delay he simply left it in his play and ingeniously, with the magic resources of his art, slurred it over. It is a supposition that, after our Coleridgean training, makes us shiver. More recently Professor Stoll, in his dauntless style, has advocated a similar view.

Now we hesitate to think such things because they involve a certain condemnation of Shakespeare. When Professor Stoll has finished with *Hamlet* there is, indeed, little left of it but a bedraggled and awe-inspiring mass [76] of wreckage. Professor Lewis is milder. His *Hamlet* still remains a noble object, but it is not quite so noble as we thought it was. It is still, in his figure, a cathedral, but it is a cathedral that begins Saxon, becomes Norman, and ends as Gothic. His view would imply as well that the masonry is not as solid as it appears: some of the pillars are filled with rubble, there is a vein of deception in the workmanship. Our impulse is to reply that it cannot be so. And yet—when Professor Nicoll, voicing again of late the reluctance we all share, speaks in these flat terms: "[Shakespeare], being a great dramatist, obviously must have striven to make such a delay, necessary as it may have been, psychologically possible": we cannot resist a lurking doubt whether the matter is to be so easily disposed of. *Obviously, must,* are strong words; *great dramatist* is a little indefinite. Even if the worst came to the worst and we were compelled to believe that Shakespeare had resorted to such stratagems as Professor Lewis suspects him of and Professor Stoll joyfully lauds him for, perhaps yet we could save greatness for the creator of *Hamlet.* The play would not be precisely the fashion of masterpiece that it is often thought to be. Though the heavens fall we will still claim it masterpiece.

But the question is hardly so serious as that. It would need discrepancies of larger magnitude than these (large as they are) to upset the greatness of *Hamlet.* In the meantime, such suggestions are at least deserving of inspection. I should like, however, to discuss the matter from a slightly different point of view.[77]

Now it is interesting, in the first place, to examine a little more closely this conception of "delay." We have noticed more than once the tendency, almost ingrained in *Hamlet* criticism, to treat the play as if it were not a work of art so much as an historical document, as if it were some kind of literal transcript from reality that we could probe into and go behind, as we would probe into and go behind a mass of law-court evidence. We have seen how such a method of investigation leads, in this instance and that, to critical mare's-nests. But I do not think it has been observed (except, in passing, by Professor Stoll) that the delay itself has suffered from a like confusing and distorting scrutiny.

This is a matter of great importance. Delay in real life is one thing; in a drama, another. It is, I suppose, indisputable that one is more impressed by the delay in *Hamlet* when one reads the play than when one sees it; and more still than when one reads it, when one reflects upon it afterwards. A remark of Hudson's is noteworthy. He says that "he has learned by experience that one seems to understand *Hamlet* better after a little study than after a great deal." He draws the inference, how absurd to imagine that we can comprehend this play in a hurry! The inference, of course, is very sound. But the opposite deduction also has its truth, namely, that the only way to grasp the entire *Hamlet* is to understand it quickly, in an embracing impression. Our great handicap (as well as advantage) is that we write with wisdom after the event. One could even suspect that many of the chief difficulties of this play are of the kind [78] that occur to one in afterthought. It is assuredly so with this one. Says Professor Nicoll: "Obviously the first thing which strikes us is the fact that the hero delays so long in achieving his revenge." *When* does it strike us? It strikes us when, in calmness, and after the hurrying scenes have run their course, we begin to reconstruct it all in our minds as it might have been in real life. It is then that we begin to remember things. It is then that the impression of the delay grows on us so powerfully.

It must be emphasised that delay in real life is one thing, in a drama quite another. We know quite well that Hamlet delays two months or so before he kills the King. How do we find this out? We find it out by putting two and two together. We hear from one character in the drama that the old King has been dead not quite two months. Then another character, later, in an unguarded moment, lets slip the information that the King has now been dead "twice two months." We pounce on this. We subtract. Then we follow Laertes. We find that he has been in Paris some time and is now wanting supplies. We collect the evidence bit by bit, we calculate, we reach our conclusions. They are conclusions that, if *Hamlet* were a piece of real life actually occurring, could not be questioned. As it is, they cannot be questioned. Only, they may or may not be of use to us. Laertes could wander all over Europe and yet Hamlet, as far as our impressions go, could in that time have been living a mere two days. In some dramas such things perhaps do not happen; in Shakespearean dramas it is a mere fact that they do. We are here in an Einstein [79] world, where time has strange oddities, where intervals are a delusion and durations a snare. What does it matter that a month or two have gone by between Acts I and II? They have gone by, but not noticeably where Hamlet is; somewhere in another plane of the drama they have gone by.[1] Hamlet at the end of Act I has announced that he will presently put on an antic disposition; in the first scene of Act II we see the initial consequences: he has frightened Ophelia. What has he been doing with himself all the time? It is like asking for news from the fourth dimension. Of course we know that he did several things. He had time to disarrange his attire, and it was perhaps in this interval that he took Horatio into his confidence. But the point to be made is that the interval (apart from one or two such suggestions made about it) has really no dramatic existence. Delay does not exist in a drama simply because [80] it is (as it were) embedded in it. The delay that exists in a drama is the delay that is displayed. Delay, in any case, does not here quite coincide with time duration, is not the same thing as a mere colour-less lapse of days. It is not enough to say that Hamlet procrastinates because, as a matter of fact, and regarding the play somewhat as an historical document, we find that he did not act for two

---

[1] It is true, of course, that Hamlet's "transformation" has been in progress some time before Ophelia is frightened by his "antic disposition." There has been opportunity for Rosencrantz and Guildenstern to be hastily sent for. Ophelia has repelled the Prince's letters and denied him access. Polonius asks her if she has given Hamlet any hard words "of late." I feel, however, that such indications are mere "embedded" delay compared with the powerful impression made by Ophelia's report. Professor Bradley complains that people think that "Hamlet's visit to Ophelia was the first announcement of his madness." It *is* the first announcement of it in the play and arrives as the immediate sequel to Hamlet's revelations, a few moments before, of his intentions. It is hardly to be wondered at that "many readers and critics imagine that Hamlet went straight to Ophelia's room after his interview with the ghost." The point is that if Shakespeare had in mind strong "delay" values just here, he was no dramatist, for he has not conveyed them.

months or so. If he procrastinates, it is because he is shown procrastinating. To put it another way, it is not sufficient that delay
should be negatively implicit in the play; it is necessary, for its
dramatic existence, that it should be positively demonstrated. The
delay, in a word, exists just inasmuch as and just to the degree in
which it is conveyed.

It seems to me that if this principle is held in mind, the problem of *Hamlet* looms rather less large. There is, to begin with,
less delay to account for. I do not mean merely that we can cease
tormenting ourselves with the puzzle of Hamlet's occupations
during those mysterious months. Certain scenes and passages
which have often been dragged into the problem and made part
and parcel of it are seen to have no real relevance to it. It does
not, for example, concern us in the slightest that Hamlet, when he
ought to be killing his uncle, calmly lectures the players on the
intricacies of their art. "How characteristic," says Bradley, "that
he appears quite as anxious that his speech should not be ranted as
that Horatio should observe its effect on the King." As if Shakespeare were beyond stopping a plot for a moment or two to
interpolate (dramatically) some other piece of material [81] that
interested him! All this while, of course, Hamlet is delaying. He is
delaying while he converses with Ophelia, he is delaying while he
welcomes Rosencrantz and Guildenstern, he is delaying while he
interviews his mother in her closet. But, of course, in our impressions, he is doing nothing of the kind. How, in the absorption of
so much present interest, could we be conscious as well of an
inaction beneath the action; how, in the fascination of so much
happening could we spare a thought for what is not?

Unless our thought is jogged. It is, in that scene with the
mother, where suddenly, in the midst of Hamlet's passionate outburst, the Ghost appears (III, IV, 106):

HAMLET. Do you not come your tardy son to chide,
          That, lapsed in time and passion, lets go by
          The important acting of your dread command?
          O, say!
GHOST.   Do not forget: this visitation
          Is but to whet thy almost blunted purpose.

Such a passage constitutes a violent reminder. And then there are
the famous soliloquies.

The grand problem of *Hamlet* is this: to know exactly how much "delay" there is in the play. I do not mean, to know precisely how long Hamlet delayed, but to know precisely how important in the design of the play the "delay" motive was meant to be. The question, "Why did Hamlet delay?" assumes the other question as solved; but it has never been solved, perhaps is insoluble. One thing, however, seems to be growing clearer: that [82] the motive is not the only motive in the play; that perhaps it is not the central (for we have seen that another competes formidably); that perhaps it is not even a major motive. To go so far may well seem extreme; but it is interesting, once again, to look at the facts.

We have noticed the difficulties in the scene that follows the disclosure of the Ghost. No criticism is sound that ignores the suggestions of imperfect adaptation in this scene. I feel that to approach such a scene in the calm confidence that Shakespeare, seeing that it is such an important scene, *must* therefore have expended his most careful work upon it, *must*, if we had only eyes to see, have made everything clear, is to invite disaster. There are no *musts* about it. Shakespeare ought to have been careful, but if we observe signs that he was not, what can we do but put ourselves on our guard? The antic disposition provides us with something like a false clue at the start; it seems to direct us along the old road of melodrama, although we are presently, in this new play, to swing off at a very wide angle. But if one knew nothing about the play beyond this scene one would imagine that Claudius was a formidable person, difficult to get at, and that the revenge was to be fraught with many dangers against which Hamlet, by these mysterious proceedings, was taking precautions. In short, as we have seen, this incident seems a piece of the old design that was never quite adjusted to the new. It is like a piece of primitive rock projecting through more recent strata. And our only protection is to recognise that this may be so and to beware, accordingly.[83]

At the end of the scene, however, comes the significant couplet:

> The time is out of joint: O cursed spite,
> That ever I was born to set it right!

That it *is* significant, one cannot doubt. But one wishes one could decide precisely in what way. It is a groan at the hatefulness of

existence. Life itself has become a burden to Hamlet (and we
know, partly, why). Under the burden that weighs him down,
duties of revenge, like all other duties, might well lose some of
their imperiousness. He is not savouring his revenge (for the
savour has gone from all things); he is not anticipating it (as we
may imagine his prototype doing) with gusto; we get the impression that he may not, for all his earlier outburst, "sweep" to
it. But there is nothing, if we remember the indications we have
already had of his state of mind, very puzzling about all this. Nor
is it clear why we should be obliged to draw from the words the
further inference, namely, that he is already feeling twinges of
inadequacy, fearing that he will not, for some reason that he
scarcely knows himself, be equal to his task.

Now comes an interval, but we will dispense with conjec-
tures as to how Hamlet spent his time. He put on the antic disposition. The next act goes along. There are no rifts where "delay"
might lurk, for all rifts are loaded with dramatic ore. And it is to
be remembered that we are really not yet in a position to know
what Hamlet is proposing to do about his revenge. "Delay" cannot yet (unless we have second sight) have entered [84] our heads.
We come, then, at the very end of the act, to the "O, what a
rogue" soliloquy.

What is to be made of this? It would be absurd to attempt to
minimize the effect of this passage. There is plenty of "delay"
here. And yet it would be, perhaps, just as false to Shakespeare's
purpose to underscore heavily all its suggestions. It is so easy to
make a "pet" of a passage and then to turn the whole play round
until it fits in. How Coleridge did that with Hamlet's few remarks
about the "pale cast of thought" and the "thinking too precisely
on the event"! However weighty this utterance or that may seem,
we are still bound to consider *all* the facts, and while we are
contemplating one set to bear in mind the others. It is worth
noting, to begin with, that the soliloquy is prompted. We are not
compelled to imagine that Hamlet has spent all the interval writh-
ing over some strange torpor that has beset him. The impression
is rather different. In any case, as we have seen, it is difficult for
us to imagine precisely what Hamlet is doing when we do not see
him, and when we do see him he is generally engaged in something that effectively prevents our thinking of his delay. The
soliloquy, however, does not clearly imply that Hamlet has been

brooding over inadequacy. Rather, this strange behaviour of the
player impresses his imagination with a startling contrast. That
the actor should have broken down in his speech, shed real tears—
"and all for nothing"—while Hamlet himself, with such a living
motive, peaks like John-a-dreams and says no word—what a
queerness in life! Well, we have had hints of another trouble that
is [85] on Hamlet's mind and that might possibly affect his reactions to his new calamity. Are we really made to feel, by the
speech, that it is strange that Hamlet has not yet acted? Do we
concur in his wonder at himself and join with him in his self-
reproaches? A Shakespearean soliloquy is often naïve: and our
responses must be naïve; but surely not quite so naïve as that.

It is to be remembered, too, that the soliloquy is not entirely
one of self-blame, although no doubt it is our impression of the
self-blame that chiefly remains with us. But the impression, though
it is by no means neutralised, is a good deal modified by the concluding lines. We have noticed before just how we seem obliged
to take these lines which contain the proposal for the play-scene.
They do jar, rather, with the lines that have preceded them. It
would be pleasant if we could feel that that jar was significant in
the sense in which Professor Bradley accepts it. But it is altogether
too much of a risk. It seems much more likely, as we have seen,
that what we have here is a slight bump in the highway of the
plot. Shakespeare has left a little gap between two surfaces. Trav-
elling at speed, we scarcely notice it; when, in our leisurely sur-
veys, we slow down, we feel it.

The soliloquy, then, paves the way (a little roughly) to the
play-scene. But we have, intervening, another soliloquy, the "To
be." Now this is not, properly speaking, one of the soliloquies of
procrastination, although we may allow that it has a relevance for
that motive. But its place is rather by the first soliloquy of the
play, the "O, that this too too solid flesh would [86] melt." Certainly it is profoundly revealing of Hamlet's mood and, if we
have yet begun seriously to wonder why Hamlet delays, furnishes
us with a tolerably adequate answer. Hamlet, in his despair, is
contemplating a cutting away of the very basis of ethics. For what
does this imposed duty, with all other duties, depend on but the
assumption that life is worth living: an assumption that Hamlet is
now on the verge of denying? The feeling that vengeance (or
anything) is worth while presupposes an active belief in life.

Hamlet (and we have been given means of knowing why) has almost lost that belief. The point seems to be that so far as the play has gone, there has been, what with one thing and another, not much occasion for surprise in Hamlet's behaviour; nothing, surely, that cannot be received, on our data, without much difficulty; nothing that has really assumed problematical dimensions.

But we have still, of course, the "pale cast of thought" to dispose of. After Hamlet has finished talking about the whips and scorns of time, the fardels, and the dread of the unknown that induces us to continue bearing such trials instead of making our quietus, he draws the moral (III, i, 83):

> Thus conscience does make cowards of us all,
> And thus the native hue of resolution
> Is sicklied o'er with the pale cast of thought,
> And enterprises of great pith and moment
> With this regard their currents turn awry
> And lose the name of action.

What really does he mean? We are still debating this.[87] Is it just moralising? Or has he, when he says "enterprise," some very particular enterprise in mind—his own, say, of revenge? I would only suggest that there is at least reason for caution. He has not, in the earlier portions of the speech, been thinking of his revenge: at any rate, that has only been part of the "sea of troubles" from which he is considering taking refuge. The sweep of the thought grows wider as he proceeds. The lines in question are like a normal, and somewhat impersonal, generalisation: a philosophical tag to his discourse. They are, in so far, very characteristic of Hamlet, who (like many another Shakespearean character, but in a way all his own) delights to pass from the particular to the general. One thinks of his disquisition to Horatio on the "heavy-headed revel" of the Danes—a speech that does not appear in the Folio, for it is not part and parcel of the plot;—how there he proceeded from his special censure to a wide-reaching conclusion (I, iv, 23):

> So, oft it chances in particular men,
> That for some vicious mole of nature in them,
> As, in their birth . . .

and so on. It is not denied, of course, that such extra-dramatic utterances (for though they are still dramatic they are extras) often

yield much matter. Among them are some of the most pregnant
lines in Shakespeare. It has often been observed how much of the
essence of the Shakespearean tragedy is held in the nutshell of this
very passage (I, iv, 31):

> Carrying, I say, the stamp of one defect,
> Being nature's livery, or fortune's star,— [88]
> Their virtues else—be they as pure as grace,
> As infinite as man may undergo—
> Shall in the general censure take corruption
> From that particular fault.

And perhaps these other lines of Hamlet's about the resolution
sicklied o'er contain some suggestions of what Shakespeare deeply
meant to convey about him. But that, again, is something that we
must judge from the play as a whole.

The play-scene satisfies Hamlet. He has no more excuse for
doubting the authenticity of the Ghost. Now surely he must do
something. Well, he does. When he finds the King at prayer he
nearly kills him; when he hears him behind the arras he *does* kill
him. As it turns out, it is Polonius he has killed, but that is not
Hamlet's fault. I know that this seems like burlesquing the sequence, but what can we do? That the deep design which Bradley
detects in this series of incidents is really intended I feel we have
simply no ground for inferring. Or almost none. All the elements
are natural except one. Hamlet's inflamed hate, his savage postponement of the act, the sudden thrust as the "rat" stirs behind the
curtain: all this hangs together and bears one meaning on its face
and one only. And then the Ghost must needs bring back our
doubts.

I do not think any passage in the play is more tantalising
than this second exchange between Hamlet and the Ghost. The
suggestions are so interesting and yet leave us so perplexed. Hamlet's behaviour in the last quarter of an hour or so has been clear
and consistent.[89] It has been like a recovery. He has roused himself from his broodings to act; he has acted drastically. Yet now he
greets the returning Ghost with shamefaced apologies (III, iv,
106):

> Do you not come your tardy son to chide,
> That, lapsed in time and passion, lets go by
> The important acting of your dread command?

The Ghost endorses Hamlet's self-censure:

> Do not forget: this visitation
> Is but to whet thy almost blunted purpose.

Now this is the kind of thing that makes *Hamlet,* as a drama, so exasperating. We have been following Shakespeare's lead with good intentions and with every care. We must still believe, in spite of Professor Bradley, that it *was* his lead that we followed. And this is our reward! "Blunted purpose"; "lapsed in time and passion." It is some consolation to find that critics who base their theories on "blunted purposes" are themselves discomposed by this passage. Mr. Clutton-Brock will have nothing to do with it. He resorts to "survival" from the old play. In any case, I see no clear way out of the trouble except (the last ludicrous and desperate measure left us) to refuse to take very much notice of the lines. Shakespeare deserves it. It amounts to this: which passage shall we notice? If we take full notice of this one, then we must suspect, in the immediately preceding incidents, dramatic intentions which our impressions do not convey to us. But the conflict of suggestions leaves us very dissatisfied. We know, of course, that the Ghost [90] is speaking from his own point of view. From his point of view, the deed has yet to be done: what Hamlet has planned, what Hamlet has otherwise accomplished, are all irrelevancies. But this does not satisfy us. What tantalises us is our very definite notion that the Ghost is speaking, also, from Shakespeare's point of view, and that when Hamlet says, "lapsed in time and passion," Shakespeare also means lapsed in time and passion. That is our characteristic difficulty with *Hamlet:* to square meanings that will not square; to decide amidst apparently conflicting intentions precisely what it was that Shakespeare did intend. At least it is best to recognise that the difficulty exists.

It recurs, though perhaps in a slightly less insistent form, in our next "delay" passage, which is also our last. We have already seen that to press for reasons—dramatic, psychological reasons— why Hamlet sails for England is to press for what was, as far as we can judge, not supplied. Hamlet sails for England for motives, not of his own, but of Shakespeare's: or perhaps, we may say, of Kyd's. But he does something in Shakespeare that he had probably not done before. He pauses on the way to England to express surprise at himself for going there. We have now to grapple for a

moment with the second great "procrastination" soliloquy: the
"How all occasions do inform against me" (IV, iv, 32).

It is perhaps worth noting that this soliloquy, like the "O,
what a rogue," is prompted. It is not an unstimulated outburst, a
welling-up of self-torturings that must find expression and release. No, again a curiosity [91] of life has struck Hamlet's imagination: the spectacle of this Prince Fortinbras marching with his
army

> To all that fortune, death and danger dare,
> Even for an egg-shell

while he himself, with what "excitements of his reason and his
blood," has done nothing. It is strange. But, again, is it really
strange to us? Fortinbras is, for the moment, a symbol of exhor-
tation to Hamlet. But do we really think that Hamlet ought to be
like Fortinbras? Does Hamlet himself, while he uses Fortinbras as
a "spur," not see ironically through and through this delicate and
tender prince who finds quarrels in a straw and leads twenty
thousand men, for a fantasy and trick of fame, to fight for a plot

> Whereon the numbers cannot try the cause,
> Which is not tomb enough and continent
> To hide the slain?

But, certainly, the "spur" was there; the occasion informed
against Hamlet. Professor Lewis and, after him, Professor Stoll,
elude the obvious suggestions of this speech very ingeniously.
They regard the passage as, roughly, a kind of stratagem on
Shakespeare's part. After all, Hamlet had been delaying now for
some time; the delay would presently begin to be noticeable. The
English voyage, in particular, might well provoke questions. So
Shakespeare, as it were, grasped the nettle of the difficulty and
anticipated our doubts by putting them in Hamlet's own mouth.
He also put promises in Hamlet's mouth. Hamlet, even if he has
done not much [92] yet (we must remind ourselves that he has
done several things) assures us that he will do something soon—

> O, from this time forth,
> My thoughts be bloody or be nothing worth!—

and with this reassurance we sit back contented and agree to overlook his remissness. But Shakespeare was, for once, too clever. He
stilled, perhaps, the doubts of his audiences. But the seed sown

was to rise up against him: every seed a commentator. And the result of his ingenuity has been the problem of *Hamlet*.

Such a view (Professors Lewis and Stoll differ slightly in their treatment) may well hold some of the truth. We can feel fairly sure that it does not hold all of it. The speech, whatever plot devices it may further, still emphasises a state of mind. But when we ask what elucidation it furnishes of this state of mind, the answer is not so clear (IV, iv, 39):

> Now, whether it be
> Bestial oblivion, or some craven scruple
> Of thinking too precisely on the event,—
> A thought which, quarter'd, hath but one part wisdom
> And ever three parts coward,—I do not know
> Why yet I live to say "this thing's to do,"
> Sith I have cause, and will, and strength, and means,
> To do't.

He has will and strength and means; that is definite. The "bestial oblivion" and "the craven scruple of thinking" are, I think, for all the reams of commentary, doomed to remain indefinite to the end of time. Perhaps that was just what they were meant to be— for we come to this suspicion in the end. Did Shakespeare wish [93] not to pursue that particular motive any farther? After all, we have been shown, apart from "bestial oblivion" and "craven scruple," a good deal of what has been going on in Hamlet's soul. We remember the tremendous pre-occupation that was on him before the Ghost arrived. We know that his thoughts, since the play began, were never single; that there was always that other matter, that other burden. Is "bestial oblivion" the corollary of that other so strong necessity to remember? As for "craven scruple," we do not know what it means. But it seems hardly necessary that we should. Hamlet has delayed because he has had something else (that other thing) to think about. Perhaps the problem requires no further answer than that.

For (and here I return to the primary question) is the problem pressed? There is, concerning this same soliloquy, one other point to be observed. It is not in the First Quarto play. More than that, it is not in the Folio play. That means, apparently, that it was not the custom to speak it in the acting version; it is not now the custom to speak it in the acting version. Now there are, in

our play, only two great soliloquies that strongly suggest procrastination, that strongly raise the problem of delay. This is one
of them. The other is the soliloquy at the end of Act II: "O, what
a rogue." I will not attempt to decide which of these two soliloquies is the weightier. Professor Bradley, with some suggestion of
hesitation, votes for the earlier. If either had to be dispensed with,
better, he feels, that it should be the later. But how important the
second soliloquy is,[94] especially for a view of the play such as
Coleridge's, or Bradley's, may be gauged from the several lines we
have been discussing. It is, from all such points of view, a passage
of enormous importance. It is one of the twin-pillars of "delay."
Now it is easy to say that our concern is merely with the Second
Quarto; that the play, as cut down for acting, means nothing to
us. It does mean something. The omission of the soliloquy means
this: that if Shakespeare intended his play to be, above all, about
procrastination, if he meant it above all things for a study in
"delay," he was misunderstood almost at the beginning. The
actors of his own time misunderstood him; or, if they understood
him, decided that it was of no use trying to convey his meaning. I
suppose it is obvious that no performance of *Hamlet* ever has succeeded, ever will or can succeed, in conveying that meaning.

This is not to deny procrastination. Of course there is procrastination. But it is not everywhere in the play, the play is not
compounded of it, it is not the theme of themes: at least I fail to
see how it can be considered so. The "How all occasions" soliloquy is the last clear and obvious suggestion of procrastination that
we have. The fifth act is full of varied interest. Hamlet returns. In
the second half of the act the current of events becomes a swirl
and we are swept to the culmination. And when we look back
over the course of the play, it is not on one long delay that we
think. The changing spectacle, the absorbing story, have left us
space only now and again for a glimpse of these doubts and hesitations. They are there, they are in the design; they are not the
design.[95]

I would suggest, then, that the question "Why did Hamlet
delay?" instead of being *the* question about Hamlet, is a question that in our immediate experience of the play (which is our
all-important experience) does not, after all, very seriously arise.
No one can deny the positive indications of delay; they are not,

however, quite so numerous or quite so urgent as one might be
led to think from some of the critical accounts; and their cumula-
tive effect is not, perhaps, so powerful as has been assumed. The
play is not dyed in delay. Now that means, simply, that the problem of the inaction recedes. It does not vanish. But it becomes less
obtrusive.

Nor does it seem necessary, even if we suppose that the
inaction is accounted for, by Shakespeare, rather less certainly,
with rather less logic, than it is accounted for by Coleridge and
Bradley, that we should rush into a kind of critical atheism, proclaiming the shattering of our belief in the dramatist. Dramas are
of many kinds. We have no reason to require of Shakespeare that
every play should match a set technique. The inaction (as much
of it as is dramatically urgent, as much of it as Shakespeare per-
mits to become stuff of the drama) is accounted for, when all is
said, with fair sufficiency. It does not worry us, unless we let it
worry us. We take it in our stride. And it was surely open to
Shakespeare,[96] when he wished, to keep motives subdued, as it
was open to him, when he wished, to enforce them.

We still, of course, have our difficulties: plenty of them.
Some of these, as we have seen, seem inherent in the design. The
play, from one point of view, is a tremendous *tour de force*. An
old plot is wrenched to new significances, significances, in places,
that to the end it refuses to take. It was, perhaps, inevitable that
the play should show signs, in fissures and strain, of all this force-
ful bending. There are other difficulties that we can hardly venture
to account for. Motives vaguely indicated ("blunted purpose,"
"lapsed in time") fade, seem somehow thwarted in their working
out. We are left to surmises. Chords are sounded, dimly, suggestively, then become blurred. We seem to gain partial visions of
intentions not clearly formulated. (How it would have helped us,
supposing Shakespeare strongly meant "delay," if he had made
Horatio give a hint, in aside of just four words! Indeed, the failure, in such a case, to make use of Horatio for explanatory comment—never needed more than here!—is well-nigh incredible.)
But what would *Hamlet* be without its puzzles: the eternal piq-
uancy of its imperfection?

Imperfection. For the play, after all, is just a play: a work of

art with a design that is deceptive and intricate and somewhat misleading. We are discouraged if we cannot trace the design as evenly
as we could wish, we are disappointed if we find the pattern a little
mixed and bewildering. But at least we must keep to the design as
it appears, abide by the patterns as we find them.[97] Nothing is to
be gained by compelling system from what is not system. If the
filaments are not everywhere tight, it is not for us to tighten them;
if the design relaxes, we cannot put it right.

But there is an inveterate temptation to try. We are for ever
discovering new causes for Hamlet's inaction. Professor Nicoll
the other day discovered one more. He suggests that a chief cause
was Hamlet's ambition, or rather, his fear of his ambition: more
precisely, his sincerity. The King speaks once of Hamlet's "pride";
Hamlet himself makes a remark to Rosencrantz about "lacking
advancement," he declares, again, to Ophelia that he is "proud,
revengeful, ambitious"; and later (v, ii. 65) refers to the King as
one who has "Popp'd in between the election and [his] hopes."
Hamlet, then, has a strongly ambitious spirit, distrusts it, and fears
that if he murders his uncle it may be, deep in his heart, for his
own ends. So, he delays. Surely it will not do. Those few wisps
of suggestions, artificially put together, make in the total design a
thread that is absolutely invisible. Nothing is more obvious than
that such an idea was never in Shakespeare's head. No, it seems
pretty clear that we can find out no more secrets about Hamlet's
motives. We persist in digging for them; what happens usually is
that our spade goes through the other side of the drama.

Is it, finally, of very great moment that we must admit these
difficulties? The play, in spite of its discrepancies, has a fine harmony. Can we look usually [98] in Shakespeare for the precise and
narrow consistency that distinguishes the work of some other great
literary craftsmen? Invincible logic of plot was scarcely his special
glory. How different is, say, a novel by Henry James, the technique so deliberate, the fashioning so conscious; the work *sound*
through and through! Shakespeare is rarely *sound* in that sense:
how majestically careless, in comparison, he can be! He gives us
things that were beyond James's range: he does not give us just
that. To look for it is rather to wrong him. We know what, among
other things, he has given us in *Hamlet:* the portrait of a man

who seems to express (and the more in his sufferings and his disasters) all that Shakespeare found of greatest beauty and worth in
the human spirit. There is no one, in history or in literature, like
Hamlet. All that humanity is, all that humanity might be, seem
figured in him. It is no wonder if we find it a task of some difficulty to pluck out all the mysteries of his soul.[99]

Wit, Humor, and Shakespeare

By John Weiss

John Weiss, from "Hamlet," in *Wit, Humor, and Shakespeare*
(Boston, Roberts Brothers, 1876).

IT IS POSSIBLE to have Hamlet played in
a style so greatly absorbed as to obliterate our knowledge that the
father's custom is to take his cue from the climax of his son's
speech and to appear. Then we reproduce the thrill that Shakespeare felt when he sat alone with awe and silence, and they
suddenly drew him to their ghost.

I recur now to consider the nature of the oblique and enig-
matic style into which Hamlet has fallen. It is not a deliberate
effort to sustain the character of a madman, because such a person
as Hamlet could find no motive in it: he could not need it to mask
his desire to avenge the ghost, for he is Prince, an inmate of the
palace, and supernaturally elected to be master of the situation.
He says he has "cause and will and strength and means to do't." I
conceive, then, that his mind, driven from its ordinary gravity,
and the channel of his favorite thoughts diverted, instinctively
saves itself by this sustained gesture of irony; and it appears to be
madness only to those who do not know that he is [165] well informed of the event, and is struggling to set free from it a purpose.
And why should a man of such a well-conditioned brain, a noticer
of nice distinctions, have selected for a simulation of madness a
style which, nicely estimated, is not mad? He could not calculate

that everybody would interpret this difference from his usual deportment into an unsettling of his wits; for the style shows unconsciousness and freedom from premeditation. If he wished to feign distraction, he would have taken care to mar the appositeness of his ironical allusions, which are always in place and always logical. And, if he was half unhinged without knowing it, his speech would have betrayed the same inconsequence. Nowhere is he so abrupt, or delivers matter so remote from an immediate application, that he seems to us to wander, because we too have been admitted to the confidences of the ghost, and share that advantage over the other characters.

Since this essay was written, I have found, in the highly suggestive "Shakspeare-Studien" of Otto Ludwig, the following remarks, which are closely related to my own treatment of the subject, and provide some additional reflections:—

"Hamlet's subjective tendency is so predominant that we are surprised when he alleges no motive for assuming madness; nor is it elsewhere accounted for. It would have served his purpose much better if he had feigned a comfortable and contented, rather than an unsettled, mind. And, on the whole, one cannot at any point detect a reason why he chooses any active dissimulation.[166] For he merely needed to remain undiscovered.

"We never hear him once reflecting upon his intention, though he runs to reflection on all topics. Just after the apparition, he merely remarks to his friends that, if he should appear to them to do strange things, they need not remark upon it so as to betray his object." Ludwig here alludes to the lines,—

> As I, perchance, hereafter shall think meet
> To put an antic disposition on.

Hamlet tells them not to seem too wise about it. The theory of premeditated madness rests upon this passage, and upon one other, which will be noticed. But suppose that Shakspeare did at first entertain a purpose, borrowed from the old chronicle, of disguising Hamlet in some unusual vein, the psychological necessities of his character decided what that vein must be, as they also decided against the old chronicle in the matter of introducing a ghost. And Hamlet's mental quality is really shown by the vein into which it imperatively runs. He was overmastered and completely occupied by this mood of indignation at all the villainous cants of a smiling world. The temper grew so compactly beneath Shakspeare's pen that he could not interpolate into it any amateur simulations. The poet would not, if he could, have so diluted the terribly gathering sincerity which left that epithet of "antic" beached high up and disqualified for floating on its tide.

On Elsinore's platform, Hamlet felt that the sudden [167] complication would put him into strange behavior; he did not know exactly what, but he perceived it coming on. Such a man estimates himself more shrewdly than the crowd imagines. He was aware of a mind that over-refined and idealized, and of a disposition to avoid too close realities. Any hint of nature or society sufficed to sequester him in a monologue. But now he felt some modification passing through him; it is scarcely yet articulate, but it is inevitable to a man of his quality. Hamlet may call his mood by whatever phrases suit the different emergencies; but, in the main, it is the breaking-up of his mind's customary exercise into ironical scorn at discovering the rottenness of Denmark.

The Greek word εἰρωνεία, whence our Irony is derived with its special meaning, had not yet been modernly grafted on the Saxon stem. Ben Jonson says:—

> Most Socratic lady!
> Or, if you will, ironick!"

For the words *irony, ironick,* were at first used in English, and quite sparingly, to express the method of Socrates in conducting an argument; that is, by eliciting from an opponent his own refutation by asking him misleading questions. The words, in any sense, are not found in Shakspeare. Lord Bacon, in one instance, uses *irony* nearly in the modern sense; and that is Socratic only so far as a thing is said with an intent the reverse of its ostensible meaning.

The other passage upon which the theory of premeditated [168] madness rests occurs in the great scene with his mother, Act III. 4, during which she becomes convinced that Hamlet is out of his senses by seeing him kill the good Polonius, and hearing him rave as if he saw a spectre. She was the earliest of the critics and experts who are profoundly convinced of his madness. At the close of the scene, it occurs to him to avail himself of her misapprehension to procure continued immunity from any suspicion of

design against the King. How shall he do this,—how contrive to
clinch her conviction of his madness, and send her reeking with
it to inform the King? His subtle intelligence does at this point
invent the only simulation of madness that the play contains. He
is just about to bid the Queen good-night: "So, again, good-night."
Then the device occurs to him: "One word more, good lady"; and
the Queen, turning, says, "What shall I do?"

> Not this, by no means, that I bid you do:
> Let the bloat King tempt you again to bed;
> Pinch wanton on your cheek; call you his mouse;
> And let him, for a pair of reechy kisses,
> Or paddling in your neck with his damned fingers,
> Make you to ravel all this matter out,
> That I essentially am not in madness,
> But mad in craft. 'Twere good you let him know.

This is the very craftiness of a madman, to try to convince people
that, if he ever seems to be insane, it is for a sane motive. Hamlet
reckons that the Queen is so deeply imbued with the idea of his
insanity as to interpret this disclaimer of his into the strongest
confirmation. Hamlet, moreover, not only seems to be [169] accounting for symptoms of madness, but to be making a confidant of his
mother; he begs her not to betray the secret object of his strange
behavior. This seems to her to be the very quintessence of madness, to confess to her that he is feigning it out of craft, and to
suppose that she would not apprise her husband, who must be the
special object of that craft and most in danger from it. He must
be indeed preposterously mad; so in parting she pretends to receive his confidential disclosure:—

> Be thou assured, if words be made of breath,
> And breath of life, I have no life to breathe
> What thou hast said to me."

She may safely promise that, when she means to repair to the
King with quite a different version of Hamlet's condition, the
very one upon which he counts to keep the King deceived. And in
the next scene she conveys her strong impression to him:—

KING. What, Gertrude? How does Hamlet?
QUEEN. Mad as the sea and wind, when both contend
      Which is the mightier. In his lawless fit,
      Behind the arras hearing something stir,

He whips his rapier out, and cries, "A rat!"
And in his brainish apprehension kills
The unseen good old man.

She is the mother of the physiological criticism which issues
from insane asylums to wonder why Hamlet is not an inmate:
and Hamlet himself, by deceiving his mother, furnished to psychological criticism the text that he was mad in craft. Between the
lines of the genuine Hamlet you can read that Shakspeare belonged to neither school.[170]

Hamlet gives us unconsciously an opportunity to infer his
ability to frame the incoherences which real madness suggests to
one who would feign it. It occurs directly upon the Queen's suspicion, who, being unable to see her husband's ghost standing in
her chamber, exclaims,—

This is the very coinage of your brain:
This bodiless creation ecstasy
Is very cunning in.

Hamlet, repelling the insinuation, says,—

It is not madness
That I have uttered: bring me to the test,
And I the matter will re-word, which madness
Would gambol from.

And herein he implies that as he can construct the phrases of sanity, being all the time of a sound mind, so the soundness would
serve him to invent the *non sequiturs* of madness. If, then, he
purposed to feign it when he said that perhaps he might hereafter
put on an antic disposition, the reader may ask why so subtle a
person did not carry out his plan. No doubt, it occurred to him
that, as he travelled towards his purpose, his demeanor must be
of the kind that would cover up his traces. But he could baffle
Polonius and the other spies by the natural penetration of a mind
that suspicion had sharpened. Those emergencies did not call for
any style of feigning. It is enough for him to finger the ventages
of a recorder and invite Guildenstern to play upon it; the latter
understands that he knows no touch of Hamlet, and leaves the
heart of that mystery to be voiced by the varying breaths of
critics.[171]

When Hamlet explains to Polonius that he is reading slanders, and then describes the old man himself as having a plentiful lack of wit together with most weak hams, yet holds it hardly fair to have it thus set down,—"For yourself, sir, should be old as I am, if, like a crab, you could go backward,"—Polonius, who is nothing if not satirical upon himself, muses apart, saying, "Though this be madness, yet there's method in 't"; and there he blundered as patly into Shakspeare's secret as he did into his own death.

And why do so many actors make Hamlet appear to be conscious of the manœuvre to throw Ophelia in his way that the King and Polonius may mark his tone from the place where they hide? Shakspeare has left no loophole for this supposition that Hamlet, observing the trick, assumes a tone of flightiness towards Ophelia, in order to throw off the spies and make them infer that he is mad. The scene being over, the King is wrong when he says,—

> Love! his affections do not that way tend;

but right when he adds,—

> Nor what he spake, though it lack'd form a little,
> Was not like madness.

Of course it was not; and the whole scene with Ophelia is ruined for Shakspeare's purpose by this modern contrivance of the theatre to deprive Hamlet of his spontaneous and uncalculating mood.

Otto Ludwig notices that his madness is "alluded to by Ophelia as having broken out between the first and [172] second acts; and that is another strange thing in Shakspeare. Then, too, the style, if it was dissimulation, is such as to bring to pass the opposite of what he seems to have intended. So far from being disguised by it he is rather betrayed. And what is the use of any feigning when he does things like that of contriving the mock play? For that betrays him to the King more than it does the King to him. It makes the situation all awry, because the King must now know on what footing he is with Hamlet. At all events, the courtiers keep telling how danger is threatened to the King from Hamlet: they have no means of fathoming the King's offence. They merely presage some danger to the King, and they manifest no surprise. Hamlet must be conscious that he would be in great

peril if the King knew that he knew every thing; the King would
be put on his defence, and he was quite capable of contriving another murder to forestall retribution for the first one. Why, then,
does he keep on feigning? Yet we do not observe that he hits
upon any expedients to meet this possible case; it does not even
occur to him before he concocts the trial-scene."

Ophelia thinks that she sees

> That noble and most sovereign reason,
> Like sweet bells jangled, out of tune and harsh,

because she cannot understand his unflattering talk that appears to
be disclaiming any regard for her and any desire to marry her. In
all those sentences that make such a coarse rupture with love and
soil the previous sentiment of their intercourse, there is no trace
of a distracted [173] mind. How could we expect this maid to be
prepared to entertain such monstrous irony? It was as much
Shakspeare's intention to have him misunderstood as to represent
him so occupied by the sweeping scepticism that follows the disclosure of villainy. This irony of the most sombre kind, the mental mood that corresponds to such a harsh awakening, was not
customary with Hamlet, who was by nature mirthful before this
murder happened.

And notice how this ironical tone is kept up by him all
through Ophelia's misconception, into which she falls because
Hamlet's mood is too overpowering, and she thinks he has a
wrecked brain from which she can rescue nothing to enable her to
claim the salvage of loving him. When he meets her after many
days of unaccountable neglect, she returns the few remembrances
which were messengers of the happier hours of his affection, but
he casts discredit upon these sacred tokens. He never meant them,
in fact he never gave her any thing. But she says, "Yes,"

> And with them words of so sweet breath compos'd,
> As made the things more rich.

Has the bloom been rubbed from them, and their perfume lost?
Then, says the self-respecting maid, tearing the presents by bleed-
ing roots out of the heart where they had lodged to fructify, take
them again,

> For to the noble mind
> Rich gifts wax poor, when givers prove unkind.

"I did love you once," he says. "Indeed, my lord,[174] you made me believe so." Hamlet is enraged at his own love, and appears to have discarded it, for that too may smile and be a villain, or hers may. "You should not have believed me: for virtue cannot so inoculate our old stock, but we shall relish of it." That is to say, if I had felt true love grafted on my stem I should have received and imparted its flavor of sincerity. But nothing is sincere: "I loved you not."

Hamlet's observation of human nature had furnished him with elements which only needed provocation to develop into this uncompromising irony. His mother, married to that satyr of an uncle,

> Or ere those shoes were old,
> With which she follow'd my poor father's body,

might well cast a slur upon the sex in his opinion, and prompt the text which cynics use, "Frailty, thy name is woman,"—all but Ophelia: it does not include her until all life's illusions vanished with the ghost. Then she would do well not to walk in the sun, and would be safest in a nunnery.

Previous to that, he had dispatched a missive to her, which is commonly supposed to have been written on purpose to foster the notion that he was mad. But its tone does not seem to me to have been rightly interpreted. It begins in the style of Pistol: "To the celestial, and my soul's idol, the most beautified Ophelia." Then comes a verse fit for a valentine,—

> Doubt thou the stars are fire,
> Doubt that the sun doth move;
> Doubt truth to be a liar,
> But never doubt I love.[175]

So far the mocking spirit of his irony does not fail him. But the mood changes, for this was written just after the scene in Ophelia's chamber when he seemed to bid her an eternal farewell. Remembering this, he breaks the tone and adds, "O dear Ophelia! I am ill at these numbers: I have not art to reckon my groans; but that I love thee best, oh! most best, believe it." So with impetuous emphasis he confessed afterward upon Ophelia's grave. Nothing could more precisely convey to us his mental condition than this mixture of moods.

In the churchyard scene, we observe that Hamlet recurs unconsciously to his ordinary mental disposition, because he is alone
there with Horatio, whose grave and silent friendship is con-
genial. It is the foil to Hamlet's restless speculation; it calls a truce
to the civil war between his temper and his purpose. He is paci-
fied in the society of Horatio, who gives him a chance to recur to
his native mental habit. As he naively pours out his thoughts, how
little does Horatio answer! as little as the ground beneath their
feet, less laconic than the lawyer's skull. He is a continent upon
which Hamlet finds that he can securely walk, the only domain in
Denmark that is not honeycombed with pitfalls. Turning toward
Horatio's loyal affection, he feels a response that is articulated
without words. As little need the forest reply to her lover save in
dumb show and in obscure reflex of feeling.

The artless nature solicits confidence: its still air disarms and
dissipates the unrelenting irony. Then we see that Hamlet was
naturally more inclined to that use [176] of satire which indicates an
ideal far lifted above the methods by which men live. He puts that
fine sense into the skulls of the politician, the courtier, and the
lawyer, and we acknowledge the satirical tone of an exalted mind.
And this lends to that scene a feeling that in it Hamlet recurs to
himself, and resumes the usual tone which always advertised him
to his friends. To them his long maintenance of ironical behavior,
broken by so few sallies of his healthy satire, was additional confirmation of his madness because it was so unusual with him. Old
friends remembered nothing of the kind; they were first puzzled,
then convinced, and we saw that Polonius hurried to show his
insapiency by attributing the craze to love for his daughter. 'Tis
very likely, they all thought, for they could refer to no other
probable cause for it.

It is by unconsciously remanding Hamlet to Irony that Shakspeare has expressed the effect of an apparition, and of the dis-
enchanting news it brought, upon a mind of that firm yet subtle
temper. Lear's noble mind tottered with age before grief struck it
into the abyss of madness. Constance stands before us, like Niobe,
all tears, or sits with sorrow; but she was a too finely tempered
woman to drip into craziness, till health, hope, and life broke up.
Shakspeare has not represented any of his mature and well-
constructed natures as capable of being overthrown by passion

the most exigent or events the most heart-rending. They preserve
their sanity to suffer, as all great souls must do to make us worship
them with tears. So Hamlet, being incapable of madness [177] and
lifted above the necessity of feigning it, gives to every thing the
complexion of the news which has revolted his moral sense,—that
is, the King, his uncle, is not what he seems; his own mother's
husband does not appear to be a murderer. The State of Denmark
is rotten with this irony. No wonder that his brain took on the
color of the leaf on which it fed. Oh, every thing is not what it
appears to be, but only an indication of its opposite, and must be
phrased by contradiction! He is really in love with Ophelia, but
this irony conceals it. With the mood into which he has been
plunged, his own love is no more worth being seriously treated
than is old Polonius, whom he knows excellent well,—he is a
fishmonger; that is, not that he is a person sent to fish out his
secrets, as Coleridge would explain it, but that he is a dealer in
staleness, and yet not so honest as those who only vend stale fish.

If we return to a period in the play which follows closely
upon the scene of the taking of the oath, Ophelia herself will discover for us the turning mood in Hamlet's character. The time and
action of the piece allow us to suppose that he soon went from
the oath-taking to visit Ophelia. Naturally, he turned from that
bloodless and freezing visitation to see life heaving in a dear
bosom and reddening in lips which he had love's liberty to touch.
The disclosures of the ghost had worked upon him like a turbid
freshet which comes down from the hills to choke the running of
sweet streams, deface with stains of mud all natural beauties, and
bury with the washings of sunless defiles the meadows [178] span-
gled with forget-me-nots. His love for Ophelia was the most
mastering impulse of his life: it stretched like a broad, rich domain, down to which he came from the shadowy places of his
private thought to fling himself in the unchecked sunshine, and
revel in the limpid bath of feeling. How often, in hours which
only over-curious brooding upon the problems of life had hitherto
disquieted, had he gone to let her smile strip off the shadow of his
thought, and expose him to untroubled nature! The moisture of
her eyes refreshed his questioning; her phrases answered it beyond philosophy; a maidenly submission of her hand renewed his
confidence; an unspoken sympathy of her reserve, that flowed into

the slight hints and permissions of her body, nominated him as
lover and disfranchised him as thinker; and a sun-shower seemed
to pelt through him to drift his vapors off. But this open gladness
has disappeared underneath the avalanche of murder which a
ghostly hand had loosened. He ventures down to the place where
he remembers that it used to expect him; but we know that it has
disappeared. His air and behavior announce it to us. The catastrophe seems to have swept even over his person, to dishevel the
apparel upon that "mould of form." In this ruin of his life
Ophelia is the first one buried; for she was always more resident in
his soul than maintained within a palace, and his soul is no longer
habitable.

Polonius has just been giving those scandalous instructions to
his pimp to waylay the Danes in Paris, and, by insinuations of ill-
conduct in Laertes, worm out [179] of them possible admissions of
its truth. He wants to know how his son is spending money in the
gay capital, how many times he gamed, was overtaken in drink,
or visited "a house of sale." The pimp is to draw on his fellow-
countrymen by pretending that Laertes is given to all these things:
he knows the man; 'tis the common talk about him at home; you
cannot surprise him by any thing you say. Says the old manœuvrer:

> See you now;
> Your bait of falsehood takes this carp of truth:
> And thus do we of wisdom and of reach,
> With windlasses, and with assays of bias,
> By indirections find directions out.

No wonder that Hamlet in the churchyard, kicking the pate of a
politician, called it something "that would circumvent God." The
state-craft of old Polonius has lived so long without a change that
its garments are dropping from its limbs. Now see what an indecent forked radish it is. But the scene is eminently in its place,
and has nothing incongruous with what transpires before or after;
for the incident is cunningly contrived to prepare us to find him
applying his principle of the windlass and indirect purchase to
the relation of Hamlet with his daughter; and it breeds in us a
contempt for the notion that the Prince has been made mad by
love.

Ophelia enters to her father:

> Oh, my lord, my lord! I have been so affrighted!

Then she describes Lord Hamlet entering with garments all disordered,[180]

> And with a look so piteous in purport,
> As if he had been loosed out of hell,
> To speak of horrors. . . .
> He took me by the wrist, and held me hard;
> Then goes he to the length of all his arm;
> And, with his other hand thus o'er his brow,
> He falls to such perusal of my face,
> As he would draw it. Long stay'd he so;
> At last,—a little shaking of mine arm,
> And thrice his head thus waving up and down,—
> He rais'd a sigh so piteous and profound,
> That it did seem to shatter all his bulk,
> And end his being. That done, he lets me go:
> And, with his head over his shoulder turn'd,
> He seem'd to find his way without his eyes;
> For out of doors he went without their help,
> And, to the last, bended their light on me.

Polonius decides that it is the very ecstasy of love. Yes, it is, but
ecstasy that has made an assignation with despair. The two feelings meet at the rendezvous of Ophelia's description, where they
display to us the yearning scrutiny that a man throws into the eyes
of an expiring love: it is too passionately dear to be surrendered
into the inane; it is too selfishly personal to be consistent with his
future purpose. For he had married a bride at midnight who is
still expecting him. It is the consummation of one murder by
another. For such a bridal as that, to leave her cheeks on which
the color comes and goes between her love and his renunciation,
"like heralds 'twixt two dreadful battles set," seems to shatter and
end his being. But let him to fall to such persual of her face as he
may, he sees the complexion of the ghost through each warm feature; and its pallor stands even there to wave him apart to an [181]
interview in which all seeming becomes debatable, for rascally
things may smile. He shades his brow, and his eyes are two mag-
nets which he detaches from her heart, as he surrenders his last
confidence in a stale and unprofitable world.

The irony reaches its most powerful exercise in the second
scene of the third act, where Hamlet avails himself of the arrival
of play-actors to test the King with his mouse-trap of an interlude.

The Athenian mechanics played Pyramus and Thisbe with the simple intention of contributing their duty and homage to the nuptials. We see the humor of its juxtaposition with courtly scenes and weddings. But Hamlet, in his interlude, pretends amusement and mimics a murder to conceal his knowledge of the real one. "No, no, they do but jest, poison in jest; no offence in the world." His light talk with Ophelia is nothing but the audacity of excitement and expectation. His baffling of Guildenstern with the pipe; his making Polonius see a camel, a weasel, and a whale in a cloud, —covers the dreadful necessity which drives him, in the witching time of night, to that upbraiding of a mother, and that second meeting with a dead father, which will make men's breath bate and their veins creep while English is spoken in this world.

What other mood than Irony could a soul with such a secret for its guest spread for entertainment? Too strongly built and level to be cracked with the earthquake of madness; too awfully over-clouded to sparkle with imaginings of wit; too daunted and sad-dened with [182] the thought of a dear father in purgatorial flames to break into the geniality of Humor,—all his mirth lost of late, there is no resource, no method of relief to the mind that is strained to live with dissemblers and swear vengeance to a ghost, but to dissemble too with an irony as ruthless and sweeping as the crime. He saves his wits which might otherwise justify suspicion and go all distraught, by unconsciously assuming that love, mar-riage, chastity, all honorable things, and friendship too, are crazes, and he that banters them alone is sane.

But when he knows that the grave, near which he stood and satirized the careers which men pursue, was another piece of irony, since Nature by keeping Ophelia alive and beautiful really meant death by her, it destroys his own tendency to be ironical, and he breaks forth with an intense sincerity; then we take the point of his previous behavior.

> I loved Ophelia: forty thousand brothers
> Could not, with all their quantity of love,
> Make up my sum.

And as his soul was thus ample in its love, so was it in all serious and ennobling things,—too much so to grow deranged, enough so to create the concealment and defence of all his innuendo.

The tone recurs when Osrick is introduced, and makes a speech full of pompous platitudes about Laertes,—"an absolute gentleman, full of most excellent differences, the card or calendar of gentry," and so on. Hamlet mimics the style; and you would think he was just such another natty phrase-monger as Osrick, whose [183] macaronic manner he assumes to indicate his aversion from it. "Sir, his definement suffers no perdition in you; though, I know, to divide him inventorially would dizzy the arithmetic of memory, and yet but yaw neither, in respect of his quick sail. But, in the verity of extolment, I take him to be a soul of great article; and his infusion of such dearth and rareness, as, to make true diction of him, his semblable is his mirror; and who else would trace him, his umbrage, nothing more."

I wonder that the psychologists have not greedily picked up this obscure and fantastic passage as a specimen of his craft in feigning.

But Osrick belonged to the prosaic sort of minds which took up so readily with the theory of Hamlet's madness; all of them incapable of irony, therefore not competent to fly into his meaning; limited, like the dodo and other wingless birds, to running along the plain appearance. "Your lordship speaks most infallibly of him," says Osrick.

So Hamlet could sport, who went towards his death with a presentiment which his soul was great enough to put aside, and also give him breath to say how great it was: "We defy augury: there is a special providence in the fall of a sparrow. If it be now, 'tis not to come; if it be not to come, it will be now; if it be not now, yet it will come: the readiness is all." No crotchet of real or assumed madness could lurk in the repose of such a man. [184]

The Heart of
Hamlet's Mystery

By Karl Werder

Karl Werder, from *The Heart of Hamlet's Mystery* (1859–60),
translated from the German by Elizabeth Wilder (New York,
G. P. Putnam's Sons, 1907).

*A*LL *THE LEADING CRITICS,* with
Goethe at the head, advance the idea that Hamlet is at fault on
account of some subjective deficiency or weakness. If he had not
been just the man he was, if he had been fitted by nature for the
task imposed upon him, he would immediately have taken another
and more direct course to accomplish it. He himself is the obstacle; he procrastinates from his own nature, and thus complicates the situation and drags everything out of place by giving it
a direction wrong in itself and ruinous to himself and others.

For my own part, I must flatly dissent from this conclusion.
Let me ask, first of all, would Hamlet have dared to act as these
critics almost unanimously demand that he should have done?
Can Hamlet, or can he not, so act? It is certainly a pertinent question. I maintain [41] that he could not have thus acted, and for
purely objective reasons. The facts of the case, the force of all the
circumstances, the very nature of his task, directly forbid it; so
absolutely that Hamlet is compelled to respect the prohibition, even
when his reason, his poetic and dramatic, yes, even his human
judgment, would decide differently. The critics have been so absorbed in the study of his character that the task imposed upon
him has been lost sight of. Here is the fundamental mistake.

What do the critics require of Hamlet? That he should attack the King immediately and make short work with him, in-

deed, the shortest possible. He is not to feign to be crazy; not to
draw out his tablets, but rather his dagger; not to cry "Adieu,
remember me," but "Death to the murderer!" He should go to
the King at once and slay him. He can do this the first time he
sees the King, if it be the very next hour; the opportunity is always at hand, nothing is easier than to take advantage of it. But
what is to follow the dagger-stroke? Then, say the critics, he is to
call the court and [42] people together, justify his deed to them,
and take possession of the throne.

And how is Hamlet to begin to justify his deed? By telling
what his father's ghost had confided to him, say the critics. But
does not this imply a very strange idea of Hamlet's public, of the
Danish nobility and people before whom he must defend himself?
Is it possible that they will believe him? Would they be convinced
of the justice of his deed by evidence of this sort? The critics
have assumed that he was by birth the supreme judge in the country and the legitimate heir to the throne, whom a usurper had
deprived of his rights. Is there any proof of these assertions?
Certainly none in Shakespeare. Hamlet himself breathes no word
of complaint of having suffered any such wrong. And if such a
wrong had existed, if there had been a usurpation, Hamlet would
certainly have spoken of it, or if he had been silent Horatio and
others would certainly have referred to it. Might not the courtiers
have hinted that his madness proceeded from this cause? At the
very opening of the play, in the [43] first scene, when the possible
political significance of the appearance of the Ghost was discussed,
surely no fact bearing upon it would have been passed over! [1]
There is not the faintest hint in the play that any illegal action had
been taken against the Prince; indeed the opposite state of affairs
is clearly indicated.

How is Hamlet to justify his deed to the subjects of the murdered sovereign? He can do it only by citing the communication

---

[1] Professor Werder at this point, misled by the German word *Erbin,*
explains at some length that none of Hamlet's rights to the throne were
usurped. He asserts that the Queen was the legitimate heiress and successor to
the crown, and that the most Hamlet could hope for would have been his
election as co-regent. If Professor Werder had looked into the matter, he would
have found that Steevens, a hundred years earlier, had called attention to the
fact that Denmark was an elective monarchy. Justice Blackstone also disposed
of the idea that Claudius was a usurper.

of an apparition that had charged the King with the murder of
his brother. That is clearly too much to demand of Hamlet. It is
degrading to the intelligence of the Danish people to suppose, for
one instant, that they would have believed the story.[44]

It has been said that Horatio, Marcellus, and Bernardo could,
by their testimony, have helped him in this matter. It is true that
they had seen the Ghost—they could swear to that—but no one
except Hamlet had heard one word of what the Ghost had said to
him. All that they themselves heard was a voice from underground
which admonished them to swear upon the sword, as Hamlet re-
quested, never without his consent to talk about what had happened; so the hope of producing conviction with the people by
this means is very doubtful. They will naturally say, "Hamlet, the
only interested party, is defendant and judge at the same time,
supreme judge of his own case."

It is an absolute impossibility if he kills the King that he
could justify the deed solely upon his own testimony, and there
certainly is no other. And would not the nobles, the court, the
legislators of the kingdom, regard Hamlet as the most guilty, the
most audacious, most shameless of liars and criminals, who, to
gratify his own ambition assassinated the King, accusing his victim, without any proof whatsoever, of [45] murder in order to clear
himself from the same crime? The people would hardly acknowledge as their king a notorious regicide who could devise such a
plot for gaining possession of the throne. They would be roused
to fury against him from the very fact that he thought them foolish enough to believe his story. He would appear to them base in
murdering the King, and baser still for insulting his victim by a
most shameful and wholly unproved accusation. The very least
they could do would be to declare him insane and confine him in
chains.

Hamlet understands his own position and cares for his own
reputation very much better than the critics who have thus taken
him to task. If he had killed the King immediately, what the
critics call heroism would have served only to prove him a fool.

The Ghost himself has a better understanding of the case
than the critics. He calls upon his son to avenge his murder, but
he has by no means the passionate thirst for blood that the critics
evince. He is in no such haste, and leaves time and place to his

son. *"Howsoever* [46] thou pursuest this act" are his words. He
does not intimate that a thrust of the dagger will suffice, or that
his demands would thereby be satisfied. Even when he comes the
second time he does not blame Hamlet for his delay, as the critics
have done. Hamlet himself does that, but the Ghost says only:

> Do not forget. This visitation
> Is but to whet thy almost blunted purpose.

Moreover, the Ghost at that time does not appear as a threatening, angry form in armour, as the critics suppose, but in his home
dress.

Kreyssig says: "Hamlet, according to our idea, should have
dealt with the King without further proof, because we have
learned in the very first act of the play that the King is a murderer. Hamlet therefore would be wholly in the right in killing
him at once." As auditors in the theatre we do know this fact, but
the Danes do not know it, and the mere fact of the ghostly communication would never satisfy them of the justice of the assassination. To the audience all the details are perfectly clear, but [47]
to the actors in the play this is not the case. What would be truth
and justice by the verdict of an audience would not appear so to
the persons in the drama. Denmark is Hamlet's objective world. If
Denmark condemns him, as it must, because it is impossible for
him to justify himself before that world,—if in the eyes of that
world he must appear as a cowardly and clumsy liar and villain,
then his dramatic honour and reason, and his personal honour as a
Danish prince, are lost for ever, even though Horatio should believe in him with ten times the fervour he shows.

That an impeachment of the King would be as injudicious as
his instantaneous murder goes without saying. The result to Hamlet would be the same. But in that case the living King would
conduct the trial, and would make the alleged evidence appear still
more fabulous.

What is Hamlet to do? What is his actual task? A sharply
defined duty, but a very different one from that which the critics
have imposed upon him. It is not to crush the King at once—he
could commit no greater blunder— [48] but to bring him to confession, to unmask and convict him. That is Hamlet's task, his
first, nearest, inevitable duty. As things stand, truth and justice

can come to light only from one mouth, that of the crowned criminal, and if he or some one connected with him does not speak,
then the truth will be for ever hidden. That is the situation!
Herein lie the terrors of this tragedy. This is the source of Hamlet's enigmatical horror and the bitterness of his misery. The secret
of the encoffined and unprovable crime is the unfathomable
source out of which flows its power to awaken fear and pity. This
single humanly natural fact has never been perceived for more
than a century. And yet the fact is so convincing that when it has
once been comprehended it must remain for ever clear.

Why did Hamlet delay if the task could be [49] as easily accomplished as the critics insist? Alas! It is so difficult that it is
almost impossible. Shakespeare himself lets us see that he under-
tand it to be so. Claudius has no idea of confessing. Even if Hamlet should strike at him, there would be no disclosure of the truth.
Goethe naturally never thought of such an assassination. To imagine that he did is an absurdity. His view of the play was largely
that of a young man, expressed when directly under the influence
of English criticism, and he did not see the horror and the difficulty
of Hamlet's task. He did not modify his opinion afterwards because in later years he was very much occupied with other matters,
and had neither inclination nor leisure to study Shakespeare carefully.

The main point of my declaration is by no means the doubtful results for Hamlet as an individual if he had been governed by
the demands of the critics, but rather the effect such a course would
have upon the fulfilment of his task. If Hamlet had struck down
the King, without unmasking him, if he had obeyed the [50] Ghost's
prayer for revenge at the earliest opportunity by a bold dagger-
thrust, the direct result would have surely been that no one would
have believed in the apparition; its intentions would have been
frustrated, and the true punishment, which should be memorable
through the ages, would be rendered impossible. For no punishment can be real and effective unless the offender be condemned
by the unanimous verdict of his world.

The apparition did not appear for the purpose of dethroning
the King and having Hamlet succeed to the crown. The paternal
spirit asked Hamlet, as any father might ask a son, to revenge
his murder and not allow the kingly bed in which his own child

was born to be stained with infamy, not to allow injustice to triumph and villany to remain unpunished:

> If thou didst ever thy dear father love
> Revenge his foul and most unnatural murder.

Then he relates the circumstance of the crime, and continues:

> If thou hast nature in thee, bear it out;
> Let not the royal bed of Denmark be [51]
> A couch for luxury and damned incest.
> But, howsoever thou pursuest this act,
> Taint not thy mind, nor let thy soul contrive
> Against thy mother aught; leave her to heaven
> And to those thorns that in her bosom lodge,
> To prick and sting her. Fare thee well at once!

Not one word regarding the succession to the crown, not a syllable suggesting that Hamlet should thrust the King from the throne. Only the injured husband and father speaks from out the armoured figure.

If Hamlet had misunderstood the Ghost's meaning and had assassinated the King before he had unmasked him, he would really save rather than destroy him. He would make the King immortal, for the sympathy of the world would flow to him, and through all time the royal criminal would be regarded as the innocent victim of a wicked plot. Instead of being condemned he would be canonised. That his death should appear to be the result of divine justice would be impossible, for the insane act [52] would cause an impenetrable veil to fall between the light of truth and the eyes of the world. Hamlet, as the one to whom alone the truth can ever be known, would turn that truth to falsehood if he thus caused it to remain for ever unproved to the world. He would actually be a most efficient accomplice in the murder of his father, if he furnished no proof of the crime, but presented himself as the sole accuser and judge of the criminal. What Hamlet has most at heart after he sees the Ghost is *not* the death, but, on the contrary, the *life* of the King, henceforth as precious to him as his own. These two lives are the only means by which he can fulfil his task. Now that he knows the crime and is enjoined to punish it, nothing worse could happen to him than that the King should suddenly die unexposed and thus escape his deserts. Justice would

then be defeated and truth be doomed to oblivion. Hamlet must
hope that both of them will live until the time is ripe for the
truth to be disclosed, and in this hope he must do what he can to
protect and preserve his own life.

Suppose that Hamlet had killed the King and [53] thus deprived him of the fruits of the murder, or had lost his own life by
the action; or suppose that the Danes could have been so insane as
to place him upon the throne after he had murdered the King;
would revenge in the true tragical sense be satisfied? To a tragical
revenge punishment is necessary, but this punishment must be
justified and vindicated before the world. Therefore Hamlet does
not aim at the crown nor is it his first duty to kill the King; but
his task is justly to punish the murderer of his father, unassailable
as that murderer now appears in the eyes of the world, and to
satisfy the Danes of the righteousness of his action. That is Hamlet's task.[54]

The Nature of Will

By Rebecca West

Rebecca West, "The Nature of Will," in *The Court and the Castle*
(New Haven, Yale University Press, 1957).

YET HAMLET RECOGNIZES the value
of tradition. That is made clear by the courage he shows in choosing to meet the ghost and in casting off the hands of his companions when it bids him follow it and they seek to hold him
back. But he feels no real reverence for tradition. That is a very
strange scene, when he swears his companions to secrecy on his
sword, and the ghost raps upward on the earth they stand on, and
Hamlet says, "You hear this fellow in the cellarage" (I.5.151).
The root of this disrespect becomes explicable when we inquire
into Hamlet's attitude to humanity. For tradition is the distilla-
tion of human experience, and it must be condemned if humanity
is condemned; and Hamlet was disgusted by his own kind.

There are other crimes afoot in Elsinore, in the world, as well as murder. The ghost wishes Hamlet to avenge his murder and also to put an end to the unholy offense of the marriage between his widow and his murderer. But when Hamlet talks of these matters with his mother he loses all interest in that part of the command which relates to his father's murder, and in the course of over eighty lines addressed to her he devotes only three to a perfunctory mention of the fact that her present husband murdered her previous husband, and when she shows that she did not know that any such crime had been committed he does not take the opportunity of enlightening her. He simply tells her that she is behaving reprehensibly in living with her present husband, not because he had murdered her dead husband and his own brother, but because he was not so good looking as her dead husband. It is not surprising, though it is always comic, that [17] the ghost should then reappear in order to ask Hamlet to stick to the point. "Do not forget: this visitation Is but to whet thy almost blunted purpose" (III.4.110). But a revelation is made in the course of the scene. The Queen admits the charge of sensuality (III.4.88):

> Oh, Hamlet, speak no more,
> Thou turn'st mine eyes into my very soul,
> And there I see such black and grained spots
> As will not leave their tinct.

Claudius is guilty, the Queen is guilty, and so as this scene makes quite plain, is Hamlet. All that he says is smeared with a slime which is the mark of sexual corruption. His curious emphasis on the physical difference between the dead King and the living Claudius hints at a homosexual element in his nature, but that is irrelevant. Hamlet could be neither a heterosexual nor a homosexual lover. Such an egotist would be restricted to lust, for he could not afford the outgoings of love.

That has been indicated earlier in the play by his scenes with Ophelia. There is no more bizarre aspect of the misreading of Hamlet's character than the assumption that his relations with Ophelia were innocent and that Ophelia was a correct and timid virgin of exquisite sensibilities. Probably the conception would not have lasted so long in England had it not been for the popu-

larity of the pre-Raphaelite picture by Sir John Millais which
represents her as she floated down the glassy stream, the weeping
brook; for his model was his friend Rossetti's bride, the correct,
timid, sensitive, virginal, and tubercular Miss Siddal, and she
was, poor thing, especially wan during the painting of the picture,
for she was immersed in a tin bath full of water kept warm by a
lamp placed underneath, like an old-fashioned hot-water [18] dish.
We have certainly put Ophelia into the wrong category and into
the wrong century. She was not a chaste young woman. That is
shown by her tolerance of Hamlet's obscene conversations, which
cannot be explained as consistent with the custom of the time. If
that were the reason for it, all the men and women in Shakespeare's
plays, Romeo and Juliet, Beatrice and Benedict, Miranda and
Ferdinand, Antony and Cleopatra, would have talked obscenely
together, which is not the case. "The marriage of true minds"
would hardly, even in the most candid age, have expressed itself
by this ugly chatter, which Wilson Knight has so justly described
as governed by "infra-sexual neurosis." The truth is that Ophelia
was a disreputable young woman: not scandalously so, but still
disreputable. She was foredoomed to it by her father, whom it is a
mistake to regard as a simple platitudinarian. Shakespeare, like all
major writers, was never afraid of a good platitude, and he would
certainly never have given time to deriding a character because
his only attribute was a habit of stating the obvious. Polonius is
interesting because he was a cunning old intriguer who, like an
iceberg, only showed one-eighth of himself above the surface. The
innocuous sort of worldly wisdom that rolled off his tongue in
butter balls was a very small part of what he knew. It has been
insufficiently noted that Shakespeare would never have held up the
action in order that Polonius should give his son advice as to
how to conduct himself abroad, unless the scene helped him to
develop his theme. But "This above all—to thine own self be
true; And it must follow, as the night the day, Thou canst not
then be false to any man" (I.3.78), has considerable contrapuntal
value when it is spoken by an old gentleman who is presently going
to instruct a servant to spy on his son, and to profess great anxiety
about [19] his daughter's morals, when plainly he needed to send
her away into the country if he really wanted her to retain any.

   There is no mistaking the disingenuousness of his dealings

with his daughter. When Ophelia comes to him with her tale of
how Hamlet had come to her as she was sewing in her chamber,
"with his doublet all unbraced," and had looked madly on her,
Polonius eagerly interprets this as "the very ecstasy of love," and
asks her "What, have you given him any hard words of late?"
Ophelia answers (II.1.106):

> No, my good Lord; but as you did command
> I did repel his letters, and denied
> His access to me.

At that Polonius purrs in satisfaction:

> That hath made him mad.
> I am sorry that with better heed and judgment
> I had not quoted him: I fear'd he did but trifle,
> And meant to wrack thee; but beshrew my jealousy!
> It seems it is as proper to our age
> To cast beyond ourselves in our opinions
> As it is common for the younger sort
> To lack discretion. Come, go we to the king.
> This must be known; which, being kept close, might move
> More grief to hide than hate to utter love.
> Come.

This is the Court Circular version of Pandarus. The girl is not to
be kept out of harm's way. She is a card that can be played to take
several sorts of tricks. She might be Hamlet's mistress; but she
might be more honored for resistance. And if Hamlet was himself an enemy of the King, and an entanglement with him had
ceased to be [20] a means of winning favor, then she can give a
spy's report on him to Claudius. Surely Ophelia is one of the few
authentic portraits of that army of not virgin martyrs, the poor
little girls who were sacrificed to family ambition in the days when
a court was a cat's cradle of conspiracies. Man's persuasion that
his honor depends on the chastity of his womenfolk has always
been liable to waste away and perish within sight of a throne.
Particularly where monarchy had grown from a yeasty mass of
feudalism, few families found themselves able to resist the temptation to hawk any young beauty in their brood, if it seemed likely
that she might catch the eye of the king or any man close to the
king. Unfortunately the king's true favorite was usually not a

woman but an ideology. If royal approval was withdrawn from the religious or political faith held by the family which had hawked the girl, she was as apt to suffer fatality as any of her kinsmen. The axe has never known chivalry. Shakespeare, writing this play only three reigns from Henry the Eighth, had heard of such outrages on half-grown girls from the lips of those who had seen the final blood-letting. He wrote elsewhere of Ann Boleyn; and he must have heard much of the worse case, which did not excite so much compassion because the edge of the tragedy had been taken off by repetition, the case of Katherine Howard. She, who had been beheaded half a century before, was one of the Catholic Howards, a poor relative of the Duke of Norfolk, and had grown up in the attics and passages and antichambers of a disordered country seat, where maturing beauty brought her several lovers, one of whom she loved. But she did not marry him, because she was presently procured for the King, whom she pleased so well that he made her Queen. Pleasure, however, was not the most important issue involved. The marriage was a token [21] of Henry's temporary softening toward Rome. But he hardened his heart again and turned again toward the innovators of Protestantism, and so the Howards fell out of favor, and Katherine's head was cut off when she was twenty years old.

Shakespeare had pondered on such massacres of the innocent, and he had thought it one of the worse offenses of the court (and he hated courts) that by the time the innocents were massacred, they were no longer innocent. The scene between Anne Boleyn and the bawdy old lady in the part-Shakespearean *Henry the Eighth* has an obvious pathos, because he knows and we know that the girl is doomed to die by the headsman's axe. But it is even more pathetic that she is deprived not only of her life, but of a noble death; for however bravely she bore herself when she laid her head on the block, she had nevertheless found her way there by a greedy intrigue which sought to snatch profit from the fall of an authentic queen. Like Anne Boleyn, Ophelia has lost her integrity. She fiddles with the truth when she speaks of Hamlet to her father, and she fiddles with the truth when she talks to Hamlet as her father and Claudius eavesdrop; and she contemplates without surprise or distaste Hamlet's obscenity, the scab on his spiritual sore.

Surely the picture of Ophelia shows that Shakespeare, who

wrote more often of cruelty than any other great writer, was not a cruel man, and was great in pity, that rare emotion. He shows the poor little creature, whom the court had robbed of her honesty, receiving no compensation for the loss, but being driven to madness and done to death. For the myth which has been built round Hamlet is never more perverse than when it pretends that Ophelia went mad for love and killed herself. No line in the play suggests that she felt either passion or [22] affection for Hamlet. She never mentions him in the mad scene; and Horatio says of her, "She speaks much of her father." Indeed she was in a situation which requires no sexual gloss. Her father had been murdered by a member of the royal house, and she found herself without protection, since her brother Laertes was in France, in the midst of a crisis such as might well send her out of her wits with fear. For the Danes hostile to the royal house made of her wrong a new pretext for their hostility, and the royal house, noting this, turned against her, helpless though she was. Claudius speaks of a general resentment (IV.5.78):

> The people muddied,
> Thick and unwholesome in their thoughts and whispers,
> For good Polonius' death; and we have done but greenly
> In hugger-mugger to inter him . . .

When Ophelia wanders to the Castle and asks that the Queen should receive her, she is refused. The Queen says, "I will not speak with her." But Horatio tells her she is not wise (IV.5.5):

> She speaks much of her father; says she hears
> There's tricks i' th' world; and hems, and beats her heart;
> Spurns enviously at straws; speaks things in doubt,
> That carry but half sense; her speech is nothing.
> Yet the unshaped use of it doth move
> The hearers to collection; they aim at it,
> And botch the words up fit to their own thoughts;
> Which, as her winks and nods and gestures yield them,
> Indeed would make one think there might be thought,
> Though nothing sure, yet much unhappily.
> 'Twere good she were spoken with; for she may strew
> Dangerous conjectures in ill-breeding minds. [23]

Courts thus threatened had their own ways of dealing with the threats, as all courtiers knew; and Shakespeare must have heard of women thus dealt with who had been frightened into madness. Lady Rochford, who had helped Katherine Howard to meet her cousin Culpepper after her marriage, was raving mad when she went to her execution.

But neither from fear nor from love did Ophelia kill herself. She did not kill herself at all. The Queen describes her drowning as an accident. "An envious sliver broke," she says, and there is no indication that she was lying. Many things are packed into the passage which begins "There is a willow grows aslant a brook," but insincerity is not among them. These lines achieve a dramatic value often not exploited in the theater. They are beautiful and expressive verse: their sound suggests heaviness submerging lightness, the soaked clothes dragging down the fragile body they encase, the inanimate flesh grown leaden round the spirit. But the lines are also in character. The Queen is one of the most poorly endowed human beings which Shakespeare ever drew. Very often he created fools, but there is a richness in their folly, whereas Gertrude is simply a stately defective. The whole play depends on her not noticing, and not understanding; and in this passage there are samples of her stupidity. The botanical digression about the long purples is ill-timed, and the epithet "mermaid-like" is not applicable to someone saved from drowning by an amplitude of skirts or to the skirts themselves. But the fusion of perception and obtuseness in these lines, and the contrast between their distinction and the empty rotundity of all the Queen's other speeches, convince us that just once this dull woman was so moved that her tongue became alive. It is not credible that at that moment she [24] would have taken thought to deceive Laertes about the object of her emotion; nor indeed does Shakespeare suggest that she practiced any such deception.

For that Ophelia drowned herself is stated definitely only by two people: the clowns in the graveyard, typical examples of the idiot groundlings gorged on false rumor who appear so often in Shakespeare's plays. Whether we like it or not, we must admit that there is very little in the works of Shakespeare which could be used as propaganda for adult suffrage. For the rest, the priest declares that "her death was doubtful" (V.1.228), and that the doubt was enough to make it necessary that she should be buried with "maimed rites" (V.1.220). But surely we are not intended to believe him, for he is drawn as a bigot, who finds it possible to

answer her brother coldly when he asks, "What ceremony else?"
(V.1.224), and it is to be presumed that such lack of charity would
invent a doubt. Shakespeare will not allow anyone in the graveyard scene, even to the priest, to be without sin. Each of them has
helped to dig the girl's grave. Hamlet was the most guilty, for he
had been her spurious lover and a tyrant prince, giving her no
protection as a mistress or as one of his people; but it was the
whole court that had destroyed her. She was a victim of society,
which abandons principle for statecraft, for politics, for intrigue,
because of its too urgent sense that it must survive at all costs, and
in its panic loses cognizance of all the essentials by which it lives.
Even her brother Laertes was not fully aware of his sister's tragedy,
for he was tainted with the vice which Shakespeare feared most as
a distraction: he was subject to lust.

This is indicated clearly enough in the early scene when
Laertes warns Ophelia against the nature of Hamlet's courtships
and she mocks him (I.3.46): [25]

> But, good my brother,
> Do not as some ungracious pastors do,
> Show me the steep and thorny way to heaven,
> Whilst like a puft and reckless libertine,
> Himself the primrose path of dalliance treads,
> And recks not his own rede.

To this Laertes replies:

> Oh, fear me not.
> I stay too long. But here my father comes.

If Ophelia offers a *tu quoque* defense which we do not usually
offer unless we are guilty, Laertes does not trouble to put up a
defense at all. These two are no better than they should be; and
Polonius, when he instructs his servant Reynaldo to spy on his son
in Paris, speaks of drabbing and visiting "a house of sale, Videlicet, a brothel" (II.1.60), as if these were fairly certain to be
among his son's activities. When Laertes leaps into his sister's
grave, he cries (V.1.252):

> Now pile your dust upon the quick and the dead
> Till of this flat a mountain you have made
> To' o'ertop old Pelion or the skyish head
> Of blue Olympus.

For Shakespeare there was a connection between this outburst and the primrose path, the drabs, and the house of sale, Videlicet, a brothel. In his analysis of love that is not love, the hundred and twenty-ninth sonnet, he uses the word "extreme."

> The expense of spirit in a waste of shame
> Is lust in action; and till action, lust
> Is perjured, murd'rous, bloody, full of blame,
> Savage, extreme, rude, cruel, not to trust.[26]

Laertes' expressions of grief are extreme. His mind rushes away from the dead girl on too long a journey, all the way to blue Olympus, and forgets its true grief in the excitement of travel. The essence of Ophelia has again been ignored, and the waste of a human being not appropriately resented.

It is Shakespeare's contention that the whole of the court is corrupt: society is corrupt. There is a flaw running horizontally through humanity wherever it is gathered together in space. It would seem natural therefore that Hamlet should obey the ghost and punish Claudius, who controls the court, who is an emblem of society. But the flaw runs vertically also; it runs through time, into the past. For Hamlet's father, the ghost, is in purgatory, doing penance for his sins, which were of the same gross kind as those he desires his son to punish. Shakespeare tells us this, stating the fact, and again using bombast to suggest immoderation (I.5.9):

> I am thy father's spirit,
> Doom'd for a certain term to walk the night,
> And for the day confined to fast in fires,
> Till the foul crimes done in my days of nature
> Are burnt and purged away. But that I am forbid
> To tell the secrets of my prison-house,
> I could a tale unfold, whose lightest word
> Would harrow up thy soul; freeze thy young blood;
> Make thy two eyes, like stars, start from their spheres,
> Thy knotted and combined locks to part,
> And each particular hair to stand an end,
> Like quills upon the fretful porpentine.

The ghost was indeed a sinner; the voice of tradition speaks from a tainted source. The evil in the world is not the product of the specially corrupt present generation,[27] it has its roots in the generations that went before and also were corrupt; it has its roots in the race. There is no use pretending that we can frustrate our sinful dispositions by calling on tradition, because that also is the work of sinful man. This is the situation of our kind as it is shown to us in *Hamlet,* which is as pessimistic as any great work of literature ever written. The theme of the play could never appear to any reader who kept his eye on the text as the irresolution of Hamlet, his lack of the nerve which forms a hero (as Goethe put it), his failure to achieve a virtue which would consist simply of capacity for action. For what excites Shakespeare in this play is the impossibility of conceiving an action which could justly be termed virtuous, in view of the bias of original sin.

What does Shakespeare see written on the other side of the ledger? Nothing but beauty. This is the play which more than any of the others reminds us of the extraordinary advantages which he enjoyed. For it was his luck to see the human race at one of the moments, in one of the places, when it blossomed into a state of exceptional glory; and he moved among men and women who were beautiful, intelligent, learned, and fearless beyond the habit of our kind, and whose way of life, with its palaces and its pageants, was a proper setting for the jewels that they were. Here we ourselves enjoy an extraordinary advantage. Literature cannot always do its business of rendering an account of life. An age of genius not of the literary sort must go inadequately described unless there should happen to exist at the same time a literary genius of the same degree, who works in circumstances enabling him to accumulate the necessary information about his non-literary contemporaries. It happened that the Renaissance man was observed by Shakespeare. "What a piece [28] of work is man! How noble in reason! How infinite in faculty! In form and moving how express and admirable! In action how like an angel! in apprehension how like a god! The beauty of the world! The paragon of animals!" (II.2.305). Here is a coincidence. Shakespeare was himself "the paragon of animals," therefore he could describe to us the man who was "the beauty of the world." He could write this description and make the whole characer of Hamlet as shown from scene to scene bear out what he said about man.

All through the play Hamlet speaks with a quick, springing harmony recognizable as the voice of physical and mental splendor; his mind travels like lightning yet strikes below the surface, and is impulsive not in surrender to folly but in search of wisdom. How superior, to use Turgenev's words, he is in mind and temperament, how daring, how proud. In fact, Shakespeare has given us a picture of the Renaissance man, without the lacuna which makes the other attempts to portray him, which were made by the Elizabethan and Jacobean dramatists, notably Ford and Webster. They tried to depict the new man created by the new wealth of Europe, the new community and continuity of culture, the new opening of windows on far parts of the globe and on the minutiae of matter. But they fall into the trap of showing the Renaissance man at his experiments without explaining why he felt free to experiment, without bringing forward the good reasons he had for thinking that he might tamper with the existing moral world. Even Marlowe took the Faust legend for his great work, and accounted for his Renaissance man by devil-dealing; but Shakespeare in Hamlet makes the Renaissance man his own Mephistopheles, and depicts a being so gifted that he needs no supernatural being to raise him above the common lot.[29] But Shakespeare, the supreme artist observing this supreme man, immediately adds, "And yet to me what is the quintessence of dust?" And his genius has been asking that question throughout the play. Scene after scene has demonstrated the paragon of animals to be an animal, the world to be so diseased that even its beauty is infected. This speech of homage to man is indeed an example of teasing ambiguity; it can be read without irony or with irony; each reading is equally faithful to the text.

Shakespeare hopes for little from the dust. It is quite certain that he wished to present Hamlet as a bad man, because he twice makes him rejoice at the thought of murdering men who had not made their peace with God. He might have killed Claudius when he came on him at prayer. But he decided this might mean that Claudius would go straight to heaven (III.3.88):

> Up, sword; and know thou a more horrid hent;
> When he is drunk, asleep, or in his rage;
> Or in th'incestuous pleasure of his bed;
> At gaming, swearing or about some act
> That has no relish of salvation in't;

> Then trip him, that his heels may kick at heaven;
> And that his soul may be as damn'd and black
> As hell, whereto it goes.

Later on, when he tells Horatio of his peculiarly cold-blooded murder of Rosenkrantz and Guildenstern, his description of the letter he forged to the King of England shows traces of a like perverse determination to kill the soul as well as the body V.2.38):

> An earnest conjuration from the king,—
> As England was his faithful tributary; [30]
> As love between them like the palm might flourish;
> As peace should still her wheaten garland wear,
> And stand a comma b'tween their amities;
> And many such-like As-es of great charge,—
> That, on the view and knowing of these contents,
> Without debatement further, more or less,
> He should the bearers put to sudden death,
> Not shriving-time allow'd.

There would be no question at all in the minds of an Elizabethan audience that a murderer who could cheat his victims of their chance of salvation was a very bad man indeed; and indeed most of us would think with repulsion of such an action, if, through the hazards of war or dictatorship, it came within our experience.

But to this bad man Shakespeare ascribes one virtuous action; and the nature of that action is determined by his most lasting preoccupation. It is a political action. Hamlet gives his dying breath to thought for the future of his people; his last words choose a ruler for them (V.2.343):

> O, I die, Horatio;
> The potent poison quite o'ercrows my spirit;
> I cannot live to hear the news from England;
> But I do prophesy th' election lights
> On Fortinbras: he has my dying voice.
> So tell him with the occurents, more and less,
> Which have solicited—the rest is silence.

Hamlet was never more the Renaissance man—who was a statesman, a true Macchiavellian, a prince careful for the safety of his subjects. Even if one be disillusioned with the race, and suspect paragons and the beauty of the world, this is still admirable. These fragile creatures, so little changed from dust that they constantly revert to [31] it, show bravery in their intention that their species shall survive as if it were marble. Yet, all the same, how horrid is the sphere in which they show their excellence. The court was saved by its political conscience; yet it was damned by it too.[32]

What Happens in Hamlet

By J. Dover Wilson

J. Dover Wilson, from *What Happens in Hamlet* (Cambridge, The University Press, 1935).

THE ROAD TO ELSINORE
BEING AN EPISTLE DEDICATORY TO
WALTER WILSON GREG

IN THE FOLLOWING enquiry I shall take a different road from theirs [the historical and psychological critics], the road you first showed me. I shall dare to assume that Shakespeare knew his own business as a dramatist better than his critics of either school. I shall draw attention to a large number of difficulties, of which many have hitherto passed unnoticed and most have never been explained, and I shall seek a *dramatic* reason for them all. Some will refuse to yield to aesthetic treatment, and will accordingly have to be relegated to the sphere of textual criticism. But such problems, it will be found, though interesting from the historical point of view, are neither numerous nor important; aesthetically they are negligible, since, though they may perhaps puzzle the student examining the play under a microscope in his study, they disappear entirely from view when the play is acted on the stage: in other words they cannot be labelled as dramatic defects. But the difficulties I shall be mainly concerned with are dramatic problems, which [15] have arisen through forgetfulness of Shakespeare's purposes; forgetfulness due to textual corruption, to our ignorance of Elizabethan stage-effects, to the break in the theatrical tradition at the Puritan Revolution, and above all to the change in social customs and in the ordinary man's assumptions about the universe and politics which three centuries have brought with them. In brief, I shall try to show that parts of the plot have fallen into disuse through "bestial oblivion." Fortunately, there is nothing, I think, lost beyond recovery, nothing that care cannot restore to its pristine beauty and its original function. . . .[16]

HAMLET AND OPHELIA

The attitude of Hamlet towards Ophelia is without doubt the greatest of all the puzzles in the play, greater even than that of the delay itself, a fact which should long ago have created suspicion that in the course of three centuries Shakespeare's original intentions have somehow been obscured. The difficulty is not that, having once loved Ophelia, Hamlet ceases to do so. This is explained, as most critics have agreed, by his mother's conduct which has put him quite out of love with Love and has poisoned his whole imagination. The exclamation "Frailty thy name is woman!" in the first soliloquy, we come to feel later, embraces Ophelia as well as Gertrude, while in the bedroom scene he as good as taxes his mother with destroying his capacity for affection, when he accuses her of

> such an act
> That blurs the grace and blush of modesty,
> Calls virtue hypocrite, *takes off the rose*
> *From the fair forehead of an innocent love*
> And sets a blister there.

Moreover, it is clear that in the tirades of the nunnery scene he is thinking almost as much of his mother as of Ophelia.

The word "blister" in the passage just quoted introduces us to the real problem; for it refers to the branding of a harlot. Why brand "an *innocent* love" thus? Gertrude had played the harlot with Claudius; why pour abuse which [101] might be appropriate to her upon the unoffending head of Ophelia? As Dr. Bradley notes: "The disgusting and insulting grossness of his language to her in the play scene . . . is such language as you will find addressed to a woman by no other hero of Shakespeare's, not even in that dreadful scene where Othello accuses Desdemona." And that Shakespeare intended us to interpret Hamlet's speeches here, together with some of those in the nunnery scene, as, like Othello's, belonging to the brothel is, I think, incontestable. We may try and palliate this conduct by dwelling upon Hamlet's morbid state of mind, by recalling that manners were ruder and speech more direct with the Elizabethans than with ourselves, by noting that since Ophelia and the rest thought he was mad they would be ready to extenuate his behaviour on that ground (as for instance Ophelia's outspoken song in 4.5 is generally regarded as a pathetic symptom of her condition), and by emphasising the fact that she had jilted him and that he had therefore a grievance against her. Yet all will not do; Hamlet's treatment of her remains inexcusable on the ordinary reading of the story, and as such it endangers the very life of the play.

For, whatever weakness we may be expected to find in Hamlet's character, however severely Shakespeare judges him and asks us to judge him also, it is vital to his purpose that we should retain our interest in him and admiration for him right up to the end. Rob us of our respect for the hero and *Hamlet* ceases to be a tragedy; yet that is just what his unexplained behaviour to Ophelia threatens to do. There is a savage side to Hamlet, which comes out in his ruthlessness towards Rosencrantz and Guildenstern, and in the speech as [102] the King kneels in prayer, a speech that Dr. Johnson found "too horrible to be read or to be uttered." Yet this savagery, discordant as it is with our scale of values, does not detract from our general sense of the nobility and greatness of the man. But savagery towards a gentle and inoffensive child, one whom he had loved and whose worst crime towards him is lack of understanding and inability to disobey her father's commands, is a very different matter. It is, in fact, irreconcilable with everything else we are told about him.

Hamlet treats Ophelia like a prostitute; and the only possible defence for him is to show that he had grounds for so doing. What can they have been? The answer came to me, late in this enquiry, when after trying many solutions of the Hamlet-Ophelia tangle I had given the whole thing up and had ceased thinking about it. I was making the first draft of my Notes for *Hamlet* in the edition recently published by the Cambridge University Press, and asking questions, as an editor must, about the meaning of word and situation at each step I took. Presently I arrived at the point, early in 2.2, at which Polonius and Claudius devise the plot of listening to Hamlet and Ophelia behind the arras, when my attention was arrested by this line in the speech of Polonius:

> At such a time I'll loose my daughter to him.

The expression was not new to me. I had met it before in *The Tempest* at 2.1.124, where the cynical Sebastian sneers at Alonso because he would not marry his daughter to a European prince,

> But rather loose her to an African;

and in *The Merry Wives* at 2.1.163, where the confident [103] Master Page declares of Falstaff that "if he should intend this voyage towards my wife, I would turn her loose to him; and what he gets more of her than sharp words, let it lie on my head." I had met it also, listening to present-day farmers in the north of England discussing the breeding of horses and cattle; and that this was the meaning intended, a meaning that would assuredly not escape an Elizabethan audience, was confirmed to my mind by Polonius speaking of "a farm and carters" five lines later, in accordance with Shakespeare's habit of sustained imagery.[1]

But to understand the point of it and its connection with what follows, we must have the whole context before us. I quote from the Second Quarto text:

> KING. How may we try it further?
> POL. You know sometimes he walkes foure houres together
> Heere in the Lobby.
> QUEE. So he dooes indeede.
> POL. At such a time, Ile loose my daughter to him,
> Be you and I behind an Arras then,
> Marke the encounter, if he loue her not,
> And be not from his reason falne thereon

---

[1] *Vide* Introduction (pp. xxxv–xxxix) to my *Hamlet*.

Let me be no assistant for a state
But keepe a farme and carters.

KING. We will try it.

Enter Hamlet.

QUEE. But looke where sadly the poore wretch comes reading.

POL. Away, I doe beseech you both away. *Exit King and Queene.*
Ile bord him presently, oh giue me leaue,
How dooes my good Lord Hamlet? [104]

HAM. Well, God a mercy.

POL. Doe you knowe me my Lord?

HAM. Excellent well, you are a Fishmonger.

POL. Not I my Lord.

HAM. Then I would you were so honest a man.

POL. Honest my Lord.

HAM. I sir to be honest as this world goes,
Is to be one man pickt out of tenne thousand.

POL. That's very true my Lord.

HAM. For if the sunne breede maggots in a dead dogge, being a
good kissing carrion. Haue you a daughter?

POL. I haue my Lord.

HAM. Let her not walke i'th Sunne, conception is a blessing,
But as your daughter may conceaue, friend looke to't.

Everything that Hamlet here says is capable of an equivocal
interpretation reflecting upon Polonius and Ophelia. "Fishmonger," as many commentators have noted, means a pandar or pro-
curer; [1] "carrion" was a common expression at that time for
"flesh" in the carnal sense; [2] while the quibble in "conception"
needs no explaining. And when I asked myself why Hamlet should
suddenly call Polonius a bawd and his daughter a prostitute—for
that is what it all amounts to—I could discover but one possible
answer to my question, namely that "Fishmonger" and the rest
follows immediately upon "loose my daughter to him." Nor was
this the end of the matter. For what might Hamlet mean by his
sarcastic advice to the father not to let the daughter "walke i'th
Sunne," or by the reference to the sun breeding in the "carrion"
exposed to it? Bearing in mind Hamlet's punning retort "I [105] am

[1] *Vide* note 2.2.174 in my *Hamlet.*
[2] *Vide* O.E.D. "carrion", 3, and *Merchant of Venice*, 3.1.32–4.

too much in the 'son,' " in answer to Claudius's unctuous question at 1.2.64,

> And now my cousin Hamlet, and my son,
> How is it that the clouds still hang on you?—

and recalling Falstaff's apostrophe to Prince Hal: "Shall the blessed sun of heaven prove a micher and eat blackberries? a question not to be asked. Shall the son of England prove a thief and take purses? a question to be asked," [1] is it not obvious that Hamlet here means by "Sunne" the sun or son of Denmark, the heir apparent, in other words himself? And if so, "let her not walke i'th Sunne" is to be paraphrased "take care that you do not loose your daughter to me!"

What then? *Hamlet must have overheard what Polonius said to the King.* The context allows no escape from this conclusion, inasmuch as what Hamlet says to Polonius is only intelligible if the conclusion be allowed. It remains to examine the text in order to discover, if possible, what Shakespeare's intentions, clearly impaired in some way by corruption, may have been. We are left, of course, to conjecture, but even so we are not entirely without clues. Says Polonius:

> You know sometimes he walks four hours together
> Here in the lobby;

and as he speaks we may imagine him jerking a thumb over his shoulder towards the inner-stage before which the three plotters stand, their faces to the audience. Words and the action are a direct invitation to the spectators to look in that direction; and, as they do so, Hamlet enters the inner-stage from the door at the back, his eyes upon his book, quite [106] unconscious at first that his uncle, his mother and Polonius are on the outer-stage, which stands for the audience-chamber of the castle. In short, "Here in the lobby" is equivalent to a stage-direction, and marks with practical certainty the moment at which Hamlet comes in and the place of his entry. And it is the right moment; for the entry should seem unquestionably accidental, lest the audience should suspect him of deliberate spying. It would never do, for example, to let him linger in his

---

[1] *1 Henry IV*, 2.4.449–53.

place of concealment. Between the King's question "How may we try it further?" and his resolve "We will try it" there lie eight lines of dialogue. They just give Hamlet time to enter the lobby, grow conscious of voices in the larger chamber beyond, pause for a moment beside the entrance thereto, compose his features, and come forward. But brief as the period is, it is long enough for him to take in the whole eavesdropping plot and to implicate Ophelia beyond possibility of doubt in his ears as one of his uncle's minions.

Nor does the textual aspect of the matter present any insuperable difficulties. If things are as I contend, there must have been two entries for Hamlet in Shakespeare's manuscript at this point: one for the inner-stage at l. 159 or l. 161 and the other for the outer-stage at l. 167 where it now stands. Such a double-entry would have been puzzling to a compositor or a transcriber, and it is not at all surprising to find the first one absent in both the Second Quarto and First Folio texts, seeing that it might easily have been mistaken as a prompt entry,[1] while the Queen's words "But look where sadly the [107] poor wretch comes reading" would be accepted as showing which was the entry intended by the author. The omission is rendered all the more probable by the fact that both texts tend to omit important stage-directions, and that on more than one occasion such omissions occur at the same place in both editions.[2]

Hamlet's accidental discovery of the intention to spy upon him has a bearing much wider than his attitude towards Ophelia. Indeed, the manner in which it eases the general working of the plot is strong testimony in its favour. As we shall find, it constitutes the mainspring of the events that follow in acts 2 and 3; it renders the nunnery scene playable and intelligible as never before; it adds all kinds of fresh light and shade to the play scene. In a word, its recovery means the restoration of a highly important piece of the dramatic structure. For the moment, however,

[1] In preparing manuscript play books for performance prompters occasionally repeated entries in the margin a little in advance of those in the original with the intention of bringing "the characters on at the back of the stage a few moments earlier in order that they may be able to enter into the dialogue at the correct point." Cf. W. W. Greg, *Elizabethan Dramatic Documents*, p. 217.

[2] *Vide The Manuscript of Shakespeare's Hamlet*, II, 186.

let us confine our attention to the matter in hand; and see what it tells us about Hamlet's relation with the daughter of Polonius. Here its value is at once obvious, since it casts its light backward as well as forward and enables us for the first time to see these relations in proper perspective and as a connected whole.

That Hamlet was at one time genuinely in love with Ophelia no serious critic has, I think, ever questioned. Furthermore, she herself tells us that, complying with the warning of Laertes and the commands of Polonius, she

> did repel his letters, and denied
> His access [1] [108]

So far all is plain enough; but after this darkness descends, and the commentators grope for a path without a clue. Dr. Bradley, the most discerning of them all, having declared that when in doubt a critic ought to say so honestly, goes on: "This is the position in which I find myself in regard to Hamlet's love for Ophelia. I am unable to arrive at a conviction as to the meaning of some of his words and deeds, and I question whether from the mere text of the play a sure interpretation of them can be drawn." [2] He perceives that the love was "mingled with suspicion and resentment, and that his treatment of her was in part due to this cause." [3] Furthermore, he detects "signs that Hamlet was haunted by the horrible idea that he had been deceived in Ophelia as he had been in his mother; that she was shallow and artificial, and even that what had seemed simple and affectionate love might really have been something very different." [4] But when he casts about for the cause of all this he finds nothing but her "rejection" to account for it, and the inadequacy of such an explanation is clearly the root of his perplexity.

Take again his interpretation of the earliest glimpse we get of the two together, the interview in Ophelia's closet. On this he writes:

When Hamlet made his way into Ophelia's room, why did he go in the garb, the conventionally recognised garb, of the distracted *lover*?

[1] 2.1.106–7.
[2] *Shakespearean Tragedy,* p. 153.
[3] *Op. cit.* p. 157.
[4] *Op. cit.* p. 155, n. 2.

If it was necessary to convince Ophelia of his insanity, how was it necessary to convince her that disappointment in *love* was the cause of his insanity? His *main* object in the visit appears to [109] have been to convince *others,* through her; that his insanity was not due to any mysterious unknown cause, but to this disappointment, and so to allay the suspicions of the King. But if his feeling for her had been simply that of love, however unhappy, and had not been in any degree that of suspicion or resentment, would he have adopted a plan which must involve her in so much suffering? [1]

The paragraph, written for the sake of the last question which is left unanswered, displays the acumen we look for in its author. For who before Dr. Bradley has noticed that Hamlet is in 2.2 alive to the suspicions of his uncle concerning the "antic disposition" and takes steps to furnish an explanation of it? Nevertheless, he is obviously uncomfortable about the suggestion that Hamlet's main purpose in seeking out Ophelia was to hoodwink his uncle, though once again, if that were not his purpose, what was it? he seems to ask.

The double entry for Hamlet at 2.2.159 makes all clear. In marking the exact point at which Hamlet first becomes aware of the suspicions of Ophelia, it enables us to take his previous interview with her at its face value without any reading between the lines. The disordered attire was intended, as we have seen, to denote "antic disposition" and has no reference to her rejection of him though she and her father naturally suppose that it has. On the other hand, Hamlet is of course deeply hurt by her refusal to see him and by the return of his letters; and this explains his silence and the passionate scrutiny of her face: he will not speak unless she first speaks to him. Yet, though she had "denied his access," he has forced himself into her presence. Why? Put aside all preconceived [110] notions of Hamlet, derived from Shakespeare's critics and not from Shakespeare; think of Hamlet as we last saw him, in the cellarage scene, his mind tottering on the verge of insanity; and the meaning of his invasion of her closet is patent enough. Here is the full picture of him, as she gives it:

> Lord Hamlet with his doublet all unbraced,
> No hat upon his head, his stockings fouled,
> Ungart'red, and down-gyved to his ankle,

[1] *Op. cit.,* pp. 155–6.

> Pale as his shirt, his knees knocking each other,
> And with a look so piteous in purport
> As if he had been loosed out of hell
> To speak of horrors—he comes before me.

The first three lines prepare us, we have noted, for Hamlet's "antic" appearance in the next scene. But the rest! There can surely be nothing assumed or pretended here. The idea that the interview has been sought by Hamlet in order to suggest that his madness is due to his jilting by Ophelia is out of the question. Love, even "disprized love," does not cause a man's knees to knock together, or give him the look of one fresh from gazing upon all the horrors of Inferno. The lines describe the after-effects of some terrible dream or overpowering delirium, such as was known to attack melancholic subjects; and Shakespeare wrote them, I am convinced, to show us that the mental instability obvious in the cellarage scene, so far from being temporary, had grown more intense mean while.

In this condition of extreme distress Hamlet seeks out Ophelia, the woman he loves, in the hope of finding consolation and help in her presence. But she has nothing for him; and though, as she tells us,

> He falls to such perusal of my face
> As a' would draw it,

her face reflects fear alone, the fear that is still upon her as she relates the story to her father. And so, after a long pause waiting for the help that never comes, he takes his leave:

> At last, a little shaking of mine arm,
> And thrice his head thus waving up and down,
> He raised a sigh so piteous and profound
> As it did seem to shatter all his bulk,
> And end his being; that done, he lets me go,
> He seemed to find his way without his eyes,
> For out adoors he went without their helps,
> And to the last bended their light on me.

As a picture of appeal, and appeal extended to the latest possible moment of the meeting, these lines are almost unbearably poignant. To suppose that Shakespeare intended them to represent play-acting on Hamlet's part is absurd. In "sore distraction" of spirit

Hamlet instinctively turns for support to the only being left who might give it him. She fails: and the "piteous" sigh shows that he realises her failure, and that all is over between them. Thus she had rejected his love, and proved unresponsive to an appeal of extreme need. He is not yet suspicious of her; but the ground of his mind is ready for suspicion should the seed fall.

Half an hour later Polonius is retailing the scene after his own fashion to the King and Queen, and reading aloud to them one of Hamlet's love-letters. In the general bewilderment concerning the relations between Hamlet and Ophelia [112] some have even believed that this letter is intended to be ironical, and have fastened upon the word "beautified" as evidence of this, comparing it with "I have heard of your paintings," etc., at 3.1.145-7. But (i) the letter must have been written before Ophelia "repelled" Hamlet's correspondence, and (ii) Polonius's condemnation of "beautified" is sufficient to show that it is an innocent word. As a matter of fact it simply means "beautiful" or "endowed with beauty" and is so used by Shakespeare himself in *The Two Gentlemen of Verona* [1] and elsewhere. We may take it, therefore, that the letter is a genuine, if characteristic, love-letter, perhaps one of the earlier ones of the series. It begins, as Dowden remarks, "in the conventional lover's style, which perhaps was what Ophelia would expect from a courtly admirer; then there is a real out break of passion and self-pity, finally, in the word 'machine,' Hamlet indulges, after his manner, his own intellectuality, though it may baffle the reader; the letter is no more simple or homogeneous than the writer." [2]

Hamlet has little cause to love Polonius, whom he despises as a "tedious old fool," to whose friendship with Claudius he owes the loss of the crown, and who as he is no doubt aware is responsible for Ophelia's jilting of him. When therefore he overhears his proposal to loose his daughter to him he is consumed with a savage anger. From behind his "antic" mask he lashes out at him as we have seen; accusing him of playing the pandar, and hinting that the daughter he [113] has been so carefully guarding from him had better not now be left in his path. But everything he says only makes Polonius the more certain that he is mad for love of

[1] 4.1.55–6 "Seeing you are beautified With goodly shape."
[2] Note on 2.2.116–24 in the "Arden" Hamlet.

Ophelia. Hamlet notes the effect of his words, and it is this, I think, which first gives him the idea of feeding Polonius's theory as an explanation of the "antic disposition." For when the old man next enters he harps upon his daughter in his reference to Jephthah, and continues doing so until the play scene is over.

The "fishmonger" episode is, I say, a savage attack upon Polonius; but it does not, except indirectly, reflect upon Ophelia herself. What Hamlet has heard shows him that she is to be used as a decoy; it reveals nothing of her own attitude towards the scheme. That can be tested when the moment comes; and unfortunately Ophelia's conduct then confirms his worst suspicions.[114]

Problems for Investigation

Study Questions and Topics for Short Papers

RODERICH BENEDIX

1. Is Benedix correct in his claim that the action of the play takes "only a few days" if the five travel episodes are omitted?
2. Support or attack Benedix's contention that "The whole fourth act looks like an interpolation, introduced to make out five acts."
3. Did Shakespeare mar his portrayal of Laertes when he had Laertes poison his rapier?
4. Is the King an "unmitigated rascal?"
5. Do Shakespearomaniacs make *Hamlet* greater than it is? Does Benedix prove *Hamlet* a weaker play? Can you add objections to the play that Benedix does not mention?
6. Can you present a case for the use of Fortinbras at the end of the play?
7. Support or attack Benedix's assertion, "In *Hamlet* no tragic issue is necessary."
8. Make a comparative study of those critics who, like Benedix, believe the difficulties of *Hamlet* are due to Shakespeare's faulty composition.

E. VALE BLAKE

1. Blake's article is an example of how far *Hamlet* criticism can go. Make a concise statement of the kinds of errors Blake commits in this article. Can you find these same fallacies in modified form in the works of others?
2. Write a short paper demonstrating how a study of Blake's essays helps demonstrate errors in the works of other critics.

A. C. BRADLEY

1. What do Hamlet, Laertes and Fortinbras have in common?
2. Examine Bradley's refutation of the thesis that *Hamlet* is a tragedy of irresolution. Compare it with a more recent refutation of that thesis.
3. Define Bradley's use of the term *moral;* of the term *melancholy.*
4. How well does Bradley support his delineation of Hamlet's longing for death?

5. How is melancholy related to madness?
6. "But the psychological view is not equivalent to the tragic." Evaluate this statement. Compare it with the theory of Ernest Jones.
7. What is the tragic element in *Hamlet?*

CHARLES ARMITAGE BROWN

1. Using the suggestions of J. Dover Wilson and other critics, write a short analysis of Brown's gloss on this scene.

GOULD CASSAL

1. Gould Cassal, reviewing the same performance of *Hamlet* discussed by Elinor Hughes, reaches different conclusions about the play's merits. Analyze these reviews to determine the different critical principles governing each.
2. In what specific ways would treating Shakespeare's tragic characters as "typical human beings" detract from the tragic effect?
3. In what ways does our "modern fear of greatness" interfere with our appreciation of Shakespearean tragedy?

SAMUEL C. CHEW

1. Write a short comment upon Chew's theory that Shakespeare wrote on "two planes."
2. On the basis of your own reading of *Hamlet* try to answer the questions toward the end of Chew's article. What critical orientation do these questions reflect? Evaluate their importance for a spectator of the play.
3. Read the selections by Greg and Wilson. Compare your judgment of their work with Chew's judgment.

COLLEY CIBBER

1. What ideal of acting governs Cibber's praise of Betterton? Compare Hamlet's advice to the players. What other acting interpretations can you compare to Betterton's? (Use material in the text.)
2. Based on your answer to question 1, write a short paper, setting up several interpretations of the scene Cibber discusses.

SAMUEL TAYLOR COLERIDGE

1. Do you agree with Coleridge's view that Shakespeare conceived of Hamlet's story as "a mere vehicle for his thoughts"? What does such a view imply about the nature of literature?
2. Coleridge disagrees with Samuel Johnson about the reasons for Hamlet's failure to kill the king at prayer (III, iii). Who is correct? Compare other evaluations of this scene.
3. Coleridge says of *Hamlet*, "Shakespeare wishes to impress on us the truth, that action is the chief end of existence. . . ." Write an essay comparing this statement with that of another critic.
4. Compile evaluations of Coleridge by other critics in the text and draw up a summary statement of his importance, his critical position, and his value to the contemporary reader.

CHARLES DICKENS

1. Identify the scenes to which Pip refers.
2. At what or whom is Dickens's satire directed?
3. How would you improve on Mr. Wopsle's production? How would you handle his audience?
4. Compare other reports of live productions.

T. S. ELIOT

1. Attack or support the critical principle upon which Eliot bases his statement that "the *Hamlet* of Shakespeare will appear to us very differently if, instead of treating the whole action of the play as due to Shakespeare's design, we perceive his *Hamlet* to be superimposed upon much cruder material which persists even in the final form."
2. Examine Eliot's contention that "the play is most certainly an artistic failure." Does C. S. Lewis successfully counter this charge? Compare other critics who make the same charge. What is your position?
3. Eliot's term, "objective correlative," has almost become a standard term in literary criticism. Take a scene or passage from *Hamlet* (J. Dover Wilson suggests the first soliloquy) and evaluate it as an "objective correlative."
4. Is Eliot's view of *Hamlet* the same as that of Ernest Jones?

G. R. ELLIOTT

1. Contrast Elliott's view of Claudius with the view of another critic.

2. Compare Elliott's reading of the prayer scene with another reading of that scene.

3. Choose another encounter between Hamlet and Claudius; present your own interpretation of it.

JOHANN WOLFGANG VON GOETHE

1. In this famous passage Goethe presents his estimate of Hamlet. Write a short essay criticizing this selection and relating it to the critical tradition it most resembles.

OLIVER GOLDSMITH

1. Goldsmith's analysis of this famous soliloquy seems quite persuasive on first reading. Write an evaluation of this analysis showing where you think Goldsmith is right and where you think he misreads Shakespeare.

2. Does your text differ from that quoted by Goldsmith? Are the differences, if any, significant?

3. Examine carefully what the ghost tells Hamlet of the next world. Is there anything in what the ghost says to make Hamlet have less "dread of something after death"?

W. W. GREG

1. Write a paper carefully and specifically supporting or rejecting Greg's thesis that "the Ghost's narrative is not a revelation from the dead but a figment of Hamlet's brain."

F. E. HALLIDAY

1. In this essay Halliday uses the poetry of *Hamlet* as aid in interpretation. Analyze his technique carefully for its virtues and its defects. Write a short paper developing a thesis about *Hamlet* in which you employ some discussion of Shakespeare's verse.

2. Define the concept of "a tragedy of character." How does the statement, "Yet Hamlet dies on a note of certitude," relate to that concept?

3. Halliday speaks of "this synthesis of lyric, epic, and elegy." What does he mean? Do you agree? Support your explanation and your position with specific references from the play.

THE HAMLET CONTROVERSY

1. To what extent do the disputants differ in the interpretations they give the same evidence? To what degree do they cite evidence to counteract that of the opposition?
2. What does T. S. Eliot say of Hamlet's "madness"? How does his statement compare with those of Brown, Jones, and Smith?
3. In what specific ways does the question of Hamlet's real or feigned madness affect the ultimate meaning of the play?

[THOMAS HANMER]

1. Analyze the critical assumptions about the nature and function of tragedy which are the bases of Hanmer's judgments.
2. Hanmer states: "all comic circumstances, all things tending to raise a laugh, are highly offensive in tragedies." Choose a scene or passage which tends "to raise a laugh" and write a paper defending or rejecting its appropriateness to the tragedy.
3. Write your own gloss on one of the scenes or passages Hanmer discusses.
4. Collect and evaluate other views of Polonius.

ALFRED HARBAGE

1. Harbage suggests an area of meaning upon which all commentators, he thinks, would agree. What is this general area? What critics work outside this area?
2. Define and comment on the triple role of the ghost.
3. Harbage lists twelve separate theories accounting for Hamlet's "hesitation." How many of these can you identify in works you have read? Can you find any he has not listed?
4. The two most widely accepted views of *Hamlet* are contradictory. What is Harbage's solution to this enigma? Is it yours?

WILLIAM HAZLITT

1. Classify the kind of criticism Hazlitt uses in this selection. What evidence does he use? To what faculties does he appeal?

ELINOR HUGHES

1. According to this review, the McClintic production of *Hamlet* was more effective than most because it followed J. Dover Wilson's solution to the Hamlet-Ophelia problem. Take some other scholarly solution to this or another problem in *Hamlet* and describe how it would be translated into stage action.

SAMUEL JOHNSON

1. Johnson finds no "adequate cause" for the feigned madness of Hamlet. Support or attack his judgment.
2. Write a short comment on Johnson's observation that Shakespeare neglected both poetical justice and poetical probability in *Hamlet*.
3. Compare Johnson's reading of the "To be or not to be" soliloquy with that of Goldsmith.
4. Many acting versions place the soliloquy "To be or not to be" after the nunnery scene. Evaluate the effects of this transposition.

ERNEST JONES

1. Some critics have objected to Jones's interpretation on the grounds that psychoanalysis is so difficult to perform on a living character that it is foolish to attempt to psychoanalyze a fictional character. Support or defend this criticism.
2. Document your support or objection to Jones's assertion that "the grounds Hamlet gives for his hesitancy are grounds none of which will stand any serious consideration, and which continually change from one time to another."
3. Write a short paper summarizing and commenting upon the differences between the interpretation of Hamlet's soliloquy on the King at prayer (III, iii) as given by Ernest Jones, Samuel Johnson, J. Dover Wilson, and G. R. Elliott.
4. Cite evidence to prove or disprove the critical opinion that Hamlet is much more deeply disturbed by his mother's incest than he is by his father's murder.
5. Jones speaks of the "irrelevant fencing match" of the last scene. Why does he consider it irrelevant? Which critics would agree with him? Which would not?

6. Compare Jones' discussion of Hamlet's fear of death with C. S. Lewis's; with Bradley's.

THOMAS M. KETTLE

1. For what reason does Kettle advance his claim that the ghost "is the one great blot and uncombining ingredient in the play"?
2. Summarize Kettle's evaluation of Horatio and write a short paper in defense of Hamlet's friend.
3. Compare Kettle's reading of the famous "to be or not to be" soliloquy with that of Goldsmith.
4. Ernest Jones goes to some length to prove Hamlet's difficulties internal; Kettle asserts that *Hamlet* is the most external of Shakespeare's plays. Find several key passages in which these critics differently interpret the same evidence and write a short paper demonstrating which of these views you think correct.
5. If you were staging *Hamlet,* how would you portray the Ghost? Would you make him an offstage voice, a clear physical presence, or an ambiguous figure swathed in vapors? On the basis of your reading in the text deduce which critic would choose which way of portraying the Ghost; explain your deductions. In your discussion, go into details for one or all three of the Ghost's appearances.

H. D. F. KITTO

1. How successfully does Kitto refute the suggestion that *Hamlet* is a play about a man who couldn't make up his mind?
2. Draw up a definition of "religious drama" as Kitto seems to use the term. How does "religious drama" differ from a tragedy about an individual?
3. Compare Kitto's estimate of Gertrude with that of another critic.
4. What does Kitto contend is the central theme of the play?

G. WILSON KNIGHT

1. Write a short essay in which you attack or support Knight's estimate of the King's character with additional evidence.
2. Contrast Knight's interpretation of the prayer scene (III, iii) with that of two other critics.

3. Write a short essay justifying the King's action against Hamlet as an enemy of the state.
4. Knight claims that Shakespeare divides our sympathies by making the villain into a kindly uncle and the hero into a cynic. Assume this to be true and write an essay relating this division of loyalty to the final meaning of the play.

C. S. LEWIS

1. Lewis counters those critics who assert that Hamlet does not hesitate by citing Hamlet's opinion of himself. Compile and evaluate a list of such evidence.
2. At several points throughout this essay, Lewis attacks T. S. Eliot's position on *Hamlet*. Summarize his remarks and estimate the extent to which they damage Eliot's theory.
3. Elaborate upon Lewis's distinction between *Hamlet* the play and Hamlet the man.
4. Lewis makes much of the ghost's role in *Hamlet*. Compare his evaluation of the ghost with those of other critics.
5. If you agree with Lewis that the full appreciation of literature requires the child's spontaneous response, describe the way in which various interpretations of *Hamlet* inhibit this response.

JAMES RUSSELL LOWELL

1. Discuss Hamlet with respect to what Lowell calls the primary object of tragedy and the moral office of tragedy.
2. Develop Lowell's estimate of Hamlet as a man without faith, a compulsive doubter.

SIR LAURENCE OLIVIER

1. Develop a defense or attack of *Hamlet* as a film or television production.
2. Compare Olivier's discussion of audience demands with that of another critic (Hazlitt or Chew, for example). What is your own position?
3. Choose one scene from the play. How would you produce it for the stage? How would you produce it for film or television?

ROBERT ORNSTEIN

1. What critics or critical positions do you consider fit objects of the author's burlesque?
2. Can you determine the author's implicit critical standards?

EDGAR ALLAN POE

1. Compile a list of critics who commit the "radical error" Poe attacks. Evaluate their position. Develop your own position and write a defense of it.

W. TEIGNMOUTH SHORE

1. Compare Shore and Eliot on the nature of Shakespeare's failure in *Hamlet*.
2. What is the basis for Shore's observations on the ghost and Ophelia? Is such a basis justifiable?
3. Compare Goethe and Shore with respect to their reading of "The time is out of joint. . . ."
4. In a note Shore recommends that certain passages be cut in order to secure swift action. Choose one scene or passage and write a paper developing your own judgment as to whether or not it is superfluous. Compare other listings of superfluous material in *Hamlet*. What criteria determine each listing?

CAROLINE SPURGEON

1. Write an essay demonstrating the subliminal action of the imagery in *Hamlet* to underline meaning.
2. Define in your own words: image, atmosphere, iterative imagery.
3. Does your own reading of the play support Miss Spurgeon's findings on the nature of the imagery in the play? Select a critical scene or passage and study its imagery.
4. If you were watching a performance of *Hamlet* would you be aware of the imagery pattern Miss Spurgeon isolates? How do you know?

A. C. SWINBURNE

1. Does Swinburne think of *Hamlet* as a play to be acted or as a play to be read?

2. Identify the soliloquy which Swinburne so highly praises, Analyze his criticism.

3. Swinburne cites evidence for his contention that Shakespeare deliberately tried to make Hamlet seem a man of action. How convincing do you find this evidence?

A. J. A. WALDOCK

1. How well does Waldock support his assertion that "delay in real life is one thing, in a drama quite another"? What would Coleridge or Hazlitt say to his argument?

2. Compare Waldock's position on the nature of Hamlet's delay with Harbage's, with Werder's. Do they have any ground in common? At what critical instances do they part company? What is your position?

3. Compare Waldock's reading of the "To be or not to be" soliloquy with that of another critic.

4. Develop an essay based on the following statement: "It would need discrepancies of larger magnitude than these (large as they are) to upset the greatness of *Hamlet*."

JOHN WEISS

1. How well does Weiss dispose of the two passages he claims are the sole support for the theory of Hamlet's premeditated madness?

2. Weiss asserts that the text itself does not warrant the assumption that Hamlet knew of Ophelia's duplicity while her father and the King were hiding behind the arras. J. Dover Wilson holds the opposite view. Which do you find the more convincing and why?

3. Write a summary of Weiss's analysis of Hamlet's "madness."

4. Criticize Weiss's contention that Hamlet's "love for Ophelia was the most mastering impulse of his life. . . ."

KARL WERDER

1. Carefully summarize the evidence Werder lists in defense of his thesis.

2. Search out all the references to delay in *Hamlet*. Evaluate

these references in their context and test them against Werder's thesis. Then write a refutation or defense of that thesis.
3. Which critics would vehemently disagree with Werder? Which would agree with him partially or wholly? Has he altered your own conception of the play?
4. Evaluate Werder's redefinition of the nature of Hamlet's task.

REBECCA WEST

1. Compile and evaluate a list of evidence proving or disproving Ophelia's suicide.
2. Write a short essay demonstrating the importance of a correct interpretation of Ophelia's character to the final meaning of *Hamlet*.
3. Justify Miss West's statement about Gertrude: "The whole play depends on her not noticing, and not understanding."
4. Examine the evidence advanced for the proposition that Hamlet is a "statesman, a true Macchiavellian, a prince careful for the safety of his subjects." Write a short paper evaluating this proposition.
5. Develop an essay around the statement: "It is quite certain that he [Shakespeare] wished to present Hamlet as a bad man."

J. DOVER WILSON

1. Write a short paper comparing Rebecca West's view of Hamlet and Ophelia with that of J. Dover Wilson.
2. Wilson says that Hamlet's attitude toward Ophelia is one of the greatest puzzles of the play. Write a short summary statement of this problem citing specific lines and scenes.
3. Wilson, commenting upon Hamlet's speech while the King is at prayer (III, iii), finds that it does not "detract from your general sense of the nobility and greatness of the man." Comment upon Wilson's reading of this passage. What other motives can you suggest for Hamlet's speech here?

Topics for Long Papers

The following topics can be developed from a reading of the play itself and the selections in this volume. In order to supplement his research or to test his own insights, the student may wish to consult certain library materials. A basic, but by no means complete, bibliography is to be found on pages 295 to 298.

> The Causes of Hamlet's Hesitation
> Hamlet's "Hesitation" Restudied
> Hamlet and Ophelia
> Hamlet's Madness: A Revaluation
> An Approach to *Hamlet* (use an enigmatic scene or a particular character as a means of reaching a final meaning for the play)
> Plans for a Production of *Hamlet*
> A New Reading of ———————— (conduct a close reading of a particular scene or character)
> Comic Elements in *Hamlet*
> The Ghost in *Hamlet*
> Is *Hamlet* a Tragedy?
> Hamlet and His "Tragic Flaw"
> The Dramatic Uses of the Play within the Play
> The Queen: Her Guilt and Its Significance in the Play

Further topics may be extracted from questions raised earlier on the individual critics.

Suggestions for Further Reading

NOTE: Asterisks (*) indicate books available in inexpensive paperbound editions. A date in brackets represents a book's original date of publication. Selections in the text are listed below only if available in paperbound editions.†

I. EDITIONS OF THE PLAY

HAMLET, Joseph Quincy Adams, ed. (Boston, Houghton Mifflin, 1929).

* HAMLET, R, C. Bald, ed. (New York, Appleton-Century-Crofts, 1946).

* HAMLET, C. F. Tucker Brooke, ed. (New Haven, Yale University Press, 1947).

HAMLET, vol. III in *A New Variorum Edition of Shakespeare,* Horace Howard Furness, ed. (Philadelphia, Lippincott, 1877).

* HAMLET, Charles Jasper Sisson, ed. Introduction by Francis Fergusson. Commentary by Maurice Evans (New York, Dell, 1958).

* HAMLET, Louis B. Wright, ed. (New York, Pocket Books, 1958).

II. BIBLIOGRAPHY AND REFERENCE

A New Variorum Edition of Shakespeare: Hamlet, vol. IV, Appendix. Horace Howard Furness, ed. (Philadelphia, Lippincott, 1877).

Publications of the Modern Language Association of America (See annual bibliography.)

RAVEN, A. A. *A Hamlet Bibliography and Reference Guide: 1877–1935* (Chicago, University of Chicago Press, 1936).

Shakespeare Quarterly (See annual bibliography).

Shakespeare Survey (See annual bibliography).

SISSON, C. J. *New Readings in Shakespeare,* 2 vols. (Cambridge, The University Press, 1956).

III. TEXTUAL AND SOURCE STUDIES

* *Age of Shakespeare, The,* Boris Ford, ed. (London, Penguin, 1955).

DUTHIE, G. I., *The "Bad" Quarto of Hamlet* (Cambridge, The University Press, 1941).

GOLLANCZ, Sir Israel, *The Sources of Hamlet, With an Essay on the Legend* (London, Oxford University Press, 1926).

† The method of bibliographical citation follows the house style of Appleton-Century-Crofts, Inc.

GREG, W. W., *The Editorial Problem in Shakespeare: A Survey of the Foundations of the Text* (Oxford, Clarendon, 1942).

————. "The 'Hamlet' Texts and Recent Works in Shakespearian Bibliography," *Mod. Lang. Rev.*, XIV (October, 1919), 380–385.

IV. SHAKESPEARE'S LIFE AND TIMES

CHAMBERS, E. K., *William Shakespeare: A Study of Facts and Problems,* 2 vols. (Oxford, Clarendon, 1930).

* CHUTE, Marchette, *Shakespeare of London* [1949] (New York, Everyman, 1957.

HALLIDAY, F, E., *Shakespeare: A Pictorial Biography* (New York, Thames and Hudson, 1956).

* HARRISON, G. B., *Introducing Shakespeare* (London, Penguin, 1939).

* *Life in Shakespeare's England* [1911], J. Dover Wilson, ed. (London, Penguin, 1944).

SPENCER, Hazelton, *The Art and Life of William Shakespeare* (New York, Harcourt, Brace, 1940).

* TILLYARD, E. M. W., *The Elizabethan World Picture* [1943] (New York, Modern Library, n.d.).

* TREVELYAN, G. M., *History of England,* Vol. II, *The Tudors and the Stuart Era* [1926] (New York, Doubleday, 1953).

* WRIGHT, Louis B., *Middle-Class Culture in Elizabethan England* (Chapel Hill, University of North Carolina Press, 1935).

V. SHAKESPEARE IN THE THEATER

* ADAMS, John Cranford, *The Globe Playhouse* (Cambridge, Harvard University Press, 1942).

CHAMBERS, E. K., *The Elizabethan Stage,* 4 vols. (Oxford, Clarendon, 1923).

HARBAGE, Alfred, *Shakespeare's Audience* (New York, Columbia University Press, 1941).

HODGES, C. Walter, *The Globe Restored* (London, E. Benn, 1953).

* KNIGHT, G. Wilson, *Principles of Shakespearean Production* (London, Penguin, 1949).

MANDER, Raymond and J. Mitchenson, *Hamlet Through the Ages: A Pictorial Record from 1709* (London, Rockliff, 1952).

* HARRISON, G. B., *Elizabethan Plays and Players,* [1940] (Ann Arbor, University of Michigan Press, 1956).

ODELL, George C. D., *Shakespeare from Betterton to Irving,* 2 vols. (New York, Scribner, 1920).

SMITH, Irwin, *Shakespeare's Globe Playhouse: A Modern Reconstruction in Text and Scale Drawings Based Upon the Reconstruction of the Globe by John Cranford Adams* (New York, Scribner, 1956).

* WEBSTER, Margaret, *Shakespeare Without Tears* [1942] (New York, Fawcett, 1957).

VI. INTERPRETATION AND CRITICISM

* BRADBY, G. F., *The Problems of Hamlet* (London, Oxford University Press, 1928).

* BRADLEY, A. C., *Shakespearean Tragedy*, [1904] (New York, Meridian, 1955).

* CHAMBERS, E. K., *Shakespeare: A Survey*, [1904–1908] (New York, Hill and Wang, n.d.)

CLEMEN, W. H., *The Development of Shakespeare's Imagery* (London, Methuen, 1951).

* COLERIDGE, Samuel Taylor, *Coleridge's Writings on Shakespeare*, T. F. Hawkes, ed. (New York, Putnam, 1959).

CONKLIN, Paul S., *A History of Hamlet Criticism: 1601–1821* (New York, Columbia University Press, 1947).

* FLUCHERE, Henri, *Shakespeare and the Elizabethan*, [1948] (New York, Hill and Wang, 1956).

* GRANVILLE-BARKER, Harley, *Preface to Hamlet*, [1946] (New York, Hill and Wang, 1957).

GREG, W. W., "Hamlet's Hallucination," *Mod. Lang. Rev.*, XII (October, 1917), 393–421.

* HARRISON, G. B., *Shakespeare at Work: 1592–1603* [1933] (Ann Arbor, University of Michigan Press, (1958).

* HAZLITT, William, *Hazlitt on Theatre*, William Archer and Robert Lowe, eds. (New York, Hill and Wang, n.d.).

JAMES, D. G., *The Dream of Learning* (Oxford, Clarendon, 1951).

* JONES, Ernest, *Hamlet and Oedipus*, [1949] (New York, Doubleday, n.d.).

* KNIGHT, G. Wilson, *The Wheel of Fire*, [1930] (New York, Meridian, 1957).

LEECH, Clifford, "Studies in *Hamlet*: 1901–1955," *Shakespeare Survey 9* (Cambridge, The University Press, 1956), pp. 1–15.

LEVIN, Harry, *The Question of Hamlet* (New York, Oxford University Press, 1959).

MACK, Maynard, "The World of *Hamlet*," *Yale Rev.*, XLI (1952), 502–523.

MAHOOD, M. M., *Shakespeare's Wordplay* (London, Methuen, 1957).

RALLI, Augustus, *A History of Shakespearean Criticism,* 2 vols. (London, Oxford University Press, 1932).

ROBERTSON, J. M., *The Problem of "Hamlet"* (London, G. Allen & Unwin, 1919).

* SANDERS, Gerald, *A Shakespeare Primer* (New York, Rinehart, 1950).

* *Shakespeare: Modern Essays in Criticism,* Leonard F. Dean, ed. (New York, Oxford University Press, 1957).

* SPURGEON, Caroline F. E., *Shakespeare's Imagery and What It Tells Us,* [1935] (Boston, Beacon Press, 1958).

STOLL, E. E., *Art and Artifice in Shakespeare* (Cambridge, The University Press, 1933).

* TRAVERSI, D. K., *An Approach to Shakespeare,* [1936] (New York, Doubleday, 1956).

* VAN DOREN, Mark, *Shakespeare,* [1939] (New York, Doubleday, 1953).

WALKER, Roy, *The Time is Out of Joint* (London, A. Dakers, 1948).

WILLIAMSON, Claude C. H., *Readings in the Character of Hamlet: 1661–1947* (London, G. Allen & Unwin, 1950).

* WILSON, J. Dover, *What Happens in Hamlet* [1935] (Cambridge, The University Press, 1959).